AN INTRODUCTION TO THE PSYCHODYNAMICS OF WORKPLACE BULLYING

AN INTRODUCTION TO THE PSYCHODYNAMICS OF WORKPLACE BULLYING

Sheila White

KARNAC

First published in 2013 by
Karnac Books Ltd
118 Finchley Road
London NW3 5HT

British Library Cataloguing in Publication Data

A C.I.P. for this book is available from the British Library

ISBN-13: 978-1-78049-162-2

Typeset by V Publishing Solutions Pvt Ltd., Chennai, India

Printed in Great Britain

www.karnacbooks.com

For all those who have the courage to stand up to bullies and tyrants

CONTENTS

ACKNOWLEDGEMENTS

A special thank you to Clifford Davidson for persuading me to write this book and for his unwavering support to finish it.

I am very grateful to Andreas Liefooghe for his encouragement and to Birkbeck, University of London, for use of the library.

Thank you to Peter White for reading my work, over many years, and patiently listening to accounts of the challenges encountered. To John White, my gratitude for funding the research and the book.

Thank you to Susan Kahn, Alison Vaspe, Rachel Woodward, Lucy Crispin, and Sharon Toye for reading chapters and giving feedback and to Kate Jackson and Marian Armstrong for proofreading.

To the many members of OPUS (an Organisation for Promoting Understanding of Society) and ISPSO (International Society for the Psychoanalytical Study of Organisations), thank you for sharing your knowledge and expertise. A special thank you to Kay and Allan Souter for recognising the potential of my work in its early stages of development and to Paul Hoggett and Mike Broussine for supporting my research.

My deep gratitude goes to Ken Tatam and Jeni Watts for their devoted friendship.

Finally, thank you to the many anonymous contributors to the book and to all the bullies and victims who have inspired me on the way.

ABOUT THE AUTHOR

Sheila White is an honorary research fellow at Birkbeck, University of London. She has spent many years carrying out research on workplace bullying, presented papers at numerous conferences, and published in a variety of journals. Her background is in teaching and work in the voluntary sector. She is a member of ISPSO (International Society for the Psychoanalytic Study of Organizations), IAWBH (International Association of Workplace Bullying and Harassment), OPUS (an Organisation for Promoting Understanding of Society), and CMI (Chartered Management Institute).

PREFACE

Bullying scenarios are complex. They are confusing, messy, unpleasant, and destructive situations. Over time, relationships with colleagues are damaged, there is a loss of effective engagement with work, and productivity falls. Those directly involved struggle to survive and onlookers are distracted from their tasks. Ambiguity, and seemingly illogical, petty, and disrespectful behaviour, becomes the norm.

Increasingly petty conflicts are being registered as formal complaints, and in no time, legal procedures take over and costs spiral out of control.

Few of us seem immune to the dynamics of workplace bullying and many of us get drawn into its toxicity. We may find ourselves as observers of bullying—puzzled and perplexed by the confusion around us. Or we may be victims—captured, entangled, and increasingly pulled into situations in which reality is difficult to grasp; obsession with survival pervades all the crevices of our minds and our energy is drained away. Alternatively, we may have been accused, rightly or wrongly, of bullying others.

Whatever our role in workplace bullying—or interest in this complex dynamic—there is a need to make sense of what is happening and to create a narrative in which we can find an understanding for ourselves and others. The psychodynamic approaches presented in this book offer a means by which this can be achieved.

Through looking below the surface to the underlying anxieties we can appreciate not only why, but also how, bullying arises, and gain an in-depth understanding of the root causes. We can also appreciate how bullying arises from a complex interplay of factors: individuals, their interpersonal relationships, group dynamics, and organisational contexts.

By becoming aware of the deeper issues involved in bullying, we may develop a more compassionate understanding of the struggles employees face when working together in complex, 'fluid', and evolving environments. It is through our knowledge of why and how bullying behaviour arises that we can also learn how to develop organisations in which there is recognition of others, healthy engagement with work and with colleagues, and how trust, mutuality, and attunement can be fostered.

Aims of the book

There are three main aims. The primary aim of the book is to explore the hidden worlds that exist beneath the irrational and unpredictable aspects of workplace bullying. We reveal how individuals' underlying anxieties surface, how the dysfunctional nature of interpersonal relationships evolves, how impasses within group dynamics develop, and how differing styles of leadership and aspects of organisational culture provide a context in which bullying can flourish.

The second aim is to present new ways of conceptualising bullying. Three recurring themes, of space, recognition, and loss, "echo" throughout the chapters. This book presents a case for understanding bullying as follows: bullying occurs around vacuums of support within an organisation where the most negative aspects of that organisation's culture accumulate. Some individuals—potential bullies and potential victims—feel particularly vulnerable in these spaces and become trapped in a futile search for recognition. Their evolving interpersonal relationships are characterised by patterns of domination and submission. Fixed perceptions and projective gridlock ensue. The conflict is fuelled by unconscious and subconscious collusions within the group dynamics. Further bullying is an unsuccessful attempt to release the stuckness in the group, to create new meanings and to engage with reality. However, old, familiar, restrictive, and repetitive patterns of behaviour return, along with psychic deadness.

The third aim is to bridge theory and practice. Interview and observational material, collated over many years, is used to illustrate the theories, and examples are given of how practical measures can be taken both to prevent and to more effectively manage bullying scenarios.

Structure

A chapter is devoted to each of the following: individuals, interpersonal relationships, groups, and organisational contexts.

These four main chapters have three distinctive sections. Firstly, research reviews, based on bullying in workplaces and in schools, identify key features of bullying. Although reference to schools may seem rather out of place in a book on workplace bullying, researchers in schools have access to "real time" bullying scenarios and provide considerable insights into the dynamic nature of bullying. The academic field of workplace bullying has primarily been the domain of quantitative researchers carrying out large-scale surveys and very few of the researchers have entered the workplace to carry out interviews with bullies or observed bullying in action.

The second part of each of the four main chapters presents psychoanalytical theories. These give a deeper understanding of the dynamics identified in the research reviews.

The third part is shorter, and more informal, than the previous two sections. It provides answers to questions posed in the brief introduction to the chapters. These answers bring together the research theory on bullying with psychoanalytical theory to make practical suggestions for preventing and effectively managing bullying. It has to be noted, however, that there are no quick fixes. Each organisational context is different and requires different solutions. Through knowledge of the underlying issues of bullying, such as those described in this book, practitioners can find creative solutions appropriate for the situations confronting them.

Chapter Five, A case study, describes the transformation of an organisation in which bullying had been rife, into a healthy, profitable, and enjoyable place to work. The study is "analysed" using key theories from the previous four chapters.

The book is structured to enable the reader to move from section to section using the information in a flexible way, either to learn about the theory of bullying from research literature, or to study psychoanalytical theory on bullying, or, through the question and answer sections, to find out about practical measures. The chapters can be read in any order and theoretical aspects may be studied according to the reader's interests. To facilitate this, every chapter is prefaced with an introductory overview, and there are summaries of each of the theoretical sections.

Psychodynamic theories

> The purpose of Freud's lifelong struggle was to help us to understand ourselves, so that we would no longer be propelled, by forces unknown to us, to live lives of discontent, or perhaps outright misery, and to make others miserable, very much to our own detriment. (Bettleheim, 1982, p. 15)

When psychoanalysis works well, in the clinical setting, the patient has a greater self-knowledge, which Bettleheim (1982) describes as "a knowing of thyself". The patient gradually accepts that although frustrating repetitive patterns of emotional behaviour may continue to arise, they can be acknowledged; there is a reconciliation with the past. He/she gradually becomes less driven by unconscious forces, enabling an increased inner freedom of thought and choice about how to respond and relate to others (Mollon, 2002). In being better equipped to recognise the destructive patterns of behaviour and emotional responses to situations, the patient is more able to avoid becoming entrapped within dysfunctional relationships such as bullying.

Within the clinical setting there is time to explore the unconscious but in our predominantly target-driven, measurement-focussed, 24/7 organisational cultures, surviving in the here and now provides little space or time for reflection on the deeper organisational issues.

The roots of life

We only see the tops of life,
We don't see the roots—
The foundations—the heart.
We see the outside,
We ignore the truth.
Mark Smith, 1975 (aged 9).

Psychoanalytical approaches attempt to get to the truth, to that inner knowing. Essentially there are three assumptions in psychoanalysis. First, much thought and activity occurs outside of conscious awareness in the unconscious mind. Unconscious thought processes are mostly ordinary thoughts turned into ones of which we are generally unaware and it is often only through waking in the middle of a dream that we begin to question, and puzzle on, the often seemingly bizarre linkages between our conscious and unconscious worlds. Second, psychoanalysis takes a developmental view of the emotional health of adults, taking this to be rooted, to a large extent, in the experiences of early childhood. Expectations of how other individuals will respond to our needs are laid down during these first few years and continue to influence our emotions and our behaviour for the rest of our life (Mollon, 2002). A third assumption is that we use a range of defences to help us to cope with the stresses and strains of everyday life. These defences include denial, fantasy, splitting, projection, displacement, and regression.

The methods used by analysts in clinical settings have been compared to those used by archaeologists. Much of the work of psychoanalysis consists in unearthing the deeply buried remnants of the past and combining them with other fragments, from the present, that are more accessible (Ginzberg, 1980). Once all the pieces have been put together it becomes possible to speculate about the origin and nature of the individual psyche (Bettleheim, 1982). Within the analytical setting it is the unusual gesture, the repetitive use of a word or phrase, the patient's attention to a specific object within the room, or a passing remark as he/she departs at the end of a fifty-minute consultation, that give clues to unconscious processes. Deep feelings and anxieties are also revealed through transference, the process by which a patient displaces onto his/her analyst feelings and ideas. Further insights are gained through countertransference, in which the analyst can assume that his/her own emotional response is based on a "correct" interpretation of the patient's true intentions or meanings. Often this occurs when the therapist feels pressured to identify with his/her own feelings and to act out a role, seemingly on behalf of the patient.

Since its inception in the clinical setting, psychoanalysis as a body of knowledge has developed over the years and it is now applied to a wide range of different contexts, for example, interpersonal relationships, groups, organisations, and society. Increasingly, much of the theory used to analyse the irrational behaviour of individuals has been shown to have relevance in these different contexts. For many years it has been acknowledged by academics and organisational consultants that our experiences of the workplace can trigger powerful feelings, and often the issues we face appear difficult to comprehend and seem beyond our control (Gabriel, 1999; Hirschorn, 1997a; Kets de Vries & Miller, 1984;). Groups and organisations have been found to collectively "employ" similar defences to those of individuals (Hirschorn, 1997b; Obholzer & Roberts, 1994; Stapley, 2006). Also, just as individuals repeat dysfunctional patterns from their past, mistakes are often repeated in organisations, as if no lessons have been learnt (Stein, 2011). Therefore, as a discipline for the study of complexity and ambiguity, psychoanalysis is particularly useful for getting to the root causes of dysfunctional relationships such as bullying.

Organisational consultants and researchers working from psychodynamic perspectives endeavour to elicit the unconscious meanings, assumptions, and collective anxieties of employees, often through looking at the underlying motives, desires, and fantasies. In doing so they gain a perspective of a "knowing of thyself" on behalf of the organisation. Based on an understanding of the unconscious life of organisations—those unseen and immeasurable aspects—they can work with conflict, disappointment, and frustrations held by employees to foster "healing" and present creative solutions to deeply hidden problems.

Comprehensive reviews of the range of application of psychoanalysis to organisational life, and its limitations, can be found in Arnaud (2012) and Gabriel and Carr (2002). There is also an extensive body of knowledge from which organisational consultants, academics, mediators, and other practitioners can draw (see www.ispso.org).

In revealing the subconscious and unconscious processes involved in bullying, I have drawn on a wide range of psychodynamic theories from various schools of thought. My choice has been influenced by many years of research on workplace bullying and the selection has been made to provide the reader with a coherent theoretical framework which applies across the chapters.

This book does not aim to discuss the philosophical background to the theories but leaves such work to others such as Elliot (2002) and Lear (1998, 2000).

Outline of chapters

Chapter One: Individuals: bullies and victims

This chapter focuses on two of the key questions at the roots of bullying "why do bullies bully?" and "why do some individuals become victims?" A research review of bullying describes the range of behaviour exhibited by bullies, its impact on victims, and the role played by the victim. Key characteristics of the behaviour of bullies are identified as aggression, inconsistency, and envy. Psychoanalytical insights are then given into the possible origins of the behaviours of bullies and victims. Two key dynamics underlying the psychic processes are identified as the interplay of life and death and love and hate. Fundamental to our understanding of the dynamic nature of bullying are the concepts of boundaries and containment. Three further concepts, identification with the aggressor, "projective identification", and envy are presented.

In concluding this section, bullying is conceptualised as a perverse and pernicious form of projective identification in which there is an attempt to enliven psychic deadness.

The third part of the chapter brings together the research on bullying and psychoanalytical theory to answer the questions posed at the beginning of the chapter. Practical suggestions are made for ways in which victims can protect themselves from being bullied and how human resource (HR) managers can best help both victims and bullies to move forward in a healthier manner.

Chapter Two: Interpersonal relationships

This chapter forms the "hub" of the book. It gets to the core of understanding the dysfunctional relationships between bullies and victims. Key questions are: "How do bullies come to dominate victims?" and "Why do victims become so submissive?". The research review presents bullying as an evolving and escalating conflict in which the coping strategies, both active and passive, used by victims tend to fail and they become trapped. The evolutionary pattern is described in detail through "the life cycle theory of bullying" (White, 2001, 2004, 2007).

The psychoanalytical theories used to explore the hidden aspects of the research findings are drawn from two fields of psychoanalysis—attachment theory and intersubjective theory. Attachment theory looks at how the nature of our early relationships predetermine the relationships we have later in life. In intersubjective theories the key concept is recognition. We examine the two paradoxes of recognition—dependency versus independency and destruction and reality testing. These paradoxes form the foundations for relationships of domination and submission within childhood and in adult life too. Drawing on an attachment theory perspective of domestic violence, we study the perspective of the perpetrator and how his or her inner needs are met through close interpersonal relationships. Victims may, perversely, also be meeting deeper needs when trapped within relationships of domination and submission. Additional theories—repetition compulsion, authenticity, and the true and false self—explain why bullies and victims often repeat their roles.

In this chapter bullying is conceptualised as a futile search for recognition which ends in a "dance of death" for both bully and victim.

In the final section of the chapter, the theory from the research review and key intersubjective theories are brought together to answer questions posed in the introduction. Practical issues are explored, for example, how victims can protect themselves from being drawn into toxic relationships and how HR managers can help individuals to engage with their work and with each other in more productive ways.

Chapter Three: Groups

This chapter focuses on the role played by members of the group in the development of bullying scenarios.

> In reality, none of us, however isolated in time and space, can be regarded as outside a group or lacking in active manifestations of group psychology. We carry our groupishness with us all of the time and it is clear that everything is embedded in the social context of our lives, particular in the dominant primary group, the family. (Stapley, 2006, pp. 149–150)

The research review begins with the challenges faced by individuals when they first enter a group and shows how, as bullying scenarios develop, individuals take on different roles. Some group members become bystanders and others are excluded and scapegoated. This section is completed with a short description of intergroup bullying. Key questions in this chapter are: "How do the deeper dynamics of groups foster bullying?" and "Why do some individuals become stuck in their roles?". The psychodynamic theory used to present answers to these questions includes valency, transitional objects and transitional space, and shame. Further theories are Bion's classification of groups and additions to this understanding of the deeper collective processes, for example, Hopper's fourth basic assumption. This assumption closely mirrors the group dynamics of bullying in which there is fragmentation on the surface as individuals become isolated from each other and, at a deeper level, there are collusions of subservience. Subtle differences between scapegoating and bullying are illustrated with case study material (White, 2007).

In this chapter bullying is conceptualised as a futile attempt to release the impasses in the group dynamics and to create new working relationships.

The question and answer section at the end of the chapter includes suggestions on how HR managers can identify groups vulnerable to bullying and scapegoating.

Chapter Four: Organisational contexts

This chapter describes the organisational aspects of bullying, beginning with a description of the contexts of bullying from historical, social, and technological perspectives. Key questions include: "How does bullying become institutionalised in organisations?" and "When does management become bullying?" The research review starts by looking at the cultural and structural factors which facilitate the development of bullying scenarios, for example, the extremes of leadership styles. Autocratic leadership, characterised by excessive controls and monitoring, and its mirror opposite, laissez-faire leadership, are shown to create fertile environments for bullying. The research review includes a section on cyberbullying and models of dynamics of bullying, including "the contextualisation theory of workplace bullying" (White, 2007).

The psychodynamic theory returns to the topic of boundaries, first introduced in Chapter One, to explore how different organisational boundaries create the potential for bullying. The institutionalisation of bullying is explained using the concept of "social defences" and the topic of loss and mourning. When rapid changes take place in organisations but are not acknowledged by managers and not integrated into the culture and structure, deep dynamics generated by loss can create a range of problems, for example, object fixation. Fundamental to our understanding of how bullying arises within particular areas in organisations, is the topic of vacuums, those areas where there is a lack of support and recognition for employees.

Bullying is conceptualised as occurring around vacuums and where there is a concentration of the most negative aspects of an organisation's culture—the organisational "black holes".

The final section of the chapter includes suggestions on how HR managers can promote well-being and effective engagement based on a psychodynamic perspective of workplace bullying.

Chapter Five: A case study

This chapter applies various psychoanalytical theories from the previous chapters to explain the underlying dynamics of a failing engineering company in which bullying was rife. A new management team developed mutuality, trust, and respect amongst employees to create an organisation which has become a market leader in its field.

Readership

Although no previous knowledge of psychoanalysis is required, it would be helpful if the reader is open to innovative ways of looking at complex organisational dynamics. Much more than factual knowledge will be gained from the book when the reader reflects on the application of the theories in work, through observations and, in particular, through reflecting on his or her feelings.

This is a textbook for academics and practitioners who wish to have a deeper understanding of the complex dynamics giving rise to bullying scenarios. Academics, researchers, students in business schools and departments of humanities who are interested in the deeper dynamics of bullying and how dysfunctional relationships arise in organisations, may choose to adopt this book as a course text. It could also be used as a handbook for HR managers, union officials, mediators, and consultants trying to prevent and manage bullying scenarios. The in-depth explanations of the motives and dynamics of bullying may be useful for counsellors, psychotherapists, and life coaches, both from theoretical and practical perspectives, especially when trying to contextualise the group and organisational factors of bullying. Likewise, employees experiencing or witnessing bullying will gain new and valuable insights into the challenges they face day-to-day at work and, from these, find new ways of coping.

It is acknowledged that the overview of each aspect of psychodynamics may strike the expert in psychoanalytical theory as rather basic. This book is an introduction to the topic, written to inspire readers to find out more for themselves about bullying and psychoanalytical theory. There is ample material available for the reader to pursue the theoretical concepts in more detail elsewhere, for example, courses are available through the Tavistock Consultancy, OPUS, and the Institute of Psychoanalysis in London. It is hoped that new researchers will be inspired to take up the challenge of working in a very complex, but worthy, area of work and that the academic community will have the courage to support innovative research. Practical advice and further theoretical ideas will continue to be available from www.whybulliesbully.com.

CHAPTER ONE

Individuals: bullies and victims

Introduction

The aim of this chapter is to present in-depth insights into the motives and behaviours of bullies and victims. We begin with a review of research into bullying and then use psychoanalytical theories to explore the root causes of bullying from an intrapsychic perspective.

The first part of the chapter, the review of the research into bullying, starts with the derivation of the word "bully" and how its meaning has changed over time. Victims' perceptions of bullying behaviour and how it impacts on them in the short and longer term are described. Then we look at the part played by victims. As there is no consensus on this topic amongst researchers, a range of views is presented, from the victim being a victim by chance to victims lacking resilience as a result of childhood experiences or alternatively being vulnerable because they differ, in some way, from the rest of the group. The behaviour of bullies is described in terms of three key characteristics: aggression, inconsistency, and envy. Key points are illustrated with case-study material.

The second part of the chapter explores some of the unconscious and subconscious processes which can help us to understand why and how bullying arises. There is an acceptance, in this intrapsychic perspective, that insights into early childhood development, in particular the mother-child relationship, can explain aspects of the adult psyche. (The term "mother" refers to the primary carer and is not necessarily the biological mother).

Various psychoanalytical theories explain the origins of the aggressive, inconsistent, and envious nature of bullies and why some individuals succumb to their attacks. Whilst describing the theories, an argument is developed for conceptualising bullying as a particularly perverse and pernicious form of projective identification.

Starting with the underlying dynamics of projection—the interplay between the life and death instincts and love and hate—we can begin to understand how bullying is so damaging. The rhythms of life and death go awry and "death" dominates in the form of psychic deadness. This concept helps us to appreciate an individual's ability, and inability, to reflect on his/her actions and the impact of those actions on others. When trying to survive at work, to cope with feelings of psychic deadness and with anxieties about their relationships with others, bullies can be seen to use the primitive defence known as splitting. This creates a polarised view of the world. Mediators, and others who attempt to resolve conflicts, often notice that the bullies accuse victims of being "the bully". The accusations of role reversal are explained through the concept of the paranoid-schizoid position. Another key dynamic underlying projective identification is the interplay of love and hate. In bullying this also goes awry. Hate creates a distance between bully and victim, a distance which bullies can exploit to their advantage.

Key concepts for understanding why some individuals lack resilience to being buffeted by the demands made by others are boundaries and containment. A description is given of how boundaries are first formed in the early years and how the nature of these boundaries influences future relationships. The concept "identification with the aggressor" shows how bullies may have been subject to aggression in childhood and how they continue, later in life, to act it out in the workplace. Having outlined the background theory to projective identification, this concept is explained along with its importance to understanding the intrapsychic processes of bullying. Finally, there is a description of the dynamics of envy, the main motive ascribed to bullies by victims.

The third section of the chapter brings together the theory on bullying and psychoanalytical theories to answer the following questions:

- Why do bullies bully?
- Why are some bullies more aggressive than others?
- How do they bully?
- Why do some bullies become victims and some victims become bullies?
- Why are some victims badly damaged by their experiences, whereas others are relatively unscathed?
- What can employees do to protect themselves against being bullied again?
- How can HR managers help targets and bullies?

Research review

What is bullying?

The noun "bully" has its origins in the sixteenth century Middle Dutch word "*boele*" when it was used as a term of endearment and familiarity, applied to either gender. It implied that the bully was a sweetheart, darling, or lover (Websters, 1986). In England, following the late medieval era the word "boele" meant a fine fellow" and "blusterer". By the mid-nineteenth century "bully" had taken on connotations of intimidation, threats, and an overbearing demeanour. "Bully" was used to mean a liar, pitiful wretch, unscrupulous individual, or someone to be feared. Today the noun "a bully" generally refers to "an aggressive person who intimidates or mistreats weaker people" (*Oxford Concise Dictionary*, 2004). However, remnants of the original and positive meaning of bully linger in the phrase "bully for you", which expresses approval for a daring action, whilst the Dutch meaning of "*boele*" has also evolved and today has diverse colloquial meanings referring to, for example, a person who has committed adultery, to live outside marriage, a darling, to cheat, to mislead, an executioner, a hangman, and an untidy mess.

In the workplace and in schools the term "bullying" covers a wide range of behaviours, extending from teasing to violent assault. The behaviours are usually categorised as overt and covert. Overt behaviours include physical threats and verbal abuse such as ridiculing and constant criticism. Covert actions of bullies include lying, spreading malicious rumours, and undermining performance at work by denying individuals information and access to basic materials to carry out their tasks effectively. Employees' workloads may be unmanageable, opinions and views ignored, and their tasks may have impossible targets and deadlines. Employees may be excessively monitored. Sudden changes to routines may be made which are unpredictable and appear illogical. Alternatively, procedures may be adhered to with such vehemence that the rigidity belies basic common sense especially when it is to the detriment of customers and colleagues. Individuals may also be excluded from the social group, sidelined by colleagues, scapegoated and isolated. Bullying effectively portrays targets as undesirables (Einarsen, 1999).

There is general consensus amongst researchers that bullying is not a one-off incident but occurs over a period of time. It is usually ongoing and escalatory.

Victims

The impact of bullying

Victims describe bullying behaviour as insulting, demeaning, patronising, humiliating, offensive, and aggressive (Keashley & Jatic, 2003).

Some victims express feelings of fear and dread. For example, a financial analyst in a multinational company said,

> Bullying is a continuous fear of failure which tends to develop into a very high anxiety state. You are continually concerned, far more than normal, that what you are doing is right, so you tend to exist in a state of constant anxiety, and fear.

A temp in a UK sales office said,

> Bullying is like being on a knife-edge of fear and dread. When you get up every morning and drive to work and you get that sinking feeling. When you get there and open the door—it swallows you up. The dread is almost worse than the experience. When you are away from the place you almost exaggerate it, whole weekends are spent dreading Monday—thinking about it all the time, imagining things.
>
> Bullying destroys your life. You can't relax, you can't enjoy yourself, you can't take pleasure in the things you used to enjoy because your whole life away from the place is spent thinking about the place and dreading going back.

A nurse in an NHS hospital described how a new colleague came into his ward and started changing things.

> He appeared to take an instant dislike to me for some reason. I just felt he was victimising me for some reason I couldn't understand. He made me feel quite on edge. I said good morning to him at first but he wouldn't say good morning. He would mutter something then straight away pick up the phone. The ten minutes handing over to him were hell because he wasn't listening. I felt that I shouldn't have been there.

Victims often feel powerless to do anything to help themselves and gradually become worn down. They tend not to like themselves, to worry, to feel unsafe and sad, and believe that others would be better off without them (Berthold & Hoover, 2000).

A theatre technician in an NHS hospital who was being bullied by her line manager described bullying as intimidating and degrading.

> It knocks your self-confidence and makes you feel worthless so you feel you can't do anything. It makes you hate yourself. It gives you a very negative feeling about yourself.

A teacher described the powerlessness of her situation when she said,

> You know you are mismanaging the situation; you are obviously not good enough. It's this feeling there is no way out. There is nothing you can do, you are just not good enough.

In the long term, hostile actions threaten a person's identity to the point where this is diminished (Einarsen & Mikkelsen, 2003). Employees targeted with workplace bullying liken themselves to vulnerable children, slaves, prisoners, and heartbroken lovers (Tracy, Lutgen-Sandvik, & Alberts, 2006). A victim described the long-term impact of bullying:

> "I'll never be the same again, never. It's like everything's been taken out of me, I mean esteem, I've got no self-esteem now like I used to. I think it is something you never get over". (Kelly, 1999, p. 78)

An employee in a social services department said,

> Bullying gets to the core of you. It's soul destroying. It eats, takes all. It erodes your confidence to the extent you don't know how to fight back.

Physical health often suffers too. Victims complain of headaches, feeling sick, disturbed sleep, palpitations, and loss of energy. Others experience stomach problems, aches and pains as well as panic attacks. Many become irritable, lack motivation, and have pent up feelings of anger. They may lose the ability to concentrate and become hypersensitive to situations. Some become emotionally exhausted (Agervold & Mikklesen, 2004).

A teacher, in her first teaching post, said,

> The final showdown was when I was called in to the head's office and given the sort of dressing down that might have been expected of an eleven-year-old kid who had done something really dreadful at home and whose parents were out to teach the child a lesson. The end result was that I was a complete quivering heap. She [the head teacher] completely and utterly demoralised me to the extent that I went home and a doctor had to be called. It was such a trauma that I have never stopped revisiting it. I don't think I understood it at the time and I have never lost wanting to understand it.

The effects of bullying behaviour do not end with the exit from the workplace. It is very difficult for some victims to turn off the intrusive thoughts, which researchers describe as "thought terror" (Leymann & Gustafsson, 1996). The threat is repeated or relived in some way, such as in nightmares (Tracy, Lutgen-Sandvik, & Alberts, 2006). Outcomes may also include posttraumatic stress disorder (PTSD) and general anxiety disorder (GAD). PTSD was first identified in war veterans when it was found that fight and flight instincts were constantly active, long after the threat had been removed. Levels of PSTD were found to be even higher for victims of bullying than those for train drivers who had run over and killed suicidal individuals (Leymann & Gustafsson, 1996).

Some victims describe bullying in terms of death, as a fight in which the target is "killed", "destroyed", or "annihilated" (Tracy, Lutgen-Sandvik, & Alberts, 2006). Others complain of feelings of deadness; for example, a deputy head teacher said,

> I feel so dead inside. It is as if part of me has died.

Long-term bullying is also linked to suicide and suicidal ideation (Leymann & Gustaffson, 1996; Mikkelsen & Einarsen, 2001). Children who had high levels of self-reported depressive symptoms at the age of eight were likely to be either bullies or victims at the age of sixteen (Souranda & Helsta, 2000). These researchers suggest that such depressive symptoms may reflect low self-esteem, immaturity, loneliness, and poor problem-solving skills.

The profile of the victim

A review of the research into the role of the personality of the victim shows a range of findings and viewpoints (Aquino & Thau, 2009). Some researchers suggest that any employee is vulnerable to becoming a victim (Einarsen, 1999; Thylefors, 1987). Little difference has been found between victims and other employees in terms of gender, age, and position within organisations (Hoel & Cooper, 2001). The destruction of the personality of the victims of workplace bullying is seen as a consequence of the bullying, rather than due to pre-existing personality factors (Leymann & Gustafsson, 1996).

Other researchers make clear links between experiences in early childhood and in school life. Bullying is the outcome of a complete pathway of influences that begins in the family and extends to bullying in the child's peer group (Smith & Ananiadou, 2003). A longitudinal study of bullying and victimisation found that almost all the boys who were victims at the age of sixteen had also been victimised at the age of eight (Sourander & Helsta, 2000). Among the girls, from this study, about half of those who were victims at age sixteen had been victims at the age of eight. No explanation is given for the gender difference; however, as the researchers associate victimisation with internalising problems and as girls traditionally discuss their emotions more openly than boys, it could be surmised that the girls may have found the help they needed to change their roles.

Other researchers suggest a link between childhood and adult life. Victims may have had experiences in childhood, or afterwards, which predispose them to being bullied in the workplace (Adams, 1992; Randall, 1997). They fail to develop resilience (Bowes, Maughan, Caspi, Moffitt, & Arseneault, 2010; Waddell 2007). Resilience refers to a relative resistance to environmental risk experience or the overcoming of stress or adversity (Rutter, 2006). A significant correlation has been found between victimisation and styles of parenting; parents of victims tend to be intrusive and demanding to such an extent that the children are offered little opportunity to control, or influence, social situations (Ladd & Kochenderfer-Ladd, 1998). Children who are brought up with a passive social orientation, and a restricted sense of autonomy, have little opportunity to practise assertive interpersonal skills. In schools, once bullying has become established, low levels of maternal warmth and lack of sibling support fail to buffer children from the negative outcomes of bullying (Bowes, Maughan, Caspi, Moffitt, & Arseneault, 2010). There is evidence that some victims come from over-protective families who may not help a child to develop assertive social skills and coping strategies to deal with minor teasing and provocations, thus making them more likely to become targets for bullying (Smith & Myron-Wilson, 1998). When children are not given the opportunity to play positive roles in family power games, they lack tactical awareness and have a naivety which may continue well into adulthood. For example, a victim accused of various misdemeanours, even though he felt that he had followed the rules and done the "right" thing, said,

> I didn't realise people deliberately tell lies until I was in my fifties.

The first report on the association between school and workplace bullying showed a significant relationship between roles in school bullying and the experience of workplace victimisation (Smith, Singer, Hoel, & Cooper, 2003).

> It is paradoxical that many of the adult victims of bullying who present themselves to me and to my colleagues for counselling keep saying, "I don't know how this could happen to me". Yet for the most part, they do have this understanding because that behaviour has been happening to them for years and goes back to childhood. (Randall, 1997, p. 89)

Workplace bullying is traumatic because it is unexpected and always perceived as undeserved and unjustified (Keashley & Neumann, 2005). It occurs when an employee's well-being is harmed by an act of aggression by a colleague and when fundamental psychological and physiological needs are unmet or thwarted. These needs include a sense of belonging and a feeling that the victim is a worthy individual, together with the belief that he/she has the ability to predict, and in some ways to control, his/her environment, and can trust others (Stevens & Fiske, 1995). At a deep level, bullying disrupts an individual's ontological security, including shaking or destroying important values and beliefs about the world in which we live (Lutgen-Sandvik, 2008).

Victims in the workplace tend not to use their internal power or identifiable resources to prevent abuse (Ishmael, 1999). They have been found to be submissive and non-controversial, preferring to avoid conflict rather than face up to it (Coyne, Siegne, & Randall, 2000). Victims are also often conscientious, traditional, dependable, and reserved, with a preference for quiet and familiar surroundings. Although this personality profile reflects someone who will be an easy target, it does not prove that personality is a cause of bullying (Coyne, Siegne, & Randall, 2000).

Adams (1992) refers to the placatory position of the victim and his/her masochistic behaviour in which the victim repeats a pattern of hurt, thereby recreating an earlier relationship with a parental figure.

A personal assistant to a senior executive in a large organisation said,

> My boss shouts at me. My father used to shout at me and if anyone shouts at me I am a wreck. She [her boss] treats me like a child. She has the ability to make me feel terribly inadequate and I know that I am an extremely adequate person in every other aspect of my life. When I go to the office in the morning, I am really charged up because I have a plan for the day and she walks in and she can just blow it out of the window. She can say one word to me and destroy me. But other people can come in and I don't experience that.

A former bank employee, recalling the bullying by her boss, said,

> I never believed I would be bullied but my boss was just like my mother.

Victims with a long history of victimisation have been found to be attacked more frequently than those with a shorter history (Einarsen & Skogstad, 1996). However, besides factors relating to childhood, bullies often pick on individuals who are different from their social group. Some employees may be at risk of being bullied at work due to social, demographic, or personal factors (Zapf & Einarsen, 2003). Characteristic of the behaviour of bullies is singling out individuals who are having difficulties in their lives such as a bereavement, caring for a sick child, or a home relocation (Crawford, 1999). Newcomers to organisations are particularly vulnerable to becoming victims (Rayner, 1997; White 1998). They are unfamiliar with working practices and may take time to understand the cultural norms and values and to adjust to their new roles.

Individuals with a disability are often targets of bullying. For example, high levels of bullying are found amongst children who stammer (Hugh-Jones & Smith, 1999). These researchers found that children, who experience "severe" bullying were over fifteen times more likely to report that this had affected their schoolwork than those who experienced only mild bullying. In a retrospective study of adults who stammered it was found that the majority had experienced bullying and reported long-term effects, predominately affecting personal relationships (Hugh-Jones & Smith, 1999).

A university lecturer, wheelchair-bound as a result of brittle bone disease, was bullied by a professor over a number of years. The professor referred to the lecturer, in front of other staff, as "hell on wheels". He got a colleague to sit in on her classes and mentor her, not to report on the quality of her work but for the professor to claim that her teaching was so bad that she needed an assistant with her. The results of the lecturer's teaching assessments were manipulated so that her strengths were ignored and the few weaknesses highlighted. When the question of tenure came up, staff colluded with the bully. However, with encouragement from her dean and family, she hired a lawyer with an interest in the rights of women and the disabled and successfully filed a grievance against the university which resulted in granting of tenure, albeit belatedly.

Other university staff are not so successful in gaining support and winning their cases. In a survey of bullying and harassment in UK universities only twenty-three per cent of cases were upheld, the conclusion being that no bullying or harassment had taken place (Academic, FOI, 2011).

Some victims spend many years and considerable amounts of money in trying to gain an apology from the workplace where they have experienced bullying. A few are successful in winning substantial amounts of compensation through the legal process. Those who demand an apology from bullies may bring further damage to their mental and physical health, and fighting for justice often contributes to an escalation of bullying (Zapf & Gross, 2001). Other employees who distance themselves from the situation, both physically and psychologically, have less long-term damage and are better able to move on.

Summary of characteristics of victims

The impact of bullying behaviour on individuals varies considerably. Some victims escape relatively unscathed whilst others are traumatised for years. Many are worn down, lose self-confidence and self-esteem. Amongst the research community there is little consensus on the role played by victims, with views ranging from the victim being a victim by chance, to the stance that the victim is vulnerable as a result of being different from the group or lacking in resilience as a result of childhood experiences. Evidence shows that some victims lack social awareness and the skills required to cope with the aggressive and negative behaviour displayed by a bully. Others may be distracted from the threats around them by personal issues originating from outside of the working environment. Fighting back can be successful, but can also lead to further conflict and increased stress for the victim, particularly if the bullying has become well-established.

Bullies

There is evidence, going back many years, that bullies in schools tend to come from dysfunctional families, in which there is little sense of love, support, and belonging (Rigby & Slee, 1991). It has been recognised that in these families violence may be common and discipline inconsistent (Olweus, 1993). Fathers who were aggressive, and had bullied others at school, are likely to have sons who are bullies (Farrington, 1993). Bullies are more likely than other students to spend time at home without adult supervision (Berthold & Hoover, 2000).

Bullies frequently see their families in terms of power relationships. It seems almost inevitable that a child who learns to perceive relationships in terms of battles for power will re-enact those power relationships in school (Smith & Myron-Wilson, 1998). Once established, early childhood patterns of behaviour continue throughout childhood. For example, aggressive attitudes among middle school students predict subsequent aggressive behaviour and bullying over the course of the school year (McConville & Cornell, 2003). About half the boys who bullied at the age of sixteen had bullied others at the age of eight. However, this pattern was not as pronounced amongst girls, as only one out of four girls who were bullies at the age of sixteen had bullied others when they were eight (Sourander & Helstela, 2000).

Direct links have been made between parental involvement with children and bullying. Inter-parental discord significantly lowers a child's self-confidence and heightens his/her chance of being involved in delinquent behaviour and becoming an instigator of peer conflict (Christie-Mizell, 2003). Lack of parental involvement contributes significantly, and independently, to bullying behaviour in adolescents (Flouri & Buchanan, 2003). These researchers found that, even after divorce, a father's ongoing involvement continues to protect against children externalising problems, for example, working out their angst on others. Involvement of fathers is even more important when the mother's involvement with the child is lacking. Yet, if a child has a higher self-concept, parental discord has less of an effect (Christie-Mizell, 2003).

Although bullies seem to get their "kicks" from bullying others, they have been found to be more unhappy at school than other students and report feeling alone (Forero, McLellan, Rissel, & Bauman, 1999). Bullies are more prone to depression and have higher levels of suicidal ideation than victims (Kaltiala-Heino, Rimpelä, Marttunen, Rimpelä, & Rantanen, 1999). Workplace bullies have been found to be high in social anxiety, low in social competence, and low in self-esteem (Einarsen, Raknes, & Matthieson, 1994).

Aggression

Children who feel ignored, or sidelined, by a parent figure, can develop a psychological strategy whereby aggression is an attempt to win love (Adams, 1992). The fury of being ignored, and getting no response, can provoke anger and this may be dealt with by getting at others. In adult life, bullying can be a continuation of this pattern and reflects an individual's fear that he/she is not lovable (Adams, 1992).

> "I would even go so far as to say that people deprived of love in childhood may have a greater need of power, or even a greater need to be famous where ambitions are linked to gaining power, to compensate for the powerlessness they felt as a child." (Adams, 1992, p. 74)

A significant difference was found between workplace bullies and non-bullies in terms of aggression, with bullies being significantly more competitive, assertive, and confrontational than non-bullies (Seigne, Coyne, Randall, & Parker, 2007). Workplace bullies tend to be dominant, defensive, and aggressive (Glasø, Nielsen, & Einarsen, 2009). One characteristic of bullies is their love of rules, possibly because the rules were broken for him/her when he/she was a child (Woods, 2006). A workplace supervisor, venting his anger on a subordinate, is an example of a bully's lack of emotional control (Zapf & Einarsen, 2003). For example, a financial analyst in a large multinational company described his boss as aggressive and extremely task-orientated. He said,

> The boss was so bull at a gate, almost uncontrollable. So much so, that he once came in to the office with his arm bandaged up where he had tried to cut a hedge with a flymo [a grass cutter].

Bullies show a lack of empathy (Seigne, Coyne, Randall, & Parker, 2007). They have a less sympathetic attitude towards victims than other employees and a higher approval of bullying behaviour in general (Ireland, 1999). Through interacting with an aggressive, dysfunctional family environment, children grow up to copy and "enjoy" aggression and perceive it as the norm. When aggressive tendencies have not been inhibited, the child does not develop the same awareness of right and wrong as other children (Johnson & Lewis, 1999).

A senior executive in a bank described her boss as an egomaniac. She said,

> Once he has decided something is to be a certain way and has recommended that to his boss, he is very determined that nothing should change that. He is determined he won't be shown to be wrong or be seen to have made a mistake even though he caused me ill health.

If an act of aggression or victimisation effectively produces a desired outcome, then bullies tend to see that act as justified (Arsenio & Lemerise, 2001). They are less aware than other children of the possible negative consequence of their solutions to social problem-solving situations. Compared to other students, bullies are more morally disengaged (Perren, Gutwiller-Helfenfinger, Malti, & Hymel, 2011).

One bully, a head chef, claimed: "If I can make a remark that puts someone down, it makes me feel powerful" (Adams, 1992, p. 89). "It certainly never occurred to me that I bullied anyone, although I did notice that one chef was so knocked flat after I'd had a go at him that I couldn't get any work out of him for the rest of the day. I'd see him shaking all right, but I didn't realise it would destroy him" (Adams, 1992, p. 88).

Bullying is less about ignoring or denying the feelings of those they are hurting and more about self-preservation (Sutton, Smith, & Swettenham, 1999). Using a set of stories to access the cognitions and emotions of seven-to-ten-year-olds, these researchers found that bullies performed well in understanding emotions in stories. This suggests that if bullies possess the skills to read the emotional responses of others, they could be at an advantage in avoiding detection, or choosing the most effective time to bully others. They could maximise victims' vulnerability and minimise the chance of hurt to themselves (Sutton, Smith, & Swettenham, 1999).

An administrator in a public sector organisation said,

> There have been incidents where the boss has ripped into an individual for better or worse and you think—wow! That shouldn't have happened. That was the wrong place at the wrong time. I got the feeling that it was done deliberately as a lesson to us all, almost as a public flogging. It was not only designed to chastise the individual but also to be an abject lesson to the rest of us.

Researchers in schools found that bullies conceptualise themselves as being superior and powerful and that they have a high opinion of themselves (Bjorkqvist & Osterman, 1999). Both boys and girls scored highly on dominance and idealising dominant behaviour, thereby wanting to be even more dominant than they thought they were (Bjorkqvist & Osterman, 1999). In the workplace a significant difference was found between bullies and non-bullies in terms of independence, indicating that they prefer to "go it alone" (Seigne, Coyne, Randall, & Parker, 2007).

The manager of a large project, and an overt bully, described how he could become stressed, not by the size of the task in hand, but by the calibre of his staff. He described them as

> sad people who burden him with silly hidden agendas ... They need to open their minds and see the world and behave better. I have to challenge them and their obsolete ideas. They carry baggage; I have no baggage. They are very slow. They are weak on business plans. My business plan is an exception. When they come across me there is a big clash. Some are still asleep. They believe they know everything but when put on the spot they blame everyone else. I could run with half the number provided I had a choice of who I had—but I inherited them.

Bullies often seem unable to make realistic judgments about the intentions of other people, at times viewing their intentions as hostile (Randall, 1997). In being motivated by revenge, they hold very favourable attitudes towards the use of violence and other forms of aggression to solve problems (Randall, 1997). Employees who had been accused of bullying others had little insight into the severity of their behaviours and reported feeling that the judgments against them were unfair and too harsh (Jenkins, Winefield, & Sarris, 2011). When bullies' needs conflict with those of others, they are willing to initiate intentional aggression that they would otherwise consider unacceptable, and yet, when the tables are turned and bullies are the targets of provocative behaviours, they appear to have the same concerns with moral intentions as their peers (Arsenio & Lemerise, 2001).

Inconsistency

Bullies are impulsive, follow their own urges, and are careless of social rules (Byrne, 1999). Targets of workplace bullying claim that bullying is like a game in which bullies create the rules and then change them without notice (Tracy, Lutgen-Sandvik, & Alberts, 2006). Bullies tend to have a Jekyll and Hyde character, charming to some individuals and evil to others (Adams, 1992). They are two-faced actors (Tracy, Lutgen-Sandvik, & Alberts, 2006).

A victim said, "In public she [the bully] would be really kind to me but on my own she was just horrible … I couldn't come to terms with the incongruity of it" (Kelly, 1999, p. 114).

Other employees describe their abrasive bosses as having favourites, being nice to superiors but treating others badly, having blacklists of colleagues, or being in the dog-house (Crawshaw, 2007).

These inconsistencies in behaviour create confusion and generate fear.

A financial manager in a public sector organisation said,

> My boss [a bully] wants to constantly see how people react to certain things and whether changing course has any impact or not. There is a general indecisiveness and even decisions are indecisive—that's a contradiction. The boss is one of the most decisive people I have worked for but there is vagueness to it as well. You get the headline but the detail behind that is not clear.

Staff of a production company dreaded visits by their managing director (MD). He picked on and lambasted employees over seemingly petty and often easily explained variations in procedures. On several occasions he singled out individual managers, took them outside, pinned them against the wall and spoke abusively to them. Yet on other occasions the MD would go over the top in praise of his employees. Staff dreaded his visits, not just because of his violent outbursts and aggression, but because his behaviour was unpredictable and inconsistent. They were constantly concerned about his mood swings. Due to his ownership of the company, this MD had few constraints on him to conform to legitimate controls. He could be confident that no one would challenge him, being in a position whereby he could easily "dispose" of his victims.

One victim made sense of her experiences of being bullied by equating it to the movie *The Matrix*, in which the main character lives in a dream world that is distinct from the real world where his oppressors live (Tracy, Lutgen-Sandvik, & Alberts, 2006).

Envy and jealousy

Envy is one of the most common reasons given by victims to explain the motives of bullies (Seigne, 1998; Vartia, 1996).

Bullying by a head teacher was triggered when one of her staff moved to a house which was bigger and more expensive than hers. The head teacher visited the house to give the teacher a moving-in present, but soon afterwards isolated the teacher from colleagues and became very critical of her work. The teacher was the third victim in that school in a case of serial bullying which continued until the head teacher lost her job.

Envy can lead to hostility if a victim's advantage in a situation is seen by bullies as unjust and unfair (Smith, Parrot, Ozer, & Moniz, 1994). Bullying is a kind of personal retaliation that can be explained as a self-regulatory mechanic of self-esteem protection (Zapf & Einarsen, 2003).

A theatre nurse described how her line manager began to psychologically bully her and then physically attacked her. She said,

> He didn't like the idea that I was so ambitious. He had been there a long time. The course I was doing was a management course. I wasn't on a management grade and he was. I think he felt jealous that I was doing this course and getting paid for it and taking the initiative.

Bullying can involve blocking a colleague's chance of promotion, the removal of opportunities of work for the victim, and plagiarism (Crawford, 1999). The aggressive nature of the theft leaves the person feeling vulnerable and invaded just as if one had been robbed (Crawford, 1999).

A university lecturer was undermined by a professor for fifteen years. Her ideas were stolen, lies were spread about her, and she was denied information and promotion opportunities. In trying to understand the motives of the bully, she said,

> She [the professor] was an only child and she felt that she was a disappointment [to her parents] that she wasn't a boy. She was very bitter about the public school system and she felt that English universities were run by ex-public school boys. There were a lot [of public school boys] in the department but she didn't pick on them, she picked on me [one of the few women). I found that incredibly bizarre. One lecturer thought it was jealousy. I was young, I was bright and somehow it was something about me. Far from being supportive of another woman, she seemed to make sure I was going to go through hell.

Bullies often pursue victims in a predatory manner, constantly watching and pursuing in a manner which, to the observer, seems obsessive and absurd. In cases of predatory bullying the victim has personally done nothing provocative that may reasonably justify the behaviour of the bully (Einarsen, Hoel, Zapf, & Cooper, 2003).

The MD of a large engineering company, a local lad who had risen through the ranks, was well known for his autocratic manner and bullying behaviour. Over a number of years he relentlessly bullied a junior colleague, who was much admired by colleagues for his talents. The junior had moved into the area and was from a very different background to the MD, was better educated and with an accent different to most of his fellow employees. Colleagues generally acknowledged that he had key skills essential for the organisation to develop yet the MD tried numerous ways to get him dismissed. A board member, recognising the potential difficulties this could cause to the company, intervened and had the junior employee moved to a subsidiary company. However, undeterred the MD continued his pursuit and relentlessly tracked him down. Eventually the talented employee left the organisation for another company, out of the area.

Summary of the characteristics of bullies

From the research, a picture emerges of a bullies as individuals whose behaviour can range from being very aggressive to very covert. Overt bullying, such as aggression, appears to be an attempt to "kill off" others as quickly as possible. Envy, a key motive of bullies according to victims, is more likely to occur over a period of time and is about identifying with the talents of others, stealing and spoiling them. The characteristic of inconsistency generates confusion and fear in others.

Psychoanalytical theory: intrapsychic processes

In this section we look beneath the dramas described above to reveal the unconscious and subconscious processes involved. The following theories describe why and how bullies bully and how some individuals become victims. Three key concepts form the foundation of an understanding of the root causes of the behaviour by both bullies and victims. These are: the life and death instincts; love and hate; and boundaries and containment. A further three concepts are introduced. These are: identification with the aggressor; projective identification; and envy.

Life and death

To understand the roots of bullying we need to look at the very early stages of development of the intrapsychic processes: the first few weeks of life. This is a time when individuals are primarily concerned with survival. The newborn baby's emotions and his/her view of the world are largely unintegrated and the ego is in a state of constant flux (Benjamin, 1988). Emotional states oscillate from one extreme to another. There are blissful times, after being fed, but then hunger returns as a vicious attacking presence inside. These states are interspersed with sleep, an essential time of rest in a period of rapid growth. Being totally dependent on others, it is through crying that the baby signals his/her distress, need for feeding, and preservation of life.

In these early stages there is an ongoing life-and-death struggle. This struggle has traditionally been understood in terms of biological forces, a life instinct and a death instinct. Death instincts strive towards the reduction of tensions with the aim of taking the living to an inorganic state (Laplanche & Pontalis, 1967). Life instincts, on the other hand, preserve existing forms and create new ones (Laplanche & Pontalis, 1967). Until we are faced with potential death and trauma for ourselves, we tend to be unaware of how our life and death instincts operate.

Life and death instincts never lose their independent existences but act simultaneously and co-operate with each other in a wide variety of ways (Eigen, 1996).

> Life feeds on death and death on life. Life deflects death outward for a time. Ambition, the will to power and mastery, sadism and destructiveness, are some indications of variable life-death drive fusions. Life holds death captive, directs its attention toward objects, and makes death want things, persons, places, positions. It is as if life attracts death's interest, fascinates death, and busies death with diversions. The deception, masquerade, and rerouting take effort. Systems wear themselves out by the working of sustaining them. One dies, in part, from exhaustion. (Eigen, 1996, pp. 6–7)

The implication of deadness, in Eigen's terms, is not just a physical death but also a psychic death. It is the sort of death, and feelings of deadness, which victims of bullying describe, as in the review above—"*I feel so dead inside.*" From time to time we all experience feelings of deadness within, but these are generally balanced by the life instinct which enlivens those feelings and takes us out of a state of depression.

Within our psyches, the degree of deadness varies. In some individuals it does not consume much psychic space, others have pockets of deadness that are relatively constant and hence they become used to living with areas of deadness (Eigen, 1996). However, for some people the sense of deadness is pervasive. Pervasive deadness occurs when the life-death interplay, the rhythm of life, goes awry. Energy can no longer flow along the neurological pathways and the capacity to reflect, to play, to make associations, and to develop a sense of reality is lost. Individuals who lack psychic space also lack the ability to access their feelings. When deadness is pervasive, it is as if "the music" of the psyche has been turned off. Death works by sucking life away. Eigen (1996) describes how this occurred within one of his patients. "It was as if she had to stay alive until there was nothing more for death to eat" (Eigen, 1996, p. 7).

A damaged psyche tries to reconstruct itself but images, and narratives, lead nowhere. The unconscious may not be able to heal itself (Bollas, 1997).

The literature on bullying suggests that bullies and victims have higher level of depressive tendencies than others. Suicidal ideation is higher among victims and bullies compared with non-victims and non-bullies: however, suicidal ideation was found to occur most often amongst the bullies (Kaltiala-Heino, Rimpelä, Martunen, Rimpelä, & Rantanen, 1999). From these findings we may imply that bullies and victims lack a healthy interplay of the life and death instincts and have relatively high levels of psychic deadness. When under stress their working lives could become a life and death struggle, a fight for survival.

Splitting

One of the main causes of pervasive deadness is constant splitting (Eigen, 1996).

"Splitting means precisely that; splitting of an 'object', be that a person, a value, or a concept, into two different parts that are exclusively identified as 'good' and 'bad'" (Stapley, 2006, p. 56).

In the first few weeks of life a baby's spatial awareness is limited. At this stage, the baby has no cohesive picture of his/her carers. The mother appears split into parts, for example, into breasts, face, and hands. These parts are very, very good when they are present and take good care of the baby, and they are very, very bad when they fail. The baby perceives his/her mother as being either very good in providing nourishment and security, or being very bad and responsible for painful hunger pangs.

Splitting is the most natural way of dealing with the world at the earliest stage of development (Stapley, 2006). As such, it is described as a primitive defence against anxiety.

The splitting between highly idealised objects on the one hand and totally bad ones on the other, helps all of us to organise our earliest experiences. The term "splitting" is also used to refer to the splitting of the ego into good or bad, and/or fragmentation of the ego. The good "objects" and good parts of ourselves are kept within us and we rid ourselves of those which are bad—such as anger and frustration—and project them outwards. This is known as *projection*. Projection is the thrusting forth into another person or group of an individual's unconscious wishes and ideas that would be painful if accepted as part of the self (Stapley, 2006). It occurs in psychic processes throughout life, not just in the early years.

Just as there needs to be a balance between the life and death instincts, so there also needs to be a balance to projections. The infant cannot just continue to project feelings outwards. He/she has to preserve feelings of safety and well-being and take in good experiences so that there is a feeling they belong. This is known as *introjection*. It is the taking in, at an unconscious and subconscious level, of "an object"—that "object" being a quality of another person, such as dependability.

Difficulties arise when splitting proliferates. This leads to "impoverishment of the ego" and dispersal of emotions resulting in a lack of emotion and unresponsiveness known as psychic deadness (Eigen, 1996). Over time an individual may get used to feeling fragmented and severed from him/herself. He/she may hold on to splitting because of its unconscious connection to emotional life, either trying to capture and make contact with the emotions being dispersed, or annihilating contact with emotional life, or even both (Eigen, 1996).

Bullies often use splitting as a defence against anxiety. They tend to perceive their world in terms of good and bad, wanting to keep the goodness for themselves and projecting their feelings of badness outwards onto others. By projecting their "bad" feelings, such as a fear of failing, on to others, they confirm to themselves at an unconscious level that those receiving the projections are "failures". At a conscious level bullies set about reaffirming their negative perceptions of a victim by denigrating him/her with constant criticism, denial of information, and other undermining bullying activities.

However, the projection only gives a temporary release of anxiety and if splitting proliferates, it leads to further impoverishment of the ego and dispersal of emotions. Psychic deadness limits space for reflection. Where there is a lack of intrapsychic rhythms within the mind, a rigidity of thought develops along with fixed perceptions.

In the most aggressive forms of bullying, the fear of death becomes overwhelming; there is a life-and-death struggle, a fight for survival. Death instincts are turned outwards, towards the outside world, in the form of rage and overt attacks on others. These actions are deflections of a "force" that would otherwise consume the self and one's body. Whilst aggression is biologically built into human beings as a reaction to danger, in self-preservation violence (such as we find in bullying) the aim is to negate the danger and to remove its sources, the fate of the victim being irrelevant (Perelberg, 1999).

Paranoid-schizoid position

When the death instinct is projected outwards, this is not the end of the baby's problems, nor, indeed, those of a bully. The next stage in the development of the baby is known as the paranoid-schizoid position, a Kleinian term. The leading anxiety is paranoid, the fear of an external persecutor. It is schizoid because the state of the ego and its "object", usually the mother, is characterised by the splitting.

Traditionally, in psychoanalysis, this stage is described in terms of the "good breast" and the "bad breast". As explained above, when faced with anxiety the ego splits itself and projects that part of it which contains the death instinct outwards into an object, which for the baby, in his/her early stages, is the mother's breast.

> Thus, the breast, which is felt to contain a great part of the infant's death instinct, is felt to be bad and threatening to the ego, giving rise to a feeling of persecution. In that way, the original fear of the death instinct is changed into fear of a persecutor. (Segal, 1973, p. 25)

At the same time as the death instinct is projected outwards, the life instinct is projected into the "good breast". This occurs to create "an object" which will satisfy the ego's instinctive striving for life as the baby needs to feel loved both by an external object (the mother) as well as the internal good "object". The integration of these two objects gives rise to feelings of being alive, being loved, and capable of loving others.

In the evolution of thought over the years about the paranoid-schizoid position, there has been an appreciation of the further complexities of the interplay of life and death. Whereas Klein explicitly ties anxiety to the death instinct, Eigen (1996) suggests that anxiety can float freely between death and life. For those who lack the feeling of feelings, anxiety may be enlivening, yet it is also the case that many individuals with high levels of psychic deadness cannot bear any rise of emotion, including anxiety (Eigen, 1996).

When under stress, a bully projects his/her anxieties, such as a fear of failure, outwards onto a target. The bully then takes action, for example, denying the victim information to carry out his/her work, in order to reinforce the perception that those feelings now reside in that "object", the victim. However, if the bully is particularly anxious, he/she fears the return of those projections. As the victim cannot be trusted to keep the projections, he/she has to be controlled and monitored.

Mediators are often faced with bullies who claim that they are the victims. This role reversal, although puzzling, is an example of the paranoid-schizoid dynamic. The bully perceives, at an unconscious and subconscious level, that his/her "badness" resides in the victim and becomes paranoid about it returning in a persecutory manner. In the mind of the bully, the victim is then perceived as being threatening. As the bully lacks the ability to reflect on his/her feelings, perceptions become fixed and the victim appears, in the mind of the bully, to turn into the aggressor.

Love

> Love is not just a feeling or a discharge of energy, but an emotional orientation to the world. That orientation demands that the world present itself to us as worthy of our love. That is for the world to be lovable. (Lear, 1998, p. 153)

During the second quarter of the first year of a baby's life, the life-death struggle diminishes. The young child increasingly relates to the world in terms of feelings and begins to recognise his/her agency. Although the baby begins to develop his/her own likes and dislikes, he/she is still very dependent upon a caring figure for protection, and introduction to the surroundings and to his/her own emotionality. The mother's function at this time of absolute dependence mainly involves keeping the baby safe from unpredictable and traumatic events and meeting the baby's physiological needs by appreciating how the baby is feeling (Piontelli, 1985). The baby's inner world gradually emerges based on a broadening experience of the world together with concurrent neurological development.

As the splitting, which has so far ordered the baby's psyche, lessens, the baby becomes aware that feelings of love and hate come from the same person, the mother. The baby is now faced with an ambivalence—he/she loves and hates at the same time. It is at this stage that introjected love can bring stability to the ego. In healthy relationships there is a greater emphasis on introjecting good things into the internal world, replacing the impulse to project bad things out. This is known as the *depressive position*. (To the reader unfamiliar with psychoanalytical concepts, this term may be confusing, as it has little to do with "depression" as widely used in society).

> With the decline in reliance on projection there is a greater opportunity for awareness of the state of the internal world and, in turn, of the external world—the first entails acknowledging unwelcome aspects of oneself; the latter entails recognising the better qualities of the external world. (Hinselwood, 1991, p. 144)

In the life-death and love-hate interplay of a nurturing environment, the good "object" is introjected and integrated into feelings of self. When a good "object", which loves and protects the self and is loved and protected by the self, is established within, then a basis is created for trust in one's own goodness. This is the foundation for self-confidence and self-esteem. Winnicott (1971) describes this as a "good-enough mother within".

> I would suggest that a securely established good object, implying a securely established love for it, gives the ego a feeling of riches and abundance which allows for an outpouring of libido and projection of good parts of the self into the external world without a sense of depletion arising. The ego can then also feel that it is able to re-introject the love it had given out, as well as take in goodness from other sources, and thus be enriched by the whole process. In other words, in such cases there is a balance between giving out and taking in, between projection and introjection. (Klein, 1955, p. 144)

Freud tells us little about love, but implicit in Freud's emerging thought was the idea that love pulls us in two directions (Lear, 1998). First, there is a regressive force by which we yearn to re-establish a previously existing unity. Second, there is a creative force working in the opposite direction and seeking something new. Lear (1998) elaborates on these two forces with reference to the myth of Aristophanes and to the thoughts of Diometa in Plato's *Symposium* (Hamilton & Cairns, 1961).

Aristophanes' myth describes how humans are descended from hermaphroditic creatures, cut in half by Zeus to curb their wild behaviour. According to the myth, we all long for our other half so we can heal the wounds of human nature. Love, the name for desire and pursuit of wholeness, impels us to abolish the boundaries with others and restore a lost unity. As love is regressive, there is a tendency for us to return to earlier stages at which we have received gratification and love, and the unity that an individual is thereby impelled to seek is with his/her own past (Lear, 1998).

This regressive force, however, is balanced by a creative one. Love also pulls in the opposite direction to higher, more differentiated, unities so that life can be prolonged and brought to higher development. Socrates' teacher, Diotema, introduces the idea of platonic love, which starts with an appreciation of beauty in a human being, leading upward to spiritual and universal love. Diometa also adds to Aristophanes' concept by suggesting that love is directed neither at the half, nor the whole, unless that part turns out to be "good". Love is the need to get hold of "good" and possess it forever, creating images of virtue and immortality like those of the gods. As Lear (1998) argues, a human is not divine and not immortal and so love's desire is frustrated. Propagating upon the beautiful, both in body and in soul, is the best effort mortal humans can make to achieve their immortal aim.

We can assume, from the research review, that bullies and victims may have lacked the love of adult caring figures in their early years. They failed to develop a capacity to love themselves. Victims, who had their feelings repressed in childhood, are driven by their search for love to try to create new relationships, a wholeness, but in doing so, repeat the patterns of their earlier relationships. With a lack of agency in childhood, a restricted sense of autonomy, and practice in taking control and influencing others, they relate to those who challenge them by behaving submissively. Bullies are also on a search for the love they were denied in childhood but, based on their early experiences of power games, they see relationships in terms of achieving what they desire at the expense of others. They lack empathy. When attempting to attain "immortality", like the gods, workplace bullies may become obsessed with personal targets and financial gains as objects of their affections, rather than working with others to collectively achieve results. The personal needs come to the fore (Thylefors, 1987).

Hate

In our desire to love, and to be loved, we face a dilemma. One of the paradoxes of love is that we can only develop emotionally and become fully individuated selves within an intimate relationship (Mann, 2002). Love is risky, as it closes down the psychological distance between individuals and involves a type of dependency which can feel too threatening and bring pain and frustration (Mann, 2002).

> The problem with love, one might say, is that it necessarily stirs up hate too. To love someone is to depend on them, and therefore to hate them when they frustrate us, as they inevitably do, and to hate the fact of our dependence. (Gottlieb, 2002, p. 68)

Hate creates distance from others and erects barriers against the potentially destructive nature of intimate contact with the other. It is more persevering than anger, which tends to be transient. Although it creates a space between individuals, hate also enables the individual to keep contact with others since it still maintains a passionate connection. It offers an intensity of experience, enlivening the deadness within. Hate revitalises and galvanises and gives the ego a sense of strength (Hoggett, 2001). Yet when hatred binds the individual to the hated object there is no getting beyond the wish for vengeance, the wish to destroy the object. Christopher Bollas (1985) coined the term "loving hate", which describes a situation where an individual preserves a relationship that can only be felt to exist where love would seem to be unavailable, such as that characterised by abuse or neglect.

This perversity can be seen in the bully–victim relationship. A victim may prefer being hated to being ignored or abandoned. Unable to access his/her own feelings, perhaps as a result of a repressed childhood, he/she is unable use hate towards others in a constructive defence. On the other hand, a bully uses hate to create a distance between him/herself and the "hated" object, the victim.

Returning to the baby, as he/she begins to perceive the mother as a whole, there is a greater awareness that the mother is separate and not under the baby's control. The baby may also feel anxious that his/her hatred and attacks on the "bad" mother have damaged, or destroyed, her. His/her dread now is not of the annihilation of his/her own self, as it was in the paranoid-schizoid position, but rather of loss of the good object, the mother, because of his/her hatred and imagined attacks on her. This loss poses a devastating threat to his/her fragile sense of security, particularly as the baby now feels responsible for hurting or damaging the mother. This can feel catastrophic because his/her whole sense of well-being now depends upon the persecution of the loved mother in the external world and the good object in his/her internal world. The baby feels guilty.

Guilt has numerous tones to it, strung out along the spectrum from mourning, reparation, and pained remorse, to horrendous and persecuting punishment. The ability to cope with this range of emotions depends on whether or not the child felt loved and securely held. If the child felt unloved those emotions will resurface throughout life, as described in the section on loss and mourning in Chapter Four. The child who feels loved may feel full of guilt and remorse but will be able to strive to make things better, to repair and restore the loved object within him/herself. When the child reaches this stage, he/she is said to have attained the depressive position. This is when the object is loved in spite of its bad parts.

Attaining the depressive position is a developmental step. It is also an uncertain one, as it can be a lifelong task. When challenging events in life are encountered, even those from a nurturing background, who have developed inner feelings of love and care, may find themselves regressing and holding polarised perspectives. However, where there is psychic space, rather than psychic deadness, these individuals will ponder their thoughts and feelings and consider alternatives. Adults who felt anxious and unloved in childhood are less likely to cope with painful feelings of loss and the potential fear of punishment and retaliation, and may more easily regress to the paranoid-schizoid position.

Within times of change and upheaval in the workplace we all become anxious to some degree. Excessive and continual change, extreme expectations from others, and inconsistency, can easily tip the most stable of us out of the depressive position and trigger a struggle within us to contain and manage our emotions. Those employees who become bullies are likely to feel particularly insecure at these times and to split their world into good and bad. Hate helps them to distance themselves from others and from their unwanted aspects of themselves. The victim can be destroyed without conscious feelings of guilt.

Boundaries and containment

These two concepts help us to understand how some individuals are resilient to the stresses imposed by other employees and generated from within the cultures and structures of the workplace, whilst other employees are more vulnerable.

To understand how some individuals are able to set boundaries for themselves and are able to contain and work through their own anxieties whilst others have difficulties with these actions, we need to go back to a time before a child is born, to the foetus. Within the mother's body, the foetus experiences the close and sustained support, and at-oneness, with the muscular and containing object, the uterus. However, at birth the baby loses that container and protection and is exposed to the outside world.

The baby needs to develop an equivalent emotional skin or boundary of his/her own. To do this the mother needs to provide a range of sense-based nurturing feedback responses, experiences that can be introjected, or internalised, to shape a contact barrier or boundary. The baby then gradually acquires that very capacity for containment that was initially the function of the mother. Within a nurturing environment the child is able to develop a sense of his/her own reality and boundaries and has, in Winnicott's terminology "a good-enough mother" within (Winnicott, 1971). He/she develops permeable boundaries and can begin to distinguish his/her internal reality and the external world as being different.

However, when a mother is emotionally unreceptive and unable to process the introjections and projections from the baby, she fails to accept, absorb, and transform the baby's experiences into meaningful ones. Her baby is likely to form weak boundaries and be overwhelmed by his/her experiences of the world. The baby will be unable to develop any proper psychic holding capacity and hence will be unable to form a clear identity of him/herself. Without proper boundaries, or a containing skin, the baby lacks a personal filtering or selection system. New experiences, people, and events challenge the young child and throw him/her into confusion, disintegration, and bewilderment.

When boundary formation is not based on the introjections of a loving carer, the child may develop various defences, such as using physical rather than psychic objects for containment. The baby, or young toddler, may come to be over-reliant on physical objects to hold him/her together. For example, in a long-term study of two infants, Piontelli (1985) describes how the children protested with screams when a coat, or other clothing, had to be removed; it seemed as if they were losing their own skins. These children not only lacked the introjections of "good objects", there was also the absence of any receptive interested objects, such as the mother, to contain their projections The children resorted to their own bodies and bodily resources to hold themselves together in the absence of any parental caring figure inside them. With defective and leaking boundaries, which possessed no binding strength and offered no protection or containment, evacuation through the skin or through different orifices, for example, dribbling, or escape into flaccidity, seemed to be the most common ways of the children seeking comfort at the bodily level (Piontelli, 1985).

By the time these children were around two years of age, it was clear that they found it difficult to cope with life and, in particular, with change. "Living proofs of ongoing life, such as novelties, change and the presence of other people, were resented and 'attacked'" (Pointelli, 1985, p. 118). Both children looked for the known and the foreseen and went over the same old things again and again.

When boundaries continue to be weak into adult life, individuals can feel overwhelmed or flooded by energy, stimuli, drives, emotions and ideas from their external world. In response to massive flooding, an individual may shut down (Eigen, 1996). It is as if the psycho-organisation short circuits, turns off, being unable to bear its sensitivity and the blankness of too much is replaced by the blankness of nothing. Instead of too alive, we have "too dead" (Eigen, 1996).

It can be hypothesised that both bullies and victims lacked the emotional nurturing needed to form clear boundaries in childhood. They are easily overwhelmed by anxiety-provoking situations, such as changes in their working environments. Unrealistic attachments to objects, particularly to workplace tasks and goals, may be used as a means of containing anxieties. Bullies are often excessively target-driven. Victims are usually described as very conscientious and very thorough in their work; they try very hard to please others.

Potential victims, those who had little preparation in childhood for the rough and tumble of working life, find the aggressive and unpredictable nature of bullying traumatic. Their weak boundaries are easily broken and they find a bully's projections overwhelming. Lacking inner resources, unable to access "hate" and psychic space for reflection, they find it difficult to fight back.

Further theories: identification with the aggressor

Anna Freud (Freud, A., 1936), following up her father's work on projection, first demonstrated the impact of introjection of an aggressive figure in childhood in her theory, describing it as "identification with the aggressor". This theory helps us to further understand the origin of aggressive behaviours of bullies.

Again we return to early childhood experiences to get to the roots of our understanding. When a young child feels loved and securely held, a "good-enough mother" is established within him/her; the child's boundaries are not rigid, nor too open to external influences, but permeable, allowing for a balance of life and death instincts, love and hate, and introjections and projections. However, when a child lacks love and support from parents, he/she develops weakened boundaries and is likely to be overly influenced by parental figures, particularly those who show aggression and maliciousness. By introjecting external criticism, the child internalises aggression. Later when he/she feels overanxious in a given situation or threatened by others, this aggression may re-emerge. By impersonating the early aggressors and assuming their attributes, the child or adult transforms him/herself from the person threatened into the person who makes the threat (Freud, A., 1936).

For example, a child of fourteen months was observed to copy and blindly follow a tyrannical leader or any potential, or actual, persecutor (Piontelli, 1985). With a lack of clear boundary-setting and an inability to contain and work through his anxieties, this child was trying both to give in to, and to give himself up to, the tyrant so as to placate and avoid a further and possibly worse outcome (Piontelli, 1985). This child achieved a kind of illusory unity with the tyrant in a way which was all-powerful but, in a sense, he also lost himself. "Thus, abused children may become abusing parents. In the same way, abused workers may become abusing managers and leaders when they take on those roles" (Stapley, 2006, p. 54).

Projective identification

Our understanding of projection and introjection is elaborated further through the concept of projective identification. This brings together the theories above—life and death, and love and hate—to show, in more detail, the dynamic nature of the intrapsychic processes involved in bullying. Here we reach the key dynamic in the psychic processes of bully and victim.

Projective identification is a mode of communication through which we make ourselves understood (Ogden, 1992). We all use it. It evolves from a baby's early attempt to perceive, organise, and manage his/her internal and external experiences and to communicate with his/her environment (Rosenfeld, 1987). Because a young baby cannot verbalise feelings, he/she must induce those feelings in the mother. The mother introjects the baby's projections, provides containment for them and, in a healthy relationship, relays them back to the baby in a way which can be understood and valued. There is a projective-introjective flow. At an unconscious level good, or bad, aspects of the self can be identified with good, or bad, aspects of the object, and good, or bad, aspects of the object (mother) can be identified with good, or bad, aspects of the self. An array of psychic possibilities emerges in the introjection-projection dynamic (Eigen, 1996).

Projective identification describes the way in which one person makes use of another person to experience and contain an aspect of him/herself (Ogden, 1992). Essentially, it is that capacity to put oneself into another person's shoes, the earliest form of empathy (Segal, 1973). In healthy relationships projective identification is a pathway for change. When an individual is struggling with his/her feelings, these are processed by an "other" and then made available for re-internalisation in an altered but comprehensible form. The projector and the recipient of the projective identification are able to experience a range of personal meanings which make sense as they grow as individuals. This is the basis of good communication.

There are three phases in the development of the dynamics of projective identification (Ogden, 1992). First, there is a defensive phase in which an individual wishes to get rid of parts of the self, either because that part threatens to destroy the self from within, or because the part is in danger of attack by other aspects of the self. That part must be safeguarded by being held inside an "other". This serves to create a sense of distance from an unwanted, or endangered, part of the self while in unconscious fantasy keeping that aspect of oneself "alive" in another individual.

For example, a bully who gets behind with work and is anxious about reaching his/her targets will deny his/her own unbearable thoughts and feelings and project them on to others to find a suitable container for them.

In the second phase of projective identification, the individual who is projecting his/her anxieties exerts pressure on the recipient to experience and behave in a way congruent with the unconscious projective fantasy.

Unwanted feelings of anger, or hatred, projected outwards by the bully, are then seen in the victim and are quietly disowned. To ensure that the projections remain "outside" of the self and in the victim, the victim is set up to fail and is constantly monitored and controlled. This ensures that the unwanted parts of the self are kept alive in the other.

In the third phase the recipient experiences him/herself, in part, as he/she is pictured in the projective fantasy. In reality, however, what the recipient experiences is a new set of feelings differing in some ways from those which are projected. They may approximate those of the projector but they are not identical, as the recipient has his/her own feelings and interpretation of the introjections based on past experiences.

In bullying the victim may experience, for example, feelings of failure projected onto him/her. These feelings may also resonate with early childhood experiences such as those involving a repressive or aggressive parent.

When unhealthy relationships develop, as in bullying scenarios, the projective identification processes become stuck, or gridlocked. In her study of dysfunctional relationships between couples, Morgan (2004) refers to situations in which projective identification is used excessively and intrusively so that the other's separate psychic existence is denied. There is a lack of fluidity within the psyches of both individuals which is necessary in order to be receptive to the return of projected aspects of the self. Morgan (2004) describes this stuckness as projective gridlock.

To summarise, in applying the theory of projective identification to bullying, it would appear that in the early stages of bullying, the bully projects his/her badness onto a target. The bully keeps the unwanted parts of him/herself alive within that individual. This is achieved by exerting pressure on the target to experience these feelings on his/her behalf. If the target has weak boundaries, those feelings are introjected and the target then becomes a container for them, that is, a victim.

As the bullying dynamic develops there is a loss of psychic rhythms. Perceptions of the victim become fixed. The bully, who projects, for example, feelings of incompetence, perceives them in the victim. The victim is then blamed, for example, for failure and is not good enough. Projective gridlock becomes established and the relationship becomes "stuck". The pathway for change is blocked.

If the stuckness is to be released, some form of external containment of anxieties is needed for both bully and victim. This could involve intervention by HR to set very firm boundaries for the bully. As many victims feel traumatised, they need to talk about their experiences, preferably with someone who is trained to listen and to help them work through high levels of anxiety, for example, a counsellor or psychotherapist. With the skilled help of a consultant trained in understanding the group dynamics, as described in Chapter Three, the team, or group of employees, can work together to establish clearer boundaries and also offer some containment for both bully and victim.

Envy

Envy, a particularly malicious form of projective identification, is often regarded as the most destructive of emotions. "Envy is the angry feeling that another person possesses and enjoys something desirable—the envious impulse being to take it away or to spoil it" (Klein, 1957, p. 181).

Most of us have an envious side. Some of us have it in a larger or smaller measure than others. As the relation to the "good" object is deeply rooted, envy, jealousy, and greed can arise even in adults who have been loved and cared for in childhood. Feelings of envy are, however, usually transient. The good object, essential for gratitude and trust, is regained time and again. The individual who can ungrudgingly enjoy another's creative work and happiness is spared the torment of envy.

Envy can arise with actual, or perceived, deprivation or misfortune. The greater the inner need for support and attention, the more hostility is directed against the person who withholds help, or is directed towards those who are perceived to be better off, such as colleagues who have been offered training, a bonus, or promotion. The success, or attributes, of another person seem to throw into bitter relief the seeming absence of these qualities in the envious onlooker, and the other person has to be made to pay for arousing these corrosive feelings (Kane, 2008). When envy is excessive, there is a regression to the paranoid-schizoid position (Klein, 1957).

When envy is tied to the death instinct, the envious person unconsciously projects the unwanted parts of him/herself on to the other, thereby using the other as a container. The qualities of another are taken and spoilt. This can involve malicious aggression. When goodness is destroyed it is no longer felt to be good and therefore can be discarded.

Within the workplace a key factor in envy is ambition and failure to fulfil it. For example, a manager may envy the success of a new young employee who is conscientious, well-liked by colleagues and clients, and is eager to succeed. Envy is shown by the manager's contempt for the young employee's training, ideas, and enthusiasm. This results in the new employee's achievements being undermined and destroyed and the potential loss of a valued employee.

When anxiety is tied to the life instinct there is a need to invest in an image, or ideals. In the process of identifying with the other, the envious person may have an initial dependency on him/her, particularly someone who seems to be superior. This does not necessarily occur in terms of hierarchy, but in possession of a gift or talent, of that which is desirable. However, by investing in an "ideal" of the self, or of the other, there is a fear of not living up to those ideals and being let down. The potential for shame develops. The idealised object is much less integrated in the ego than the good object, since it stems more from persecutory anxiety and less from the capacity for love. If the envious individual puts someone he/she admires on a pedestal, the object of admiration may be felt to be sufficiently different so as to be out of reach of envy. This attempt to safeguard the other from spoiling envy is, however likely to fail—for the more the other is idealised the more envy he/she is likely to arouse in the long run (Salzberger-Wittenberg 1970). Over time, envy can, at an unconscious level, kill the object that the individual, or even an organisation, has come to depend on.

For example, envy can create problems in succession planning within an organisation. When the image of individuals is very much tied up with maintaining their status, each promising newcomer may be initially welcomed and even idealised. However, over time he/she may be seen to be not good enough, undermined, and rejected. Spoiling envy has the potential to create impasses within organisations and to generate stagnation.

When envy is persistent it spoils the capacity for enjoyment and gratitude. The envious individual fears that whatever is offered will be withheld or destroyed. He/she cannot enjoy the happiness of others without feeling sour. To avoid envy he/she may unconsciously choose colleagues who are not up to his/her standards. Such an individual may be capable of great devotion to others as long as they remain inferior, or worse off in some way than him/herself. Then they can be easily "disposed of" because they are "not good enough". Alternatively, he/she may defend against envy through confusion by not knowing whether what is offered is good or bad. The envious person is difficult to please and tends to find fault with everything that anyone tries to do for him/her. "It could be said that the very envious person is insatiable, he can never be satisfied because his envy stems from within and therefore always finds an object to focus on" (Klein, 1957, p. 182).

Envy undermines the very foundations on which good relationships are built—such as trust, cooperation, gratitude, and love. Deep despair is felt about the inability to love and be loveable and this in turn fuels jealousy that others enjoy better relationships. Whereas envy is bilaterally orientated—person to thing, or person to quality—jealousy involves a triangular relationship—person to person about someone else (Berke, 2012). It involves more than two individuals, and it lies in our perception that there is an "other" who might succeed in connecting with others where we have failed (Mollon, 2002).

Jealous individuals tend to be self-deprecating and dogmatic, unhappy, anxious, and externally controlled. This state unleashes obsessive feelings of unworthiness and inferiority as well as attacks on anyone who arouses self-loathing. Jealousy can erupt violently, often without warning, brutally trampling on feelings of love and trust (Mollon, 2002). The effects can be traumatising for the one to whom it is directed, particularly when a bully has quietly undermined a colleague behind his/her back to senior staff but has generally kept up a reasonably pleasant facade with the victim. By the time the victim finds out about the lies and deceit it may be too late to rescue his/her reputation within the organisation.

With the increasing need for team-based projects, greater engagement with others, and networking skills in the workplace, as described in Chapter Four, there are also greater opportunities for jealousy and envy to arise. Envious bullies are unable to value others. Whatever is offered is insufficient as he/she is insatiable and unable to show gratitude. When the "life" has been taken from a victim, another victim will be chosen to feed the bully's fragile ego.

Summary of the psychoanalytical theory

The research review identified three different characteristics of bullies: aggression, inconsistency, and envy. From a psychoanalytical perspective, underlying all these is a pernicious and perverse form of projective identification.

When bullying is particularly aggressive, there is a considerable struggle for survival. The interplay of life and death and of love and hate goes awry. The death instinct dominates and is projected on to others. Those who introject these feelings—the victims—often complain of feeling dead inside. Hate dominates over love and creates a distance between the bully and the target, further enabling the bully to "destroy" the victim. The creative aspects of love are diverted to objects such as targets which are relatively easily controlled and measurable.

Most bullies are generally inconsistent, for example, changing their minds at the last minute when plans, to all intents and purposes, have been settled and agreed. These actions are often illogical, unreasonable, and of little benefit to other employees, to the group, or to the organisation's "bottom line". The actions and behaviour of bullies create confusion and fear. Inconsistency comes from the dynamic of splitting, that most primitive of defences. The ego and objects, such as colleagues, are split into "good" and "bad". Constant splitting is a sign of a futile attempt to recapture, or annihilate, contact with emotional life. It depletes the ego.

A bully projects the unwanted and unacknowledged aspects of him/herself on to others, testing their boundaries for weakness. If a target of bullying complies with the bully and introjects the projections, he/she becomes a victim. Victims are individuals who seem unable to use "hate" to stand up to the bully. Often they are unaware, in the early stages, that they are being bullied. It tends to come as a surprise, possibly because they became accustomed to being bullied as children. They may go into denial, as it is too painful to acknowledge that this has happened before. As a result of a lack of opportunity to test out relationships in childhood they may be politically naive. Alternatively they may become very involved in what they are doing and idealise their own work and roles as a defence against anxiety. One way of denying a hateful reality is to stop thinking about it.

The victim, the container of the bully's anxieties, has to be tightly controlled and monitored to ensure that the bully's projections remain externalised and "fixed" in that container. To ensure that the victim keeps the projections, the bully sets him/her up to fail, for example by denying information, constant criticism, and other undermining activities.

Further confusion can arise when a bully accuses a victim of being a bully. When a bully fears the return of the projections, he/she may perceive the victim as a persecutor and bully. Roles are seen to be reversed. This creates many difficulties for HR managers or mediators, particularly if they are unaware of the psychic processes involved.

In the dynamics of bullying, there is loss of intrapsychic rhythms in the psyche of both the bully and the victim. A rigidity of thought develops along with a loss of reality. They are unable to acknowledge each other's perceptions of the world. Projective gridlock develops. Once perceptions have been fixed, external help from mediators, or life coaches, may be required to help the bully take a broader perspective and reflect on his/her behaviour, its impact on others, and on the organisation. If no help is forthcoming, regressive aspects of love can continue to pull bullies into repeating patterns of behaviour from their past, for example, identification with the aggressors in their childhood, such as a violent parent.

It is in the motive of envy that we see the love-hate dynamic come to the fore. Envy is a particularly malicious form of projective identification. A bully creates a sense of distance from unwanted, or endangered, parts of the self, whilst in unconscious fantasy keeping those aspects "alive" in a victim. The bully "steals" the perceived goodness, for example, talents and privileges of others, and projects the unwanted parts of his/her ego. As the victim does not have the psychic ability to process the projections and feed them back in a "digestible" form, then he/she is perceived by the bully as "bad". Projections become gridlocked. Communication breaks down, and goodness and life are taken from the victim to feed an insatiable bully. When a victim has been "disposed of" there is a return of psychic deadness within a bully which results in further splitting and the search for another victim.

Within this chapter, for the sake of clarity of explanation, the roles of bully and victim are clearly separated and defined. Yet within the workplace there are bullies who are also victims. Often they are victims of the management systems, as described in Chapter Four. There are victims who fight back but who, in doing so, may take on aggressive behaviours. Many of us have a predisposition to play the role of bully or victim and when under stress veer towards those roles within our defensive responses.

When we maintain a healthy mind and the capacity to reflect on who we are, we have an awareness of the impact of our behaviour on others. We are able to learn lessons from the past and thereby avoid getting trapped in unhealthy relationships.

Questions and answers

This section brings together the research review and intrapsychic theory, outlined above, to give answers to the questions posed at the beginning of this chapter.

Why do bullies bully?

Insecurity in change situations

Employees often become anxious when changes occur in organisations; anxiety is a natural and unavoidable emotion. It is the way in which this anxiety is managed that determines whether an individual becomes a bully. Bullies tend to be particularly susceptible to changes in the workplace. Their main concern is self-survival; the fate of others is irrelevant unless they can be exploited. Bullies feel particularly insecure for a variety of reasons: in childhood they lacked the love and care necessary to develop a "good-enough mother" within; in spite of outward appearances of omnipotence and arrogance, they lack good feelings about themselves; in childhood they were unable to establish permeable boundaries, essential for the development of clear identities and a healthy psyche. If as children they saw family relationships in terms of power games, then under stress in the workplace they regress to those patterns of behaviour, considering them to be the norm.

High levels of psychic deadness

The research on bullying indicates bullies have higher levels of depression than other individuals. This implies that their levels of psychic deadness are higher. They have difficulty in relating to their own feelings and they are unable to show empathy to others. Lacking psychic space within their minds for reflection, their thoughts easily become rigid and their perceptions of others easily fixed.

Identification with aggressors

In childhood, they may have identified with aggressors as a defence against their anxieties. In the workplace they may act out their aggression in similar ways on to colleagues, particularly if senior managers are aggressive towards them.

Regression to splitting

When stressed, they are more likely than their colleagues to regress to the primitive defence of splitting. They split their worlds and their psyches into "good" and "bad". They have to get rid of the feelings of badness by projection, and therefore test the boundaries of their colleagues until they find a suitable container for their feelings. If the target introjects those projections, he/she becomes a victim. The bullying does not stop. Constant splitting creates a further impoverishment of the ego and a repeated need to get rid of inner anxieties.

Why are some bullies overtly aggressive, whereas others are more covert in their actions?

The aggressive bully, like a serial killer, takes one victim after another. This is self-preservation violence.

When under stress in the workplace, aggressive bullies feel that they are struggling to survive. The life and death instincts dominate the unconscious dynamics. The interplay of life and death goes awry and feelings of deadness are projected outwards. The boundaries of others are tested and a container found. An aggressive bully is particularly determined to set a victim up to fail and will take whatever measures are at his/her disposal in order to do so. When a target introjects those feelings, he/she becomes a victim. Within the bully there is a temporary release of tension. However, high levels of psychic deadness return once more and another victim has to be pursued.

Aggressive bullies can be likened to the mythical figure of the Kubu. The legend of the Kubu goes back to Mesopotamia. The Kubu was the little one who never saw the sun, never sucked his mother's milk, and never knew his own name. Lacking these rituals of recognition, identity, and love, and lacking a mother's welcome into life, the Kubu is forever trapped between death and life. Desperate to compensate for this, he degenerates into a killer of other babies. He kills because of what he is—anonymous, trapped between states of being. As he is trapped, he also traps others, and by killing reproduces himself in the deadness from which he came.

In bullying the second underlying dynamic of projective identification—love and hate—also goes awry. As hate creates a distance between the bully and the victim, the victim can be more easily viewed as an object to be used and abused. "Love" is displaced onto the self or onto objects such as workplace targets or bonuses. In the ruthless drive of death and hate, a victim's demise may be comparatively swift.

The covert bully, however, is likely to be more predatory, relentlessly pursuing one particular individual for some time and inflicting emotional suffering before making the "kill".

Where we find inconsistency in bullies there is confusion between love and hate of good and bad objects and egos as described above.

Envious bullies, on the other hand, clearly identify with the perceived goodness in others, desire it for themselves, but once they attain it, they no longer care for the fate of the victim. Their behaviour is illustrated through Spenser's *The Faerie Queen* (Spenser, 1909).

> He hated all good workes and vertuous deeds,
> And him no lesse, that any like did use,
> And who with gracious bread the hungry feeds,
> His alms for want of faith he doth accuse;
> So every good to bad he doth abuse:
> And eke the verse of famous Poet's witt
> He does backbite, and spightful poison spues
> From leprous mouth on all, that ever writt:
> Such one vile Envie was, that fifth in row [i.e., as Envy among the Vices] did sitt.

How do they bully?

Essentially a bully bullies using projective identification. We all use projective identification to communicate with others, but bullies use it in a perverse and malicious way. When a potential bully feels particularly anxious, he/she often defends against anxiety through the primitive defence of splitting. Bullies split their worlds and psyches into good and bad, keeping the goodness for themselves and projecting badness outwards. They test the boundaries of others to find a suitable container for their anxieties, seeking out someone who is more vulnerable than the rest of the social group or the working group. The targets may be different from the group in some way, or have extra responsibilities at a particular time, either within the workplace or in their personal lives, or their vulnerability may come from negative childhood experiences.

When the target's boundaries have been broken and the projections introjected, the target becomes a victim. The bully has to ensure that the recipient experiences and behaves in a way congruent with the unconscious projective fantasy. Hence the bully controls and constantly monitors the victim and blames him/her for those parts of the self which he/she cannot acknowledge. If the victim does not challenge the bully, and introjects the projections, he/she accepts the description given by the bully—often one of failure. "To fail as a human being is to accept someone else's description of oneself" (Nietzsche, quoted in Rorty, 1989, p. 28). The bully's projections become gridlocked.

Why do some bullies become victims and some victims become bullies?

When under pressure, bullies project their anxieties outwards and a victim becomes a container for their bad feelings. If victims begin to fight back, their behaviour may be interpreted as aggressive by a bully. The bad feelings, residing in the victim are perceived as persecutory. Roles are then reversed, with the bully perceiving the victim as the bully, and the bully perceiving him/herself as the victim. This is known as the paranoid-schizoid position.

As bullies lack "a good-enough mother within", when they encounter other bullies more aggressive than themselves, their boundaries may be breached. They may then become victims.

> If the individual cannot take the realness, aliveness, autonomy and identity of himself and others for granted, then he has to become absorbed in contriving ways of trying to be real, of keeping himself or others alive, of preserving his identity, in efforts, as he will often put it, to prevent himself losing his self. (Laing, 1969b, pp. 42–43)

Some victims adopt victim status as a means of finding some identity for themselves and continue to play this role, throughout life, whatever context they find themselves in. Other victims are more transitory in their status and learn through their experiences of being bullied to stand up for themselves. However, as they lack positive feelings about themselves, instead of introject feelings of others, they may begin to project their anxieties as a defence against anxiety and then be perceived as bullies.

Why are some victims badly damaged by their experiences, whereas others are relatively unscathed?

Some victims are traumatised by their experiences and may suffer from PTSD. Other individuals, however, can experience similar behaviours but move on relatively unscathed. Much depends on their resilience. In psychoanalytical terms resilience can be seen in terms of the ability to set boundaries, ones which are strong enough to withstand projections from bullies. Resilience also depends on psychic space—how much space individuals have to reflect on what is happening to them.

Victims who are vulnerable due to childhood experiences in which they were unable to develop agency and had little opportunity to practise assertive social skills, may also lack tactical awareness in adult life and be naive. These individuals can be likened to Peter Pan in J. M. Barrie's story. Peter Pan was the boy who never grew up. The research on bullying shows that victims may have lacked the opportunity to develop a clear identify of their own. They were not given the chance to learn to defend themselves because their parents either overprotected them or refused to give them challenges in which they could succeed for themselves. Later in life these individuals are more easily overwhelmed by anxieties and as adults they constantly struggle to find clear identities for themselves. They remain in an immature form unless they can find sufficient nurturing to care for themselves, for example, through psychotherapy. Some take on victim status as a form of identity.

When victims find bullying particularly traumatic, they could be said to have had, psychically speaking, a close encounter with their own "death". In projective identification, the victims feel, unconsciously or subconsciously, the "deadness" of the bully. These feelings possibly resonate with their own feelings of deadness. Victims often talk about deadness, death, and dying. Death by exhaustion seems an apt term to describe the experience of some victims, particularly in the later stages of bullying.

Other victims are less traumatised because:

1. They are more prepared for the bullying and more realistic about their expectations of working life.
2. They have firmer boundaries in place and therefore have greater resilience and can more easily protect themselves from the projections of bullies.
3. They are able to get effective help from family and colleagues to stand up to the bully.
4. They are able to distance themselves both physically and emotionally from the situation.
5. They are able to move away from the bully, reflect on the experience, and learn from it.

What can victims do to protect themselves against being bullied again?

1. React faster. A victim said,

   Since being bullied, when other people have tried to bully me I have reacted much faster and called their bluff sooner. And with most bullies if you call their bluff they would probably back down.

2. Set clear boundaries. Be prepared. When the bully next starts to criticise, tell him/her this is not the moment for this type of discussion, turn your back and walk away. Alternatively tell the bully in a firm unwavering tone that he/she must stop being disrespectful. Wait for the reply, maintain an assertive stance and eye contact and whatever he/she says, reiterate your message.
3. Be professional. Do not try to describe to a bully how you feel, because bullies are not interested in the feelings of others, unless they affect their own survival. A bully will not understand, as he/she lacks empathy. If that individual had empathy he/she would not be a bully. When describing a bully's behaviour to HR staff, stick to the facts. This is not easy, as bullying is often inconsistent. Rehearse what you are going to say beforehand.
4. Find time and space to get to know yourself. There are two types of time—chronos time and kairos time. Our working lives are dominated by chronos time or measured time. Kairos time is time for reflection. Find time for yourself, ideally unstructured time to potter—to garden or to paint. Rather than darting off to rescue someone else, listen to your inner voice.

   Even when we stop to rest, our minds can go racing on, chattering away. Meditation and mindfulness have been found to improve the neurological connections within the brain.

> The important thing is to *notice* the mind's chatter, for by noticing it we come to gain control over it and eventually to quieten it. It is not a question of judging it or thinking we shouldn't be having this internal chatter. The noise is there, but just noting it will lessen its destructive effect. (Stanislaus Kennedy, 2001)

5. Rather than allow the trauma of bullying to be turned over in your mind, seek help from a counsellor or psychotherapist.
6. If you have been bullied before, your default position may be "Poor me—I'm a victim". Rewrite your story. What would you like to happen?—remembering, of course, that the bully is not going to be nice to you, whatever you do. Storytelling is a way of expressing ourselves and our world to others. It helps us to

organise our thoughts, providing a narrative for human intentions and interpersonal events.

7. Victims need to care for themselves as much as they think they would like to care for others.

   "Those that respect themselves are safe from others. They wear a coat of mail that none can pierce" (Attributed to Henry Wordsworth Longfellow).

8. Acknowledge that there are vacuums and black holes in organisations in which individuals get trapped (see Chapter Four).

9. Seek out humour, for example, watch a cartoon. This will enliven the deadness within and might get those neurological pathways moving so that you can find ways of reframing the drama. Mock the bully—quietly of course.

   Two males were bullying a female employee. They often stood over her desk giving orders, setting unreasonable time deadlines and distressing her. They refused to talk with her in a more public space. A life coach suggested she made a picture of a little man in a helmet and stick it on top of her computer, the subliminal message being that these bullies had little penises. When they next approached her she pictured them as 'little' men and this helped her to smile and reframe the situation. In feeling more confident she refused to have discussions at her desk and met for discussions on neutral territory, in a more public arena. The bullying abated.

10. Think about what the bully is telling you. This message describes how the bully is feeling. These are not your feelings and they are not your property. Draw boundaries and do not let your guard down. Be prepared for further attacks.

11. Alternative therapies, such as reflexology and Reiki, help to relax the mind and the body. Other ways of developing the psyche-soma connection, the links between the mind and body, are yoga and pilates. A greater awareness of "self" is essential in setting boundaries. Emotional Freedom Technique is helpful for setting goals for change.

How can HR managers help targets and bullies?

Many employees who are bullied are bewildered by their experiences; bullying often comes as a surprise and, being unexpected, leaves them shaken, shocked, and even overwhelmed. Some become very disoriented and confused. Do not be surprised if they tell you the same stories over and over again. This is not unusual. It is, however, a sign of trauma and needs specialist help from counsellors and psychotherapists. Whilst arranging this, gently remind victims of their own boundaries. Remind them about their areas of responsibility and in particular what is outside their remit. This offers them some containment and reassurance that they can cope.

Take reports by victims seriously. Behind a bully's facade of pleasantness a Jekyll and Hyde character will be lurking. You may have seen only one side.

When confronting a bully, give clear and accurate feedback on his/her behaviour based, wherever possible, on your observations. Plan what you are going to say beforehand. Expect him/her to create confusion in your mind. Do not fall for it, but repeat the facts. Follow up the meeting soon afterwards. Your body language needs to convey confidence and clarity (Oade, 2009).

Recognise the difference between a bully and an "over-enthusiastic" manager. The key difference is that the bully is an employee, who at a specific time, is incapable of containing his/her anxieties and has to get rid of them by projecting them outwards on to others in a way that is damaging to the recipient, and probably to the organisation too. An effective manager can contain and work through the anxieties generated within him/herself, within the group, and within the culture of the organisation.

Listen carefully to what the bullies are saying. Is their account a projection of their feelings? What is worrying them? Acknowledge that some employees have a greater need for containment and for boundary setting than other employees in anxiety-provoking situations. Bullies need support, although they rarely admit it; denial is a strong defence against anxiety. Firm boundaries need to be set and job descriptions clarified. A life coach could help the bully to reflect on his/her behaviour and its impact on others and to persuade him/her to move forward in a way which is not only constructive to him/her but also to others. The "Boss Whisperer", by Crawshaw (2007), recommends confronting abrasive bosses and asking very specific questions about their behaviours.

CHAPTER TWO

Interpersonal relationships

Introduction

This chapter focuses on the drama played out between bullies and victims. We see how their destructive interpersonal relationships evolve and become established. We find out why some targets of bullying seem to be able to cope with the psychic onslaughts of the bully, as described in Chapter One, whilst others succumb to the attacks.

The first part of the chapter is a review of the research into the interpersonal relationships between bullies and victims. Research evidence demonstrates how specific patterns of behaviours develop which evolve in stages, with victims become increasingly trapped. Coping strategies used by victims tend to be passive and/or active, but whatever course of action they take, they are often unsuccessful in finding a resolution to the conflict.

The second part of the chapter presents key psychoanalytical theories on interpersonal relationships which help us to understand how we develop our identity through each other. The theories selected are from the fields of attachment theory and intersubjective theory. Attachment theories show how our early attachments influence the formation and direction of our relationships later in life. At the core of intersubjective theories is the topic of "recognition", which is based on the premise that we are able to, and need to, recognise other individuals as different and yet alike, and as "others" who are capable of sharing our emotional experiences.

We look at how patterns of interpersonal relationships become established from the first interactions between the mother and baby. When these relationships are healthy, foundations are established for mutuality to develop. Alternatively, in unhealthy relationships patterns of negative recognition become established and these may lead to a child to dominate or be submissive in his/her relationships with others. The potential develops for a child to grow into a masochist victim or a sadistic bully. We follow these patterns of behaviour into adulthood, first from the perspective of the sadistic bully and then through the eyes of a masochist victim. Insights into how the deeper needs of a perpetrator are met through violent relationships are given from an attachment theory perspective on domestic violence by Fonagy (1999, 2001). Evolution of the sadistic-masochistic relationship in adulthood are explored through the master-slave dynamics and illustrated through Benjamin's (1988) use of a fictional story. The story gives insights into how the deeper needs of a victim may be met through bullying. The additional theories of repetition compulsion and authenticity are used to explain why bullies and victims often repeat patterns of behaviour from their past and why they may continue in these roles throughout their lives.

The third part of the chapter provides answers to the following questions:

How do interpersonal relationships evolve over time?
Why do bullies need to dominate others?
How can individuals protect themselves from becoming drawn into bullying relationships?
What measures can HR directors take to prevent toxic bullying relationships?

Research review

Models of an evolving and escalating conflict

Researchers generally agree that incidents of bullying are rarely isolated episodes but are constantly evolving conflicts which escalate over time (Leymann, 1996; Zapf & Gross, 2001). In the beginning of the conflict, victims seem to be attacked only now and then, but as the conflict escalates the frequency of attacks increases and after some time the victims may be attacked on a weekly, or even, daily basis (Einarsen & Skogstad, 1996). There is a possibility that victims can escape bullying when it first starts, but after it has become established they get stuck and, unless they have very good coping strategies, get torn apart (Thylefors, 1987).

Researchers of bullying in schools found a degenerating pattern to the evolving relationships between bully and victim (Kochenderfer-Ladd & Wardrop, 2001). In the early stages of the formation of social groups, aggressors direct their attacks toward a large number of children before focussing their attentions on a small minority, those who tend not to pose a serious threat of retaliation. These are children who prior to being bullied may have had a network of peers, or friends, with whom to play and interact. However, the longer the harassment continues the worse the victims perceive their social situation to be. Over time, victims come to believe that they are not liked and that peers are not willing to help them (Kochenderfer-Ladd & Wardrop, 2001). Workplace victims also find themselves isolated and describe their experiences of being bullied as "playing a game in which they have no rights" (Tracy, Lutgen-Sandvik, & Alberts, 2006).

Within the workplace distinctive patterns of evolution of bullying have been found (D'Cruz & Noronha, 2010; Kelly, 1999; Neidl, 1996; White, 2007). Neidl (1996) observed four stages to bullying. The first two stages are ones in which most victims try constructive ways of coping with their situation. These are known as "voicing" and "loyalty". When, after time, they perceive that problem-solving strategies fail, victims reduce commitment—the "neglect" stage—and thus enter what is known as the "exit" stage and often leave the workplace (Neidl, 1996).

From interviews with victims of workplace bullying, Kelly (1999) identifies a time before bullying begins, which he calls the honeymoon period. This is a time during which victims report having had positive professional and personal self-images, doing well at their work, and even liking the bully (Kelly, 1999). Following initial attacks by bullies, however, working life becomes a battle for survival, with victims increasingly worn down by their experiences, blaming themselves, losing confidence, and some becoming so unwell that they are unable to continue working. Some victims can no longer endure the situation and leave through choice or are "fired" (Kelly, 1999). Kelly (1999) illustrates these evolutionary stages with the following story.

Dave joined a company as a sales representative. For the first three years he enjoyed his job and achieved the status of top salesman in his area. Around this time a new manager was employed by the company. After being told of Dave's success, the manager called him a "load of rubbish". During the following year, Dave's work performance was constantly criticised, his job was threatened and he was subjected to intense and intrusive scrutiny. He was constantly criticised and verbally abused by the manager and as a result his work performance declined dramatically and his health suffered. He was unable to sleep. He said, "I'd wake up in cold sweats and I'd be awake all night. I'd get up and go into the office and sit there for hours and hours and achieve nothing". He had constant headaches, felt sick and would shake uncontrollably before visiting clients. Finally he reached the point of breakdown, when he was phoned at home by the manager and was told he would lose his job because of a small administrative error. Dave said, "That's when I cracked completely … I never stopped crying or shaking for a couple of weeks". He was off sick for eighteen months and finally retired on the grounds of ill health (Kelly, 1999).

After victims leave work they tend to compare their "old selves" to their "new selves" (Kelly, 1999). Their self-images deteriorate. In trying to come to terms with the bullying some blame, or hate, the bully, and want justice, or revenge. Others try to put the experiences behind them or use them to help others (Kelly, 1999).

Similar evolutionary patterns emerged from a study of the relationship between HR managers and victims (D'Cruz & Noronha, 2010). In this research three phases of bullying were identified. The first phase, the initial onset of bullying, was a time in which victims describe being immersed in their work and failing to realise that they were being bullied. It was only in retrospect that the victims were able to identify when their team leader began bullying. At the time they could find no apparent reason why the bully would victimise them and, moreover, they believed that irrational behaviour in a professional environment was inappropriate. The continuation of the bully's behaviour, however, made it hard for them to ignore the situation.

A second phase of bullying began when the targets approached the HR department. The HR managers assured them that their problems would be sorted out. However, over time, the HR managers began to disbelieve the targets' accounts of their experiences and blamed them for the conflict, insinuating that they had done something to invite the behaviour. In collusions between HR and bullies, targets were given a variety of labels such as "trouble-maker", "maladjusted individual", "difficult person", "misfit", or "burden to the organisation". After a few weeks of being blamed, targets felt they were going round in circles and in the absence of third party interventions from, for example, unions, they were alone in their quest for justice (D'Cruz & Noronha, 2010).

Targets of bullying described stage three, the final stage, as a period of meaninglessness, confusion, and uncertainly. They were unable to relate to the world around them, struggled to make sense of things, and withdrew into themselves (D'Cruz & Noronha, 2010).

From observations and interviews within organisational contexts White (2007) found confirmation of the patterns outlined above. Four distinctive stages were identified: an embryonic stage; trigger; a developmental stage, known as the loyalty stage; and a dance of death (White, 2007). These stages are described in "the life cycle theory of workplace bullying" (White, 2001, 2004, & 2007).

The life cycle theory

The embryonic stage

The embryonic stage is a time before the bullying has begun. In any organisation there may be potential bullies, or embryonic bullies, and potential victims, or embryonic victims. The embryonic bully is someone who has the potential to bully but has not had the opportunity, or felt the need, to do so. The embryonic victim wants to succeed through pleasing others. Both the embryonic bully and the embryonic victim may, or may not, become entrapped in the dynamic of a bullying relationship.

Trigger

Bullies and victims remain as embryos, in a latent state, until there is a suitable trigger. This may be the arrival of a newcomer to a group, the reorganisation of a department, extra responsibility for the perpetrator, or changes within a team. For many employees organisational changes are not potentially traumatic, as frustration and unhappy circumstances rouse some envy and hate in every individual throughout life. However, some individuals, such as embryonic victims and bullies, find these changes difficult to handle and become defensive. They may regress, as shown in Chapter One, to the paranoid-schizoid position and resort to splitting.

Loyalty stage

As the bully begins to test the boundaries of colleagues to find a container for his/her anxieties, victims often go into denial. They seem to be loyal to the bully, but are, in fact, becoming increasingly submissive. The group dynamic works against them too, thereby further isolating the victim from others.

Dance of death

As bullying becomes established and intensifies, victims become increasingly submissive and lose "voice". In the final stage—the dance of death—the typical victim accepts the description given by the bully—that of failure. Victims may be exhausted and unwell and often unable to continue performing effectively in their work.

There is evidence from the research review, in Chapter One, that bullying ends with further depression for the bully (Kaltiala-Heino, Rimpelä, Marttunen, Rimpelä, & Rantanen, 1999) and for the victim (Field, 1996). For a typical victim, it is as if his/her identity has been fragmented, shattered into little pieces and dispersed (White, 2004). Although bullying behaviour often only ends when the victim leaves (Adams, 1992) he/she may relive the trauma (Leymann & Gustafsson, 1996). It would appear that further attacks by bullies are more likely because of the weakening of identity. If a victim cannot re-establish his/her identity, a pattern of learned helplessness may become established and the cycle will be repeated.

Outwardly the typical bully may give an appearance of high self-esteem but inwardly the ego of the bully is impoverished through excessive splitting and, as described in Chapter One, the psychic deadness returns. Like an addict in search of a fix, the bully will seek out another victim. For the bully to live it seems as if another victim must die.

The life cycle theory of workplace bullying presents bullying as a completed cycle; however, there are variations. The cycle is often broken. It may be cut short at any stage when, for example, a victim decides to leave, or a senior manager intervenes to give support to the victim. Whilst one cycle of bullying is becoming established between a bully and a victim, another cycle may have already started with another victim. The time span of the life cycle may also vary from scenario to scenario. Just as biological life cycles are repeated when environmental conditions are favourable, so bullying may recur if relationships are facilitated by negative organisational cultures and extreme managerial styles, as described in Chapter Four. The life cycle theory of bullying is described in more detail, from a psychodynamic perspective, in the question and answer section at the end of this chapter.

Coping strategies: active and passive

In the early stages of bullying, victims find bullies' actions so subtle, circuitous, difficult to comprehend and to describe, that they do not know how to respond (Lutgen-Sandvik, 2008). Initially, they may talk to colleagues in order to try to validate their perceptions and to family and friends to help them make sense of what is happening. They try a range of different coping strategies, such as challenging the perpetrator (Neidl, 1996). Some victims cling to memories of their former successes at work in an attempt to reduce the dissonance between the bully's portrayal of them and their own previously valued identity (Lutgen-Sandvik, 2008). Even active strategies such as open discussions, or talking about the situation with the aggressor, increase the probability of negative actions against the target (Rayner, 1999).

Bullies are like tyrants: they are dependent on people giving up and feeling so demoralised that they cannot be bothered to fight. They rely on the victim feeling that it is not worth bothering to take action (Crawford, 1999).

A senior executive in a bank described how she tried to cope with a deteriorating work situation. The trigger for bullying was the arrival of architects in the building who started talking about changes to the layout of the offices, including removing the walls of her office and making the area open plan. This was the first she knew about the plans and she was shocked by the lack of consultation. Although she voiced her objections to the proposed changes, she was ignored and the building work went ahead. She said,

> There are some incredibly loud-mouthed individuals in the department who have a habit of shouting across the room. It was very annoying when they didn't react to my complaints about the process. They were unwilling to make any amendments to the proposed plan or deal with the noise problem even though I pointed it out to them. In spite of my protests, and even offers to work from home, I had to accept the situation as it was and I found it very difficult because I am a conscientious person and I try to work diligently. To have my thoughts broken into all day I found very difficult, very exasperating and frustrating.
>
> I tried complaining in a reasonable and polite fashion. I tried complaining when I got more and more frustrated. I was angry and upset and no matter what I did there was no help forthcoming. It was only after my first panic attack that I realised the toll it had taken on me. I started to think about what was really happening and realised I was being bullied.
>
> I was left with a situation which eventually made me ill. I have a record of psychiatric illness that I never had before, after a working career of almost twenty years and long-term sickness on my employment record.

Any sense of empathy by the bullies, in schools, regarding the costs of their actions to victims is missing (Arsenio & Lemerise, 2001). Also absent is any sense that deliberately victimising others, in the pursuit of desired instrumental gains, is morally wrong. Likewise, in the workplace, levels of bullying increased as attempts to understand the perspectives of others decreased, thus implying a lack of empathy by perpetrators (Parkins, Fishbein, & Ritchey, 2006). Using autobiographical narratives, Baumeister, Heatherton, and Tice (1993) found substantive differences between the accounts of workplace victims and perpetrators. Victims initially stifle their anger but later may become more demonstrative in response to provocations. These responses are then interpreted by bullies as an overreaction. Bullies tend to bracket off the event in time and regard any incident as an isolated and closed episode, whereas victims tend to look at a longer-term time frame and describe the lasting consequences and implications of bullying for themselves. Neither group seems to be aware of the differences in perceptions between them (Baumeister, Heatherton, & Tice, 1993).

The lack of empathy and the aggressive attitudes that bullies hold towards peers has been found to be associated with insecure attachment to parents (Eliot & Cornell, 2009). In questioning children as to whether they are confident that their parents will listen to them, it is clear that those who do not experience a secure home also expect peers, and others they encounter, to be unresponsive, or unpredictable in meeting their needs (Main, 2000).

A bully, however, is not a bully unless there is a victim. A victim is not a victim without a bully. The target of bullying cannot be considered a mere passive receiver of negative behaviours as his/her responses may provoke the perpetrator to take further action (Hoel & Cooper, 2001). Victims may in some ways activate bullying and initiate the negative behaviour of others (Crawford, 1999). The notion that some people seek opportunities to be bullied is distasteful to many and yet guilt, or a sense of worthlessness, can motivate an individual to consciously, or unconsciously, set up situations in which he/she will be attacked (Crawford, 1999).

Some victims have been found to provoke bullies. These are known as "provocative" victims. They tend to be rule-bound, moralistic, and well organised and therefore may induce dispute-related bullying (Coyne, Seigne & Randall, 2000). When students were asked, in an open question, why an individual was being bullied, the most frequently quoted reasons were "they do not stand up for themselves" or "they annoy others" (Chan, 2006). Some targets may participate to a certain extent in their own victimisation, since certain behavioural styles may invite aggressive action from others (Aquino, 2000). For example, victims may be highly qualified and experienced workers but may clash with the norms of the work group to which they belong because they claim to "know better", or are legalistic, insist on their own view, or have difficulty in taking the perspective of others (Zapf & Einarsen, 2003). By being overcritical, they may be a constant threat to the self-esteem of their colleagues and supervisors.

> In some cases they may actually be the "good guys" as seen from an employer's point of view. However, in practice, the management is more dependent on the group than on the victim. Therefore, because information about the conflict situation is likely to be biased in favour of the group, the management tends to take the view of the group rather than that of the victim, thus leaving the victim in a hopeless position. (Zapf & Einarsen, 2003, pp. 178–179)

Other victims tend to be mainly submissive. They are conscientious, reserved, anxious, and have difficulty in coping effectively with bullying (Coyne, Seigne, & Randall, 2000). These victims may be subject to predatory bullying, where the bully pursues the victim over a period of time.

The following employee describes how she tried to resolve difficulties between herself and her boss but acknowledged her powerlessness in changing the relationship:

> I have tried everything. I have tried sitting down with her, but never ever bringing up emotions, which is of course what it is all about. I have to sit with her and have to make all these plans on how I can become more efficient. When I am not with her I am very efficient. There's something about our relationship. There have been times when we have talked and I have said that I find it difficult to understand some of her requests because what she will do is talk to me about something she thinks I know all about but I don't. I am so terrified of her that I don't feel that I can say—I don't know what you are talking about—so I try to make it up and go off and try to find out from somebody else. It is totally dumb because it is making for bad communication and inefficiency. But what I have never been able to do when the bullying is at its worst is to sit down and say I hate working for you, I am extremely unhappy. I would give everything for the courage to say that. Every single day I could say that. I just can't that's what I would like to say to her. I am one of these people who find it very difficult to hurt someone's feelings. I would go to any length not to hurt somebody. Even though this woman treats me like a pig I won't want to hurt her.

In schools it has been found that victims of bullying do not always display signs of distress. Instead they show false emotions of "joy". These emotions appear to disguise their own true feelings and signal, in a maladaptive way, that it is acceptable for bullies to continue with their aggressive behaviour (Wilton, Craig, & Pepler, 2000). By responding in a dysfunctional manner to the attention from bullies, victims appear to show that negative attention is more preferable to them than no attention at all. When classmates are being teased by bullies but fail to show any emotional response, the bullies express irritation; the bullies do not understand if that individual is enjoying "the joke" or not (Cowie & Berdondini, 2002).

Victims seem slow to respond, and initially deny their emotions. However, even when they do react, their anger is ineffective, as they have difficulty in regulating their emotions and tend to be overwhelmed by them (Cowie & Berdondini, 2002). The researchers found that by actively engaging an already hostile bully, these victims simply prolong the bullying episode only to lose the struggle through their exaggerated displays of unregulated anger and distress responses which, in turn, are satisfying to the bully. Some workplace victims often find it difficult to take personal responsibility for their behaviour and sometimes, through lack of social skills, do not know how to deal with personally difficult situations (Ishmael, 1999).

Although some victims, in schools, reported being lonely whilst being bullied, they did not seem socially dissatisfied and this seemed to indicate that they were, in some way, unwilling to take action to fight their own corner (Kochenderfer-Ladd & Wardrop, 2001). The most lonely victims distanced themselves from others and pretended that the problems were not happening (Kochenderfer-Ladd & Skinner, 2002). By internalising their anxieties, keeping themselves to themselves, worrying or blaming themselves, victimised children may communicate weakness and vulnerability, not only to their persecutors but also to others who may have otherwise been sympathetic to their plight. In the workplace, bullying is more likely to be prolonged when employees harbour thoughts of revenge towards perpetrators and become consumed with thinking about how to get back at the bully (Muñoz-Flores, Jaca, Medina, & Guerra, 2007). Victims who fight for justice often contributed to an escalation of the bullying (Zapf & Gross, 2001).

In schools problem-solving strategies, designed to help children cope with challenging situations, are beneficial for some, but mainly the non-victimised ones. Sometimes these strategies actually exacerbate difficulties for victimised children (Kochenderfer-Ladd & Skinner, 2002). The workplace victims who were most successful at reducing the bullying were better at recognising when bullying began to escalate and they also avoided making mistakes or acting in ways which could be used against them, for example, being frequently absent from work (Zapf & Gross, 2001). By avoiding conflict in a workplace, victims could reduce the bullying. For example, those employees who distanced themselves physically from work and kept themselves mentally occupied with other activities, were less likely to be bullied (Muñoz-Flores, Jaca, Medina, & Guerra, 2007).

After leaving the workplace, either voluntarily or involuntarily, victims recall how they had to deal with the perceived loss of professional reputation, organisational identity, loss of self-confidence, and the long-term loss of core beliefs in justice and fairness (Lutgen-Sandvik, 2008). The researchers describe this in terms of a process of grieving in which victims restructured their life narratives. Some received help with processing and accepting loss from mental health professionals. Successful restructuring of identity to create a narrative which they "could live with" often took many months and, for some, even years. For others, the trials of trying to stand up to a bully were seen as an opportunity to grow stronger and a blessing in disguise (Lutgen-Sandvik, 2008).

Support within an organisation has been found to be key to resolving bullying (White, 1998). Children with best friends at school were less likely to be victims than those without a best friend (Boulton, Trueman, Chau, Whitehead, & Amatya, 1999).

By gaining support from senior managers and standing up to a bully, an engineer in an electronics department recalls how he successfully resolved an incident of bullying in which he had become a victim.

> After the first three weeks of starting my job, I began to have problems with one person. He was from a different department. The working relationship was such that I was supposed to help out the other department with problem-solving matters. It was not part of my job description, it was a kind of understanding. What happened was that he felt that I was obliged to be at his beck and call. For the first three months I put up with it, but after a while it was not a case of doing someone a favour, it was a case of being obliged to do it. He was getting more demanding. This guy was a foreman; in the company, position-wise, he was actually below me. He shouted at me a lot and there were some ridiculous requests. It came to a point that if there was a problem with a product, for example, a loose wire, you just look at it and chuck it to one side and that is that. This guy gave me every single bad part from the production floor, we're talking about hundreds. It was ridiculous. I don't know what it was—maybe he was trying to show how big he was. I took it for nine months. Basically retaliation was very easy. I wasn't under him; he wasn't even in my department. My boss and his boss were on my side in a sense as I was doing them quite a few favours in different departments. They knew what was going on. One day this guy was on the phone shouting at me, so I decided I had had enough and I yelled back at him. There was a big row and after that he didn't feel like approaching me for anything anymore. I basically cut him off and didn't do him any more favours. It was as simple as that.

Summary of the research review

Research into interpersonal relationships between bullies and victims shows how bullying follows distinctive, evolutionary, and destructive patterns. Before bullying begins there is a time when victims seem to be satisfied with their work. When bullying is triggered, often by changes in the workplace, victims tend to be unaware, or in denial, that they are being tested by the bully. Most victims initially use active coping strategies, such as trying to make sense of their experiences with family members and colleagues. When challenging a bully, their behaviour may be perceived as actively provoking the bullying. Yet victims who remain passive may also be interpreted by a bully as being provocative. Whatever the coping strategies used they are often ineffective. A lack of mutual understanding develops. Bullies, in particular, lack empathy towards their victims. As the conflict escalates, bullies increasingly dominate and victims withdraw further into submissiveness. Some victims get assistance from friends or from outside bodies, such as unions, and move on to other organisations. Those employees who distance themselves from the workplace, physically and mentally, cope more effectively and the bullying has less of a long-term impact on them than on those who fight for justice without effective support.

Intersubjective theories

Introduction

We know, from the research outlined above, that bullies try to dominate others and, in the evolution of the interpersonal relationships, victims become increasingly submissive. However, the research does not explain why victims become submissive. Nor does it explain why the patterns of dynamics of domination and submission become established.

The theories that help us to understand how these patterns become established at deeper levels are taken from two fields—attachment theory and intersubjective theory. Attachment theories focus on the propensity of individuals to make affectional bonds with others and are based on early childhood relationships. They also describe how separation and loss give rise to the many forms of emotional distress and personality disturbance, including anxiety, anger, depression, and emotional detachment (Rycroft, 1995). The "father" of attachment theory, John Bowlby, spent many years studying the relationships between parents and children to understand why some children grow up to have few difficulties in coping with life, whereas others are beset by problems both in childhood and adult years. Intersubjective theories build on these theories but focus more on the dynamic nature of the underlying and ongoing exchanges of influences in interpersonal relationships. Both sets of theories help us to trace how individuals attempt to meet unfulfilled inner needs through their relationships with each other.

A key difference between attachment theory and intersubjective theories is that central to the latter is the theory of recognition (Benjamin, 1988). Recognition has a range of meanings, such as: to identify as already known; to know again; to identify and respond to correctly. The term derives from the Greek *anagnorisis*, acquainting oneself with something afresh (re-cognition). For the purposes of this book we are using Benjamin's definition of recognition.

"Recognition is that response from the other which makes meaningful the feelings, intentions and actions of the self" (Benjamin, 1988, p. 12). Recognition is reflexive, including not only the other's confirming response but also how we find ourselves in that response. "The subject declares 'I am, I do' and then waits for the response, 'You are, you have done'" (Benjamin, 1988, p. 21).

Benjamin's theory of recognition is based on the work of Winnicott, Hegel, Mead, and Bowlby, as well as on her extensive work observing the interpersonal relationships between mothers and babies. Through Benjamin's work we can begin to appreciate how the foundations are laid for a child to become a bully, or a victim, in school, home, and the workplace. We can begin to conceptualise bullying in terms of a search for recognition. We see how patterns of domination and submission, characteristic of these roles, become established in the early years of childhood. Fundamental to this pattern are two paradoxes of recognition: first, dependency and independency, and second, destruction and reality testing.

Building on these foundations, we then look at how patterns of domination and submission are acted out in adult life from two perspectives. First, an attachment theory perspective, from the work of Fonagy (1999, 2001) on domestic abuse, shows how dysfunctional attachments meet inner needs of individuals, particularly those of a perpetrator. Second, the master-slave dynamic, originating from the work of Hegel, shows how those who submit to others may also be meeting deep needs. Then, through theories on repetition compulsion, and through the theory on authenticity and the true and false self, we develop an understanding of why bullies and victims often repeat their roles.

The first paradox of recognition: dependency and independency

> As she cradles her newborn child and looks into its eyes, the first-time mother says, "I believe she knows me. You do know me, don't you? Yes, you do". As she croons to her baby in that soft,

> high pitched repetitive voice (the infantized speech that scientists confirm is the universal baby talk), she attributes to her infant a knowledge beyond ordinary knowing. (Benjamin, 1988, p. 13)

This description illustrates a paradoxical mixture of feelings of "otherness" and "togetherness". These feelings are both mystifying and entrancing to the mother in those early days of being a parent, particularly if for the first time. The baby belongs to the mother and yet is no longer part of her, but separate.

In a nurturing environment the mother can take pleasure in the baby's existence and her connection to the baby, and the baby is able to feel both that the world is responsive and that he/she is effective. The baby's actions, such as cries and gurgles, need to have some meaning for the mother and the baby needs to know that his/her mother can understand and share his/her feelings. For example, if a child picks up a spoon as the mother requests and the mother praises the child, the child knows that he/she is able to take action independently and is appreciated. For a child to develop a positive sense of him/herself, good feelings from the mother, and about the mother, need to be introjected.

As the baby grows he/she will venture away from his/her mother and explore the world in a more independent way. The baby begins to understand that he/she has agency and is able to have an impact on his/her environment and on other individuals such as brothers, sisters, or grandparents. He/she begins to assert his/her own will and develop preferences, likes and dislikes. However, in striving for independence the baby will constantly be aware of his/her dependence on others. Although the baby needs to achieve independence, he/she must be recognised as independent by the very people on whom he/she has been most dependent. This is the paradox of recognition. At the very moment of realising our independence, we are dependent upon another to recognise it (Benjamin, 1988). A condition of our own independence is recognising the other.

True independence means sustaining the essential tension of the contradictory impulses asserting the self and recognising the other (Benjamin, 1988). When the contradictory impulses of dependency and independency are balanced, then the opportunity for mutuality develops. Mutuality is a co-evolutionary process in which there is an acceptance of sameness and difference. It requires the capacity to reflect and engage with reality. There is a dialogue between self and other and acceptance of a constant tension and continual exchange of influence. Feelings are not polarised but mixed. There is a rhythm to the intersubjective and intrapsychic dynamics which Benjamin (1988) describes in terms of a constant asymmetry of power. This involves the ability to live with uncertainty and to experience ambivalence. For example, both love and hate can be felt toward the same "object". This was referred to in Chapter One as the depressive position.

Throughout life, mutual recognition can only come from an "other" whom we, in turn, recognise as a separate person who is like us but distinct, different, and valuable in his/her own right. Mutuality requires the ability to share feelings and intentions without demanding control, to experience sameness without obliterating difference. It is the basis for compassion and empathy for others (Benjamin, 1988).

As Benjamin (1988) explains, mutuality cannot be achieved through obedience, through identifying with the other's power, or through submission. Within the workplace, mutuality cannot be achieved through creating a utopia of peace and love, a "happy-clappy" environment, or one which ticks all the HR boxes.

Conflicts can be worked through by maintaining the intrapsychic and intersubjective rhythms. Channels of communication can be kept open and others challenged in ways that recognise the other and find a shared reality. This is an ongoing process of co-evolution.

Where we find bullying, the contradictory impulses of dependency and interdependency have gone awry. The depressive position (see Chapter One) cannot be attained and there is a regression to the paranoid-schizoid position with its characteristic splitting into good and bad. A shared reality is impossible to find. Empathy is lacking.

The second paradox of recognition: destruction and reality

Returning to the early stages in a baby's development, there are numerous times when the relationship between mother and baby is tested and hence there is the potential for mutuality to go awry. Babies can feel unhappy or distressed, tired, or unresponsive. Likewise, the mother may be anxious about her new role and responsibilities. The baby's positive response can make the mother feel more positive about herself as a mother; alternatively the baby's unresponsiveness, or rejecting gestures, can damage her confidence. When a mother responds to a baby's feelings and actions in ways that have little meaning to the baby, interactions become frustrating for both baby and mother and a struggle for recognition becomes established.

In his clinical work with children and adults Winnicott (1971) came to the conclusion that there is something profoundly paradoxical about the struggle for recognition. Recognition is achieved through destruction. We find the realness of those we love through our ultimately unsuccessful attempts to destroy them.

> In a radio talk on the BBC in 1949 he [Winnicott] advised parents: "if a baby cries in a state of rage and feels as if he has destroyed everyone and everything, and yet people around him remain calm and unhurt, this experience greatly strengthens his ability to see that what he feels to be true is not necessarily real, that fantasy and fact, both important, are nevertheless different from each other". (Audard & Grosz, 2000, p. 2)

If others, such as the mother, survive without retaliating, or withdrawing under an attack, then the child knows they exist outside his/her control. The child can see the mother and others as being independent individuals as well as dependable ones. It is in the unsuccessful attempts to destroy the other that the child finds his/her boundaries and the "realness" of those who are caring for him/her. The other is seen as "real", and different, and therefore available for satisfaction.

However when the parent gives in, or is over-controlling, the pleasure of exchange is lost, along with the ability to play with the experience. The child is not able to fully engage, or be fully disentangled from the interaction with the mother. Neither separateness nor union is possible. The child can never lose sight of the mother, yet never see her clearly; never shut her out and never let her in (Benjamin, 1988). As a child struggles to find recognition, the foundations are formed for the child to opt for a role of either being submissive or domineering.

Later in life, these individuals will, when under stress, regress to their default positions. The bully tries, like the baby, to destroy those around him/her. If no one stands up to him/her and calms him/her down, that employee will be unable to find the reality of the situation and be unable, without help, to discover that reality and fantasy are different. For the behaviour to be modified, space needs to be found in which the bully can begin to appreciate that his/her perception of the situation is only one of many. There are others.

Domination and submission in childhood

The sadistic child may be over-indulged, or allowed to abuse his/her mother; hence he/she is not able to depend on others and finds them untrustworthy. When a parent fails to set clear boundaries, as described in Chapter One, the child has difficulty in processing the introjections and projections necessary to form a clear identity. He/she may become confused and live in a constant state of inner turmoil, an inner state of disorganisation. If the child experiences the parent as caving in, he/she will continue to attack others in fantasy, or reality, searching for a boundary for his/her reactive rage. As toddlers, such children may have more than the usual temper tantrums associated with frustration and the desire to manipulate the parent or carer. If the parent fails to respond by setting clear boundaries and reassuring the toddler, the child feels very insecure.

> What the child feels is something like this: When the other crumbles under the impact of my act, then my act seems to drop off the edge of the world into emptiness, and I feel that I will soon follow. In this void begins the loss of tension or boundaries, a by-product of losing the other. (Benjamin, 1988, p. 71)

Later in life when frustration levels rise and aggression comes to the surface, the sadistic child turns into the angry employee who cannot get his/her own way. Just like the raging child, the adult will try to control and dominate others in an attempt find some boundaries and containment for the inner turmoil. He/she is attempting to cope with the paradox of recognition—independency *vs.* dependency.

> Control is a way of denying dependence, of not acknowledging it and yet compelling the object to fulfil a need for dependence, since an object that is wholly controlled is, up to a point, one that can be depended upon. (Segal, 1973, pp. 83–84)

The opposite to the sadistic child emerges when a parent cannot tolerate the child's attempt to do things independently and sets boundaries too tightly. It is difficult for the child to know his/her own feelings or desires, and even to develop his/her own perspective of reality. The child is made to feel that freedom is not possible, or that the price of freedom is aloneness. If the child does not want to do without approval he/she must give up his/her will and become submissive and easily controlled by others. The submissive child continues, often throughout life, to feel the need for the parent's protection and confirmation of his/her own agency. As he/she had been unable to detach him/herself psychically and intersubjectively, the parent constantly remains omnipotent in his/her mind. These feelings of the omnipotent parent survive in two possible ways: they may be projected onto others and the child becomes submissive; alternatively he/she copies the aggressor. However, as the child is inwardly submissive, displays of aggression will not be taken to be genuine and may actively provoke attacks by a bully. Hence we have here the provocative victim. Whatever defensive mechanism is used by the masochistic child—passive and submissive, or provocative and aggressive—he/she is likely to become engaged in relationships which lure him/her into a state whereby early patterns are repeated. Reality is beyond reach. Even if the submissive child attempts to destroy the other, he/she will fail.

For both bully and victim, when the conflict between dependence and independence becomes too intense, there is a return to the early defences such as splitting. The sadistic child will externalise his/her anxieties, projecting on to others unwanted but unacknowledged anxieties, testing boundaries until a container can be found. When encountering those projections, the submissive child, having weakened boundaries, will introject the projections. The omnipotent parent in the mind of the victim is amplified by the presence of the omnipotent bully. Both sadistic bully and submissive victim lack the reflexive space to engage with their feelings. The potential exists for further defensive responses, such as projective gridlock, described in Chapter One.

Domination and submission in the adult years: an attachment theory perspective

The first perspective of domination and submission is taken from research on domestic abuse. This type of violence is similar to bullying in two ways. First, there is a continuum of behaviour, ranging from verbal abuse, through threats and intimidation, manipulative behaviour, physical assault, and even murder. Second, both bullying and domestic violence are usually perpetrated towards those with whom the perpetrator has a relationship, as opposed to random aggression towards an individual who is unknown to the aggressor.

From his observations of family life, Bowlby (1984) noted that a significant proportion of rejected and abused children grow up to perpetuate the cycle of family violence. They then may respond, in social situations, with the very same patterns of behaviour that they had developed in early childhood. Although it was mostly men who battered their wives and ill-treated their children, many of their wives came from disturbed and rejecting homes where they had been abused as children (Bowlby, 1984).

Building on Bowlby's work, Fonagy (1999) found, from interviews with violent men, that violent acts against women are often committed by men who show two particular characteristics. The first is inadequate mentalising capacities. Mentalising involves the ability to explore the meanings of actions of others, and to label, and find meaning to, our own experiences through others. It includes the ability to feel and reflect on those feelings.

The second characteristic is disorganised attachments. Children from abusive homes are frequently responded to in ways which are frightening, or confusing. It is difficult for them to acknowledge the mental state of the abusive parent because, in acknowledging the hatred implied by the parent's abuse, they are forced to see themselves as unlovable. As abusive parents commonly claim beliefs or feelings at odds with their own behaviour, this results in confusion in the minds of children. These children have no means of testing or modifying their own representations of themselves or of reality. Their thoughts are disorganised. Being unable to find their own voices and meanings in their situation, they may, at an unconscious level, attack their ability to understand what is happening. This may come across as confusion and inconsistency in behaviour and thoughts.

As adults, they tend to operate on those inaccurate impressions of thoughts and feelings that restricted their development in the early years. A marked feature of Fonagy's (1999) findings was the refusal of almost all the offenders to either spontaneously, or in response to interrogation, comment either on their own mental states or those of their caregivers. It is when they are alone and cannot escape from the torturing representations of the self within their minds, that they may feel particularly unsafe. Their inner experiences cannot be engaged with because of the lack of reflective space, and yet cannot be dismissed because they are experienced from within, at deep levels. Therefore they are likely to crave the company of others as a distraction from the inner turmoil.

Violent men have been found to establish relationships in which their partners act as vehicles for intolerable self states (Fonagy, 1999).

They project their unwanted and unacknowledged parts of themselves on to others and, like workplace bullies, manipulate relationships to engender a self-image in the other which they feel desperate to disown. For example, a man may denigrate his partner and set her up to fail. If she threatens to leave, this process of externalisation is also threatened, and he is more likely to resort to violence; violence is a final attempt to control the other. It is used because of a terror, at an unconscious and subconscious level, that the coherence of the self will be destroyed by the return of what has been externalised. This is the form of persecutory anxiety referred to in Chapter One. The container for their anxieties is about to be lost, hence the need to tighten the controls.

The act of violence performs a dual function (Fonagy, 1999). First, it recreates and re-experiences the "alien" self within the partner. Second, it destroys that "self" in the unconscious hope that it will be gone forever. When he perceives terror in her eyes, the man is reassured that the "alien" self is being destroyed within her. It is only at the moment of attack that violent men feel coherent and real (Fonagy, 1999). For the man, violence reflects the successful destruction of the woman's psychic independence. She is confirmed as an object, a mere vehicle/container, to be used for the abuser's projective needs. Soon after the attack, however, there is often a shift in the relationship. The battered woman once again becomes important to the attacker's psychological well-being and the perpetrator pleads for forgiveness. His pleas are genuine because of the man's overriding need for a relationship where this externalisation of anxieties is possible (Fonagy, 1999). But they are not an expression of love, just a crude manipulation to keep the partner captive and available to take away his underlying angst. Yet in spite of the violence, the partner may fail to understand his true motives and the game that is being played out, and interpret his pleas as genuine.

> The tragedy is that the man's need is not for his partner as a real person, and the more she is reassured by his apparent remorse and protestations of commitment, the more she relaxes and permits her individuality to emerge, the closer she brings the next episode of terrible violence. (Fonagy, 1999, p. 22)

Through these insights into interpersonal relationships occurring in the home, we can begin to appreciate the origins of the chaos that can be created by a bully. The inconsistency he/she experienced in childhood is again brought to the surface within a working environment where he/she feels under pressure. The childhood bully would have been unable to trust those around him/her, and in the workplace this lack of trust of others will turn into increasing control and monitoring of others. The act of bullying makes the bully feel coherent. The submissive responses of a victim confirm the externalisation of the unwanted anxieties and fears. However, unlike within the context of domestic violence, there is no evidence in the research on workplace bullying that the bully pleads with the victim to stay. Here the bully has a greater choice of victim and can probably find another one relatively easily.

Domination and submission in the adult years: the master-slave dynamic

As shown above, domination does not repress the need for recognition but enlists it and perverts it (Benjamin, 1988). In other words, the "other" is experienced instrumentally, becoming an object to be used and abused rather than a subject to be known (Long, 2008). Sadistic pleasure is gained through the other, whereas a healthy relationship involves being in collaboration and sharing experiences for the benefit of both individuals. The ongoing exploitation can only continue whilst one of the pair remains dominant and the other remains submissive. If the victim leaves, the perpetrator is left alone and unrecognised. The perpetrator is no longer in the role of perpetrator, the victim no longer in the role of victim.

In continuing her exploration of the dynamic of domination and submission from childhood to the adult years, Benjamin (1988) looks at how and why some individuals become locked into adult relationships in which they are treated badly. In doing this she focuses on adult sexual relationships, a time when relationships are not only shaped by events from early childhood but also provide an opportunity to re-enact the conflicts that began there. Benjamin (1988) bases her analysis on Pauline Réage's fictional *Story of O*, which tells of a woman who is enslaved and used for sexual exploitation by two brothers, or masters. Through this story, Benjamin (1988) argues that deep needs are met in the master-slave relationship, with the captive slave searching for recognition through the master who is powerful enough to bestow this recognition. The master has the power for which she longs and through his recognition she gains it, though vicariously. In the acts of violence, the slave feels that she is being reached and is able to experience the presence of another individual. The slave's "pleasure" lies in her sense of her own survival and her connection to her powerful master. As the slave increasingly becomes a dehumanised object, increasingly treated in a "rational" and "ritualistic" way, her loss of self becomes the master's gain, creating his power in which she can take refuge. In losing her own self, she is, however, gaining access to someone more powerful.

In this negative cycle of recognition, aloneness is only made possible by obliterating the intrusive other and attunement only by surrendering to the other (Benjamin, 1988). This dynamic of domination and submission is not sustainable, as the less the slave is experienced as a human subject, the more violence is deployed against her and the more she is experienced as an object—whose fate is of little relevance to the master.

> If I completely control the other, then the other ceases to exist, and if the other completely controls me, then I cease to exist. A condition of our own independent existence is recognizing the other. (Benjamin, 1988, p. 53)

Just as a parent remains omnipotent in the mind of a masochistic child, so, in the fictional tale, the master remains omnipotent in the mind of the slave. The absence of an outside world, such as family and friends, further fosters her treatment as an object of abuse.

In her analysis of the story, Benjamin (1988) suggests that the adult sadist searches for a surviving other, but this search is already prejudiced by childhood disappointments with an "other" who did not survive his/her attacks. He/she vigorously denies dependency on the other. Likewise the adult masochist continues to seek an "other" who survives, as happened in childhood. Increasingly, however, that individual feels that he/she does not exist, is without agency and has no life apart from the sadistic other. In the story the pain of violation serves to protect the slave by substituting physical pain for the psychic pain of loss and abandonment. As the sadomasochistic relationship moves towards deadness, the struggle for recognition turns into a struggle to the death for the life of the self (Benjamin, 1988). The intolerable end for the masochist is abandonment. For the sadist, the end is the death of the other, whom he/she destroys.

In her conclusion, Benjamin (1988) argues that beneath the sensationalism of power and powerlessness our deepest desires for freedom and communication can become implicated in control and submission. Agency and assertion become anchored in the context of control, retaliation, and aggression towards others rather than in mutuality and respect.

We may assume that as children, victims of workplace bullying may have had to give up their will to their parents and would not have had the chance to discover their limits and agency. With their parents remaining omnipotent in their minds, little psychic and intersubjective space would have been made available for them in which to relate to their own feelings. The sense of omnipotence remains with them into adult life: the provocative victim projects this on to others; the passive victim internalises it.

Within relationships with others, including colleagues, victims again seek out the parent figure, who survived for him/her in childhood. The attention from a bully, however perverse it may seem from the perspective of a bystander, meets the desire to be discovered. Even painful experiences are an acknowledgement by the other that he/she exists. As Benjamin (1988) implies, the victim is submissive not just out of fear, but also out of complicity with his/her own deepest desires. With boundaries weakened through childhood experiences, the victim is easily reached and discovered, just as, at a deep level, he/she always wanted. However in being reached again he/she loses him/herself in the futile search for love and recognition, becoming a mere object to be used and abused.

Victims often claim that they cannot leave their place of work, that they are trapped. Colleagues desert them as the group fragments, as described in Chapter Three. Friends cannot cope with them incessantly recounting the trauma and they may also be let down by unions and HR managers. Although not physically enslaved like the slave to whom Benjamin (1988) refers, they feel just as trapped and just as badly treated and abandoned. Even when they escape, they may find themselves in similar situations, repeating the same patterns of behaviour.

Repetition compulsion

We have seen from the research review above that bullies and victims seem compelled to repeat their roles. It is as if no lessons have been learnt from experiences and their attempts at creating a new life are futile.

The concept of repetition compulsion is illustrated by Lear (2000) using an example from Freud's game of "fort" (gone)-"da" (there).

Babies often go through a stage of throwing toys out of their cot or buggy ("fort") and seeing it return ("da"). By throwing out the toy and drawing it back, assuming that it is attached by a cord or string, the baby learns both to imagine the mother's absence and to develop the ability to tolerate her absence. The activity enables the child to learn how to test the reality of a situation. In reality-testing the child, or adult, can go back, again and again, to test beliefs, perceptions, and assessments of what can be achieved. According to Lear (2000) this is courage in the making. Courage requires an emotional ability to tolerate absence and helps to contextualise and organise the past, present, and future. The courageous person is sensitive and responsive in any particular circumstance.

When the child can only throw the toy and is not able to retrieve it, the child is stuck in the "fort", throwing away, and is unable to get to the "da". According to Lear (2000) the capacity to play has been lost and, with it, the ability to let the mind slip along paths of loose associations for the establishment of neural pathways along which energy can flow. The child who is unable to face and tolerate loss is also unable to lend meaning to what has happened. He/she cannot engage with the reality of the loss of the mother, as to do so would mean that he/she would be flooded with anxiety. The reality is too difficult to contemplate. As the child becomes an adult, he/she has difficulty in trying to hold on to negative experiences and will instead throw them away, get rid of them. No pleasure can be found in holding on to difficulties and challenges, and waiting for new ideas to emerge. That space for creativity is lost in the need to take action rather than in reflecting on what might be. Past, present, and future are governed by perversity, not courage.

In applying the theory of repetition compulsion to understanding the interpersonal relationships between bully and victim, we find another dynamic is in operation—the inability to face loss. We have already seen examples of this in Benjamin's (1988) and Fonagy's (1999) descriptions of dysfunctional and damaging relationships. However, Lear (2000) links this loss to the inability to test reality and to a lack of courage.

For the victim, the experience of being bullied is often traumatic as he/she is frequently unprepared and not aware that the bullying has begun until it is too late to take effective action. The experience can then be overwhelming and it is very difficult to find some meaning to the events. Courage cannot be found from within and, generally, little help to find a shared reality is available from within the working group. Working life becomes a day-to-day struggle for survival and there is little hope that things will make sense or turn out well. Both bully and victim, in their futile search for love and recognition, are trapped within a negative pattern of recognition, destined to repeat their chosen roles.

A senior manager, who had worked his way up from the shop floor, targeted graduates and took every chance to belittle them (Honey, 2011). If opportunities failed to arise in the normal course of events, then he created them. One of his favourite ploys was to inflict his own version of "University Challenge" on groups of graduates. He compiled a series of obscure questions to which only he knew the answers. On the rare occasion when someone answered him correctly, the manager would accuse him/her of being a geek and a "know-all". As most employees failed to answer the questions, he taunted them. Graduate turnover was high but it did not bother him. His behaviour went unchallenged by other staff. It had become the norm (Honey, 2011).

This manager seemed trapped in repetition compulsion, trying over and over again to work through his feelings of inadequacy, irrespective of the costs to the company. No one found the courage to get him to face up to this destruction, or to try to help him feel confident in his own skills and to manage those who had had different experiences from his own.

Authenticity and development of true and false selves

Further insights into the intersubjective dynamics of bullying can be gleaned through the derivation of the Greek word for recognition—*anagnorisis*—which means acquainting oneself with something afresh (re-cognition) or, alternatively, "matching on return". Anagnorisis is associated with the Greek tradition of breaking plates in tavernas at the end of a meal, a practice which long ago had a more serious and symbolic purpose. Men often spent many years away from their homelands on travels and at war. On their return they and their true loves, changed by the ravages of time, would find it difficult to recognise each other. Tradition tells us that before parting it was customary for the partners to take a plate, break it, and then for each to take and treasure his and her parts. When the traveller returned, the two halves of the plate could be matched and the pair united as true loves once again.

Although there are no broken plates in the saga of Odysseus, there are several instances of anagnorisis, one of which involved Odysseus and his wife Penelope. When Odysseus arrived home from his many years of travels, Penelope, his long-suffering and sagacious wife, did not recognise the old visitor dressed in rags as her husband. She feared he was an impostor. It was only once Odysseus had given Penelope evidence, symbolic proof special only to the two of them, that she could finally embrace him. She then knew he was the person he claimed to be. He was authentic.

> To be "authentic" is to be true to oneself, to be what one is, to be "genuine". To be "inauthentic" is to not be oneself to be false to oneself: to be not as one appears to be, to be counterfeit. (Laing, 1969a, p. 127)

When two individuals meet and they are true to themselves and to others, the two parts of the plate metaphorically fit; they meet on return. Within a true self there is an internal dialogue, an inner aliveness, which leads to an understanding of reality (Laing, 1969a). When there is a knowing of oneself, there is sufficient psychic space for the capacity to reflect and engage with reality without the need to constantly control others, or to fear the intrusion of external demands. These individuals can be attuned to others, can take pleasure in being with others and sharing feelings in a mutually respectful way.

Individuals who lack authenticity are more likely to put themselves, or allow themselves to be put, in false or untenable positions by others, and cling to external formulas and dogmas (Laing, 1969a). As we have seen in this chapter and in Chapter One, when a baby has to adapt excessively to his/her mother as an object rather than subject, the "good-enough mother" within is missing. The space, both psychic and intersubjective, which allows the infant to feel that his/her impulses come from his/her own feelings and are acknowledged by the mother, is lacking. In these conditions the baby is unable to begin to discover him/herself.

> If the individual cannot take the realness, aliveness, autonomy and identity of himself and others for granted, then he has to become absorbed in contriving ways of trying to be real, of keeping himself or others alive, of preserving his identity, in efforts, as he will often put it, to prevent himself losing his self. (Laing, 1969b, p. 42)

When reality is absorbed from without rather than discovered within, the ground is laid for the development of a "false self". Rhythms of unconscious creativity cannot become established; compliance becomes an overriding feature. Courage, that ability to interpret a situation and make a creative response, is missing. The false self is set up as real and it is this false self that observers tend to think is the real person (Richards & Wilce, 1996). Others are treated as objects rather than subjects and recognition often denied to those who are weaker or different. Those operating from a false self may live through imitation, for example, with the aggressor. Some employees may work excessively to comply with their perceptions of demands from others, whether these be managers or targets.

Those who take on a false self are traitors not just to themselves but to each other and so continue to put themselves in, or are put in, false or untenable positions by others; they cling to external formulas and dogmas. Those who deceive themselves are obliged to deceive others.

> It is impossible for me to maintain a false picture of myself unless I falsify your picture of yourself and of me. I must disparage you if you are genuine, accuse you of being a phoney when you comply with what I want, say you're selfish if you go your own way, ridicule you for being immature if you try to be unselfish and so on. (Laing, 1969a, p. 143)

Individuals caught within such a muddle do not know whether they are coming or going. They are either filling themselves with others (introjective identification) or living vicariously through the lives of others (projective identification). Their own lives come to a stop. They can no longer develop psychically or intersubjectively. They go round in a circle, in a whirl, going everywhere and going nowhere (Laing, 1969a).

When conflicts arise between those who have not had the opportunity to discover who they are or what they are capable of doing for themselves, the two halves of the plate do not meet. Rather than being able to engage with the reality of the situation, they find themselves in a muddle and there is confusion. Choices based on reality are not available since reality is not accessible. This gives rise to conflicts which are false, confusing, and complex. False conflicts draw individuals into them. The little events, the tiny misunderstanding, words misconstrued and actions taken personally, flare up and soon get out of hand.

True conflict, on the other hand, is clarifying (Laing, 1969a). Healthy intrapsychic and intersubjective rhythms allow for the development of empathy and courage and a genuine concern for the well-being of others.

In applying the metaphor of breaking plates (re-cognition) to the bully–victim relationship, we can assume that the two halves of the plate (bully and victim) were not completely formed in the early years. In continually searching for the love and recognition lacking in childhood, both bully and victim find their efforts are restricted. They were unable to develop into their true selves and emerged from childhood in a depleted form. Recognition, that response from the other that makes meaningful the feelings, intentions, and actions of the self, was lacking. In taking on a compliant and false self, they are dependent on "objects" to mirror their internal states.

The victim hopes that he/she will be reached by the other but, in continuing to feel the omnipotent power of the parent, instead again finds that omnipotence within the bully. The bully wishes to get outside of his/herself into a shared reality. Bully and victim meet as false selves, clinging on to the false self as a desperate attempt to hide the fragility beneath. Although these two false selves are complementary in their needs, they cannot be brought together to create a mutually beneficial relationship. The two halves of the broken plate cannot be matched as they are imposters not just to each other but to themselves. They fail to fit.

In meeting as false selves, they embark on a frenetic game of projecting and introjecting in a desperate struggle to find recognition. However, over time the psychic and intersubjective rhythms become rigid and gridlocked. They are back to where they started from—psychic deadness.

In lacking authenticity it could be said that both bully and victim cheat each other. Cheating is one of the colloquialisms of "*boele*", the Dutch word from which "bully" is derived (see Chapter One). Other meanings which are equally apt include "one who misleads" or "an adulterer".

Summary of the intersubjective theories

The theories above suggest that individuals may become lured into destructive interpersonal relationships out of a desire to fulfil deep inner needs.

From an intersubjective perspective bullying can be conceptualised as a search for recognition which turns out to be futile. Feelings, intentions, and actions of the self cannot be comprehended by the other and through the other. There is no mutuality, no acceptance of sameness and difference. The capacity to reflect and engage with reality does not exist in the psyche (see Chapter One).

In childhood, potential bullies may have found those around them to be unreliable and inconsistent. They would have learned a fear of dependency on others, a fear which continues throughout life, resulting in a strong desire to control and dominate others. With a lack of clear boundaries it would have been difficult for the child to find his/her own limits and this may have resulted in an expanding elation, grandiosity, and illusions of omnipotence. When boundaries were not set, the child would have to try to find his/her own limits. As a toddler he/she would throw a temper tantrum, as an adult he/she would rage at others, trying to destroy all around. If boundaries are not set and calming influences found, the paradox of recognition between destruction and reality results in further false feelings of omnipotence and distancing from the reality of others.

At a deep level within the bully there is a futile search for the survival of the other, a search already prejudiced by childhood disappointments. He/she seeks, through aggression and attempts at destruction, to break through to the other. When finding someone with weakened boundaries who is yearning to be reached, for example, the submissive employee, he/she can attempt to gain that recognition that he/she so desires. As we saw in Chapter One, the victim may have had boundaries drawn too tightly in childhood, lacked the opportunity to develop feelings of agency, and constantly seeks to be reached by others.

In Benjamin's (1988) interpretation of the sadomasochistic relationship, sadistic bullies intensify their attacks as they increasingly control and dominate the other and a masochistic victim increasingly becomes submissive. There is a loss of subjectivity as the victim becomes an object to be used and abused. Fonagy's (1999) research on domestic abuse shows that the only time perpetrators feel cohesive is in the act of violence, when the projected "alien" self can be externalised and is seen to be destroyed within the other.

The drama between the bully and victim, as between sadist and masochist, evolves into a pattern of negative recognition in which aloneness is only possible for the bully through obliterating the other and "attunement" is only possible for the victim through surrendering to the other. As we saw in Fonagy's (1999) research, after the act of violence men plead with their partners to stay so that they can, at an unconscious level, continue to externalise the "alien self". In the workplace, however, bullies have a greater choice of victims and are unlikely to make similar demands for the victim to stay. The workplace victim is only of value to the bully whilst he/she can be of use and exploited.

When bullying is not resolved "outside" between self and other, there is a breakdown of intersubjective rhythms. In the struggle for recognition, there is a lack of tension in the interaction with the other. As shown in the research review, neither side is able to engage with the reality of the other. The drama continues within the intrapsychic realm and into the world of fantasy. The victim remains "loyal", loyalty in this case being a defence against reality in the form of denial or idealisation. Perceptions of the victim become fixed and projections gridlocked. Neither bully nor victim have available the psychic and intersubjective space in which to find themselves. Splitting, into good and bad, will continue to further deplete the psyche. As the relationship tends towards "death", the individuals return to the state of psychic deadness from which they had attempted to escape. "The painful result of success in the battle for omnipotence is that to win is to win nothing: the result is negation, emptiness, isolation" (Benjamin, 1988, p. 35).

Recognition for the bully is through further domination and for the victim through further submission, through the same familiar roles. For the typical bully and victim, the search for recognition is a futile one, as courage, that ability to interpret the situation and make a creative response, is lacking. No lessons are learnt from the experiences and, if the working conditions, for example, the organisation's culture and group dynamics are favourable, the experiences will be thrown away and old familiar stories will then be repeated in patterns of repetition compulsion.

The two halves of the plate will never match on return. Unable to find their true selves, they continue to hide behind a false self. In meeting as false selves the conflict is also false. They are traitors to themselves and each other, caught in a muddle of projection and introjection, going round in circles and getting nowhere. The cycle of destructiveness ends again in "death", both psychically and intersubjectively.

In our organisations, just like Odysseus, we have a drive for self-knowledge, self-improvement, and we live with uncertainty and change. However, it is not long absences which test our working relationships and our accountability but the constant interaction, the lack of clear roles, and the need to be creative and flexible which put new pressures on relationships (see Chapter Four). "Plates" are constantly being broken, boundaries are frequently breached, and individuals become unconsciously contracted to each other. When we work closely with others, each individual's failings and weakness are exposed. With this greater awareness of the frailty of others it is easy to complain about them, to judge and to condemn. The potential for destructive relationships, such as the bully–victim relationship, is considerable.

With constant flux and demands for flexibility and creativity, conflict is inevitable. It is in our attempt to create something new that we attempt to destroy and then find reality. Thus the truth is revealed. Courage has to be found to recognise the difference between true and false conflict, to ask those difficult questions, to challenge others in constructive ways. Effective and efficient engagement with colleagues, and with work tasks, requires a constant co-evolution of workplace relationships. Healthy intrapsychic and intersubjective rhythms are needed if constant asymmetries of power are to be developed in which sameness and difference can be assimilated and the search for recognition is fruitful rather than futile.

Questions and answers

How do interpersonal relationships evolve over time?

Answers to this question are given by developing the life cycle theory of bullying, outlined in the research review. Intersubjective theories described above are incorporated with theories from Chapter One. The life cycle theory is so called because it mirrors the stages of a biological life cycle and the activity involved is an attempt, from an intersubjective perspective, to create new life, even though the end result is deadness. This version of the theory includes advice for HR managers.

The embryonic stage

Some individuals have the potential to become bullies and others have the potential to become victims. Others avoid these roles. Much depends on whether these employees have been able to develop a certain degree of authenticity in childhood and to experience permeable boundaries. Employees who have a well-developed sense of self from the early years of childhood, will resist attempts by others to invade their personal space, to define feelings, or to redefine identity without permission. The embryonic bully constantly searches for his/her limits, often through destructive behaviours, and becomes omnipotent. The embryonic victim may seek love and recognition through familiar childhood patterns of subservience and submission. He/she desires to find boundaries set by others, just as in childhood. In the mind of the potential victim, the omnipotent parent is easily replaced by the omnipotent bully.

Advice to HR managers: These embryos will only grow into their roles of bully and victim if the organisational context, for example, a culture of fear and poor communication, facilitates that development. Bullying occurs around vacuums of support, as described in Chapter Four.

The trigger

Before bullying begins is a time when victims seem content with their work and their colleagues. When organisational changes occur, the new challenges may appear threatening to embryonic bullies. These embryos may also feel very insecure, particularly when clear boundaries are not set for them and they are unsupported in their roles. Fears, from childhood, that others would be inconsistent and could not be relied upon, may be reactivated and a struggle for recognition begins. This struggle may have been ongoing in a quiet way for some time but, when triggered, then takes centre stage.

From an intrapsychic perspective the life and death instincts and the dynamics of love and hate are activated. Life pushes forwards to the production of new forms, and death moves towards repetition and conservation. As we saw in Chapter One, these do not operate independently of each other but work together. The creative and regressive aspects of love emerge in an evolving and increasingly complex dynamic of interpersonal relationships. Psychic tension builds. On an unconscious level the bully takes defensive action resulting in a regressive return to early splitting mechanisms: a process by which we imagine that we get rid of painful feelings into someone else and hope to make them feel the pain on our behalf. Splitting into good and bad is part of a bully's Jekyll and Hyde nature.

Colleagues' boundaries are tested. Once someone has been found who is more vulnerable than others, the attacks will begin in earnest. A target only becomes a victim when his boundaries are broken and he/she introjects the projections from the bully. On a conscious or subconscious level, the bully sets up the victim to fail by denying him/her information, excluding the victim from meetings, and constantly criticising him/her. The bully has to ensure control is maintained externally. The victim is monitored as the bully needs to know that "the other" is there for him/her as a container of his unwanted and unacknowledged parts of him/herself.

This is a false conflict involving the meeting of false selves. Neither are true to themselves and therefore cannot be true to others.

Advice to HR managers: When initial complaints of bullying are made, take action quickly to set boundaries for both bully and victim. Get support for both of them, otherwise they will move on to the next stage which is far more complex, messy, and costly.

The loyalty stage

This is the stage in which the dynamic of domination and submission becomes established. A victim may initially deny the reality and even idealise the bully, idealisation being a defence against envy and confusion. The confusion may come, in part, from the bully's disorganised attachments and poor mentalising abilities. The victim may respond in perverse ways to the bully's demands, seemingly either too submissive or overly aggressive—the provocative victim. It appears that whatever course of action the victim takes, the bullying is inflamed. The bully becomes convinced that the victim is one who cannot be relied upon, especially if he/she responds in perverse ways to his/her threats. The bully's need to dominate, control, and possess the victim increases. In the attacks by the bully, the victim feels that he/she is being reached, recognised, and able to experience the presence of another being. A victim's perverse pleasure is in that connection, however painful.

When the conflict between having to depend on others for recognition and independence becomes too intense, the psyche gives up the paradox in favour of an opposition. A cycle of negative recognition becomes established in which aloneness is only possible for the bully by obliterating the intrusive other, the victim. Attunement is only possible for the victim by surrendering to the bully. Within this relationship there is a breakdown of intrapsychic and intersubjective rhythms. The victim is regarded less and less as a subject and more as an object. In projecting anxieties outwards, the bully benefits from having a container of his/her anxieties, albeit temporary.

Advice to HR managers: If the victim is not being supported through counselling or psychotherapy at this stage, then the dance of death is inevitable. Move the victim. If that is not possible and he/she goes off sick, then on return strong support needs to be put in place. Courage is needed to stand up to bullying.

A dance of death

> "Everything we do is a structural dance in the choreography of coexistence". (Maturana & Varela, 1987, p. 248)

By this stage of the life cycle the interpersonal relationships have degenerated further. Interaction is further transferred to the world of fantasy and reality is lost. The intrapsychic world of the individual dominates. With the loss of recognition of the "other" there is a further loss of intrapsychic and intersubjective rhythms and projective gridlock.

As the bully–victim relationship moves towards deadness, the struggle for recognition becomes a struggle for life within the victim. Over time, victims may become exhausted, unwell, or lose confidence and be unable to continue performing effectively in their work. The intolerable end for the victim is abandonment. For the bully, the end is the death of the victim, whom he/she destroys. The temporary boundaries and containment for the anxieties of a bully are no longer available and so the victim has no more value to the bully. If neither can find the psychic and intersubjective space to learn from these experiences, or the courage to do so, they will get caught in repetition compulsion. An "inner knowing" will continue to be elusive, unless help is sought from a counsellor or psychotherapist. The bully returns to the psychic deadness from whence he/she came.

Advice to HR managers: The bully will continue to bully and the costs of high turnover of staff and loss of productivity will further burden the organisation, unless the bully receives professional help.

Why do bullies need to dominate others?

Fear of dependency

Bullies are individuals who find it difficult to depend on others, as in childhood their parents and significant others were probably not dependable or consistent in their behaviour. In the workplace they will feel that colleagues cannot be relied upon and will be untrusting of others. They will therefore resort to extremes of control.

Lack of understanding of their boundaries

Bullies tend not to know the limits to their personal boundaries, probably because clear boundaries were not set for them in childhood. They spend, and waste, their time, and the time of others, trying to find their boundaries. Working life today demands flexibility, the ability to network and engage with others. This is a problem for potential bullies. When asked to engage with others they struggle for recognition.

If the limits of their work and behaviour are clearly set, they are more likely to feel secure and be more productive.

Lack of empathy

Bullies probably lacked psychic space and intersubjective space in childhood and therefore are unable to reflect on their own feelings and engage with the feelings of others within the workplace. They lack empathy.

Need to blame others

When a bully has projected his/her bad feelings on to the victim, he/she feels better—temporarily. The "other" is a container for those feelings and can be blamed as part of the controlling process. A bully's blindness to his/her actions, may, in part, be due to an unconscious need to right a wrong done to him/her in the past. Someone in his/her history broke the rules by abusing him/her (Woods, 2006). In psychotherapy, a bully may begin to understand the meaning of his/her behaviour—taking revenge on an easier target than his/her original perpetrator.

Need to "feed off" others

A bully can be likened to a mosquito. A mosquito senses out its targets and feeds off them. After a few days (or for a bully it may be longer) it needs to feed again. Bullying enlivens the psychic deadness within the bully but it returns and he/she has to find another victim. As bullies lack reflexive space within their psyches, they have a compulsion to repeat the patterns of the past rather than engaging with reality and learning from experiences. It could be said that bullies have an insatiable appetite for recognition.

They get away with it

A bully dominates others because he/she can get away with it. The group dynamic fragments, as described in Chapter Three. Victims may submit to bullies, not merely out of fear but in complicity with their own deepest desires for recognition, their lack of agency and inability to set their own boundaries. They often claim they are stuck in a situation and cannot, for innumerable reasons, move on. They become like masochistic slaves as described in the master-slave dynamic above. Their subordination, subservience, and sadness is captured in Shakespeare's Sonnet 57.

> Being your slave, what should I do but tend
> Upon the hours and times of your desire?
> I have no precious time at all to spend,
> Nor services to do, till you require;
> Nor dare I chide the world-without-end hour
> Whilst I, my sovereign, watch the clock for you,
> Nor think the bitterness of absence sour
> When you have bid your servant once adieu;
> Nor dare I question with jealous thought
> Where you may be, or your affairs suppose,
> But like a sad slave say and think of naught
> Save where you are, how happy you make those.
> So true a fool is love, that in your will
> Though you do anything, he thinks no ill.

How can individuals protect themselves from becoming drawn into bullying relationships?

1. Acknowledge that not everyone will be nice to you. Nor will they always be honest. This is human nature.
2. Defuse a situation before it gets out of hand. Oade (2009) gives the example of a nurse who, for a while, passively tolerated snide, picky, and undermining remarks from a consultant. But being fed up with being ridiculed, she decided to take action and at an opportune moment told him, in a firm and unwavering tone, that she would like him to stop being rude to her face and cease making comments behind her back. The consultant was taken by surprise. When he

started to tell her she had got everything out of proportion, she interrupted him and told him in the same firm tone, that this was not the case and they both knew that what he had been doing was wrong. His bullying stopped and a few days later she realised he was not going to pick on her again (Oade, 2009).

3. Keep sane. The surest way to make ourselves crazy is to get involved in other people's dramas and excessive neediness—unless we are qualified to do this. The quickest way to become sane and happy is to focus on, and tend to, our own affairs. When we get caught up with the negative energy of others we wind up feeling depleted and exhausted.
4. If you find you are not sleeping, or becoming withdrawn, irritable, or tearful, get help quickly. By talking to a counsellor or therapist, you can begin to shed the false self and find your true self. Rather than being a "prostitute" to bullies, allowing them to control and dominate your life, find your own voice, the newness you were seeking in your search for authenticity; a voice which resonates with your soul.
5. Draw boundaries and let go of trying to rescue others. Focus on your own needs, be kind to yourself. Transactional analysis helps us to question and understand the roles we play in our own dramas. What role would you like to play?
6. Acknowledge that it is better to have mixed feelings about work rather than constantly wanting certainty or perfection. Reflect on the following words of wisdom:

> Of crime—none is greater than having things that one desires;
> Of disasters—none is greater than not knowing when one has enough.
> Of defects—none brings more sorrow than the desire to attain.
> Therefore, the contentment one has when he knows that he has enough, is abiding contentment indeed. (Henricks, 1989, p. 15)

7. Stand up for yourself and your work. An employee spent a year working on a project but just as she was going to present it to the board, her line manager emailed to tell her that her approach was wrong and that she needed to completely change tack. However it was too late and the presentation went ahead. During questions from the board she mentioned the email. Afterwards her line manager was livid with her and wanted no more to do with the project.

Regardless, she pressed on. Months later she found out from a colleague that her manager had been brutally criticised for his work, just before her presentation. She surmised he had probably projected his anxieties on to her, blaming her for his insecurities and his shame at being criticised. The knowledge that he had been getting rid of his feelings of "badness" on her was helpful. She felt reassured and more confident in her own work and was more able to set boundaries when he decided to challenge her again.

What measures can HR directors take to prevent toxic bullying relationships?

Be aware of the false self

When interviewing staff for vacancies beware of the "false self". If someone presents a "perfect" picture, question whether this is authentic. Can that individual acknowledge her weaknesses and be prepared to work through them? Or does he/she stick to an omnipotent stance? How flexible is the thinking? Does he/she allow time for reflection or rush into making decisions?

The costs to an organisation, and the disruption from taking on someone who may seem "ideal" on the surface, can be considerable. For example, when appointing a new head teacher, the governing body of a school consisting of mainly elderly men "fell for" a young, very attractive woman teacher. She had far less experience than other candidates. Other professional weaknesses were overlooked. Within two years the school had gone from having an outstanding OFSTED report to being put into special measures. With weak and inconsistent leadership, staff relationships deteriorated and conflicts ensued. The new head had to be replaced by temporary ones until the situation could be rescued. The distress to pupils, parents, and teachers during those two years was considerable. There were also substantive costs for the school and the local authority.

Recognise authenticity

The cognitive and behavioural aspects of authentic leadership are self-awareness, self-regulation, moral virtue, and moral actions (Beddoes-Jones, 2012). Look for leaders with ethical, pro-social, people-focussed perspectives rather than overly numbers-driven, task-focussed, goal-achievement orientations. In the ABC of authentic leadership, A is for authenticity—being true to yourself; B for bravery—having the courage to lead and to do the right thing, especially in the face of danger or dissent; C is for compassion, leading with empathy, and a concern for the physical and emotion well-being of others (Beddoes-Jones, 2012).

Be honest—forewarned is forearmed

If a potential employee acknowledges he/she has been bullied in a previous job, acknowledge that honesty and present him/her with a realistic picture of the organisation he/she could be joining. All too often, victims idealise a new situation as a defence against anxiety. They let down their "political" antenna and miss the warning signs of potential bullying. Explain the support facilities for victims, for example, buddy schemes for new recruits, EAPs (Employee Assistant Programmes), and counselling facilities, before they start work so they know how to take action early to set boundaries if the pattern of bullying starts to repeat itself.

Repetition compulsion is costly

A quick fix solution to bullying may be moving a victim but beware of how bullies tend to bully again. Repetition compulsion can drive bullies to continue to find victims. Other employees may just turn a blind eye and accept this behaviour so that it becomes institutionalised. Then the costs of lowered productivity, ineffectual engagement with colleagues and tasks, and potential mistakes can begin to mount up. Get some help for the bully, either through life coaching, setting boundaries, or providing work which is less overwhelming and may involve less contact with other employees.

Be aware of the defences against anxiety, for example, displacement

An employee in a factory had some fingers on one hand crushed in an accident with machinery. This resulted in considerable bleeding, swelling, bruising, and pain. However, her manager insisted that she should continue to work using the other hand. This was against the regulations. Eventually her hand was treated. However, when this employee subsequently developed back problems and had to take time off work, she was repeatedly ordered to return to work by her manager who refused to recognise the back problem and continued to accuse her of taking time off on grounds of her injured finger (Fevre, Lewis, Robinson, & Jones, 2011).

On the surface the manager's behaviour seems illogical. However, he may have been unable, on an unconscious level, to come to terms with the initial injury and felt guilty about it. Rather than acknowledging his guilt, he continued to try to work through these unconscious feelings and was in denial about the new reality—the back problem.

Find space and courage

Give the bully a safe space to talk about how he/she experiences the pressures being faced. Resist jumping in with solutions and let the employee explore issues. This cannot be rushed. Like the violent men interviewed by Fonagy (1999), aggressive bullies will probably talk about anything rather than their own feelings. Direct criticism will only provoke further defensive behaviour. A calm, reassuring, and containing situation with clear boundaries is more likely to produce effective change in behaviour.

One of the great challenges faced in contemporary organisations is to create an oasis of time and calm where conversation can take place. Set aside time to simply explain to a bully how you and other colleagues experience his/her behaviour. Use your own experience, for example, "When you cancelled three meetings in a row, I felt frustrated and was unable to meet the project deadline" (Sandler, 2010). Focus more on the practical outcomes rather the emotional. Give a short time for reflection. A few days will suffice. Reiterate your message. Encourage a bully to stand back and watch what happens when he/she does not constantly interfere. Discuss the worst case scenario. In a follow-up meeting, raise the questions "Did your world come to an end when you stepped back? or "Is it possible to trust others?"

Conflict is inevitable—accept it

Workplace disagreements can be expensive and yet they are inevitable. A dispute is something that you can try to solve rather than something you have to fight. Rather than finding someone to blame, let the bullies talk about what is bothering them about their behaviour or their relationship, without blaming anyone or jumping to conclusions (Chynoweth, 2011). This could be very challenging for someone who had disorganised attachments in childhood. Professional help is probably needed from counsellors or psychotherapists.

Carry out a recognition check

Many dysfunctional relationships involve competent, committed, and potentially compatible individuals who simply get caught up in a vortex of underperformance, over-monitoring, and malaise (Manzoni & Barsoux, 2004). An overly controlling style of management can encourage subordinates to disconnect from colleagues and tasks which then leads to reduced performance and increased tension. Being over-monitored and undervalued, employees lose self-confidence and avoid interactions with each other. The situation is then ripe for bullying to become established.

Look behind the HR rhetoric

The HR literature tells us much about the need for engagement but rarely explains the dynamics behind it. In brief, engagement takes place when there are healthy intrapsychic and intersubjective rhythms, when individuals are viewed subjectively rather than as objects to be measured and tightly controlled. When this happens, courage can be found to ask difficult questions and conflict can be taken as a learning opportunity.

Tune into the underlying stresses and strains before they get out of hand

Stories can be used, in training sessions, to raise issues that are hidden from view. Reframing events in such formats enables tensions to surface and potentially be resolved. Informal stories about third parties can create routes of communication that may encourage people to address difficult situations without invoking formal mechanisms. For example, simple stories based on a fairy-tale format can get employees talking about bullying issues (Coupland, 2009). Just as the plates in the

Greek legends were symbols with which partners could recognise each other's authenticity, so stories can help employees engage symbolically with the challenges they face working together.

Likewise, employees could draw pictures of their organisation. Their drawings would give access to unconscious and subconscious feelings about their workplace and raise deep issues which may otherwise be inaccessible (Broussine, 2008). This activity can stir up further anxieties but, with containment and working through of anxieties, can also create very fruitful discussions.

CHAPTER THREE

Groups

Introduction

The aim of this chapter is to show how group dynamics facilitate and moderate the incidence and nature of bullying.

The chapter starts with a review of the research on group behaviour in bullying scenarios. We look at how individuals are received into groups and the factors which influence how well they fit in. We examine the roles taken by group members. These roles are classified in a variety of ways. Most witnesses take a passive stance whilst a few become henchman and assist the bully. Very little support for victims is forthcoming from group members. Some individuals act as scapegoats on behalf of the group and are expelled. Bullying also occurs between groups.

The second part of the chapter presents a variety of theories on the unconscious and subconscious life of groups. The concept of valency is used to explore how individuals fit, or struggle to find their niche, when joining a group. During times of change, the adjustment process can be facilitated by transitional space and transitional objects. Where these are limited, the ability of individuals and groups to find creative responses to challenging situations is curtailed. We return to the theme of recognition, introduced in Chapter Two, to see how the potential for bullying can arise when individuals feel they are prevented from making a positive contribution to the group. Where there is a violation of real, or imaginary, normative expectations, employees struggle for recognition. This gives rise to shame and various related defensive responses. In the places where empathy should be there is, instead, a black hole.

Different ways of understanding the deeper dynamics of group life are outlined using Bion's basic assumptions and further categorisations, specifically Hopper's fourth basic assumption. The fourth assumption most closely describes the group characteristics of bullying scenarios in terms of the fragmentation of the relationships within the group and the deeper collusions beneath the surface. Key subtle differences between bullying and scapegoating are explored using case study material and psychodynamic theories from this chapter and Chapters One and Two.

Finally, theories on bullying and psychoanalysis are brought together to answer the following questions:

How do the deeper group dynamics foster bullying?
Why do some individuals become stuck in their roles within the group?
When does scapegoating become bullying?
How can individuals work together to change group dynamics?
How can HR managers identify groups which are at risk of developing bullying scenarios?

Research review

When interest in the general phenomenon of bullying was first aroused in Sweden in the late 1960s and early 1970s, the focus of attention was the actions of group members. It was known as "mobbing". The word "mobbing" was taken from the field of ethology where it is used to denote a collective attack by a group of animals on larger animals of another species and natural enemies of the group. Application of "mobbing" to human groups is traditionally attributed to Konrad Lorenz, who used it to characterise the action of a school class, or group of soldiers, ganging up against a deviating individual. In Scandinavian countries the term "mobbing" is still used in place of the word bullying.

Initiation into a group

It is never easy to enter a new group, and particularly difficult if a child, or adolescent, has had the traumatic experience of being harassed in another group in the recent past (Salmivalli, 1999). These children are likely to feel particularly insecure and fearful. Unfortunately their feelings are easily communicated to new classmates who may see the newcomer as a suitable target for bullying. Even when a victim moves to a completely new class where there are no former classmates, victimisation tends to start again (Salmivalli, Lappalainen, & Lagerspetz, 1998). Once a child has taken, or been put into, a victim role he/she finds it difficult to escape.

Where there are interpersonal conflicts in the working environment, there are also indications that employees, who are not part of an inner group, are excluded, thereby making it difficult for them to be integrated into the workplace community (Maier, 2008). In a study of skilled migrants in Australia, in-groups appeared to be favoured at the expense of out-groups when seeking access to employment in the workplace (Ramsay, 2008).

Research by Collinson (1992) into working life in UK factories, shows that humour was often used to initiate newcomers. Apprentices had to negotiate a series of degrading and humiliating initiation ceremonies, or rites of passage. One apprentice was made to sing Christmas carols to the rest of the workforce as part of his initiation, an act which he described as "bringing me out of meself". Other initiation rites were less pleasant and more degrading. Even the researcher was tested. One day, unbeknown to him, workers stuck flowers made from paper cups on his back. Such pranks were viewed by the perpetrators as "learning about taking a joke" and "being a man". Exposure to a joking culture not only instructed new members on how to act, and react, but was also a test of the willingness of the newcomer to be part of the group and to accept its rites and rituals (Collinson, 1992). Evidence of ridiculing and teasing of new recruits was also found in the Fire Service (Archer, 1999). This behaviour served to indoctrinate the new arrival into the group and was usually defended on the basis of being "character-building".

In schools, as children adapt to new social groups, bullying may be one way in which young adolescents manage peer and dominance relationships. Research shows that when children first transfer from primary to middle schools bullying increases (Pellegrini & Long, 2002).

After the initial few months bullying declines as more pro-social and co-operative strategies are used to consolidate status, make friends, and reconcile former foes.

Roles

Most insights into the roles taken by witnesses of bullying are from observations in schools. In one study eighty five per cent of children were involved in bullying scenarios and their behaviour ranged from active participation to passive onlooking (Atlas & Pepler, 1998). Another group of primary school children spent one fifth of their time in the playground joining in as henchmen to copy the bully's behaviour and abuse the victim, and about half their time reinforcing the bullying behaviour by passively watching (O'Connell, Pepler, & Craig, 1999).

Four different roles have been identified in bullying scenarios: assistants, re-enforcers, outsiders, and defenders (Salmivalli, 1999). Some children eagerly join in the bullying when someone else has started it and then act as assistants to the bully. Others, known as re-enforcers, may not attack the victim but offer positive feedback to the bully, for example, by coming to see what is going on and thereby providing an audience. They may incite the bully by laughing and making encouraging gestures. Outsiders tend to stay away and not to take sides with anyone, yet by silently approving they allow the bullying to continue. Defenders comfort the victim and try to make the others stop their bullying behaviour (Salmivalli, 1999). Similar roles have been found within the workplace. Most witnesses to bullying are passive, which conveys messages to bullies, participants, and targets that incivility is acceptable (Van Heugten, 2010).

In the literature on bullying in the workplace, a passive witness is known as a bystander.

> "A bystander is the descriptive name given to a person who does not become actively involved in a situation where someone else requires help". (Clarkson, 1996, p. 6)

The few witnesses of bullying who offer support to the victim tend to do so hesitantly (Van Heugten, 2010). In a study of union members in the UK, it was found that colleagues rarely offered overt support; union officials typically responded by providing indirect support and yet the onus to resolve the bullying tended to be placed on the victims (Mawdsley, 2012).

In attributing roles within workplace bullying scenarios four different groups were identified (Power, Lee, & Brotheridge, 2008). These were pure perpetrators who report to have bullied others but not to have been bullied; pure targets who report to have been bullied by others but not to have bullied others; hybrids who report to have been bullied by others as well as to have bullied others; and observers, who report neither to have been bullied by others nor to have bullied others but may have witnessed negative acts (Power, Lee, & Brotheridge, 2008). The minority of witnesses, who act as allies of the bully, may have been friends of the bully when they first joined the organisation, or may have been seduced into friendship via sexual relationships, or financial, or status-related, inducements (Van Heugten, 2010).

Although children are aware of bullying going on in their schools and claim that they want to do something about it, their words rarely turn into action (O'Connell, Peplar, & Craig, 1999; Salmivallii, 1999). Peers only intervene to prevent the bullying in around ten per cent of cases (Atlas & Pepler, 1998; O'Connell, Peplar & Craig, 1999). Targets of bullying in school tend to be most vulnerable when they are alone. Sixty-five per cent of bullying in a classroom context occurred when the children were involved in solitary tasks as opposed to those led by the teacher or group activities (Atlas & Pepler, 1998). However, even if teachers were present they only intervened in approximately one in six incidents of bullying in the playground and one in five in the classroom. This lack of intervention provided a tacit message to bullies that "they can get away with it" (Craig, Pepler, & Atlas, 2000). Likewise, in the workplace the most relevant factor in explaining the antecedents of bullying behaviour was managers' lack of attention to it (Cangarli, 2010). In the Fire Service, complaining about bullying behaviour was seen as disloyal and, with few complaints, managers and union officials kept the abuse of power at a distance (Archer, 1999). Ninety-five per cent of the respondents in a UNISON survey (2009), carried out by Portsmouth University, thought workers were too scared to report cases of bullying. Bystanders fear becoming victims themselves, or fail to recognise that certain behaviours constitute bullying (Paull, Omari, & Standen, 2012).

Colleagues who witnessed bullying acted by ignoring the event, and its impact, as if nothing had happened (Cilliers, 2012). Even family and friends who initially seemed shocked by victims' reports, later claimed they were unable to help and accused the victims of "overreacting" and being "oversensitive" (Cilliers, 2012).

In deciding who is responsible for bullying, witnesses have been found to use three types of moral schemas: defender, persecutor, and commuter (Bloch, 2012). The defender is an individual who gives a positive and empathetic view of the victim and describes him/her as having positive social and work-related characteristics. The prosecutor schema sees the victim as deviating from the norms of the workplace and creating his/her own problems. The commuters are less fixed in their interpretations of bullying, switching their attributions of blame between the victim as a deviant and as normal. Victims' colleagues can suddenly change their opinions after talking to the bully (Mulder, Pouwelse, Lodewijkx, & Bolman, 2008).

Slander and insults are used by bullies to change group members' perception of the victim (Strandmark & Hallberg, 2007). When a bully ignores victims, excluding them from meetings, their standing is devalued within a group.

> I tried to do my work but was completely isolated. When they saw that I was unable to cope with the situation and had to go home to get away from every one, they increased the pressure on me. They made a rule amongst themselves forbidding anyone to talk to me or greet me. (Strandmark & Hallberg, 2007, p. 9)

The more the victim is viewed as responsible for initiating the bullying, the less bystanders are willing to help. Even seemingly helpful interventions by a colleague may further highlight the fact that the victim is experiencing difficulties and also show that the victim is weak and unable to defend him/herself (Bloch, 2012). The intervention may then result in the victim further losing his or her social standing. For example, a line manager described her dilemma in trying to help someone who was a potential victim within a department where bullying was rife.

She said,

> There is someone who works for me who has a lot of anxieties, gets very agitated and almost unintentionally refuses to do things, or doesn't listen, when you are trying to explain things. I think why am I bothering? I do get annoyed. She is very good and she knows her job but then she panics and thinks she can't cope and what she tells people isn't correct. Her former line manager just tried to shield her and help her along. I don't think that would do her any good in the long run. I'm trying to get her to help herself.

Where group support for victims in schools is formalised, or more covert, this may help the victim. Support systems, promoted by schools, in which children take on the role of defending the victim, are effective in reducing the negative effects of bullying for victims and create a socio-emotional climate of care (Naylor & Cowie, 1999). A longitudinal investigation found low levels of victimisation amongst children who have reciprocated friendships (Boulton, Trueman, Chau, Whitehead, & Amatya, 1999). Likewise in the workplace, the higher the levels of support from family, friends, workplace colleagues, particularly managers, and unions or professional bodies, the greater the chance that bullying would be resolved or the damage to victims limited (White, 1998). A study of bystander behaviour within call centres in India found that, with the help of friends and colleagues, victims were able to identify and label the conflict as bullying, make the decision to leave, and successfully move to other organisations (D'Cruz & Noronha, 2011). Support is more effective when the supporting person, such as a union representative, is not directly involved in the bullying process and when the victim and the supporter have shared values (Strandmark & Hallberg, 2007). Whilst unions may have limited power to alter management solutions to bullying, there was some evidence that where they fostered a collective response to allegations of bullying, perpetrators were more likely to be held accountable (Mawdsley, 2012).

Victims found that once they had decided to resign and made this known to their colleagues, previously silent bystanders began to change roles and offer their support (Van Heugten, 2010).

The following description of a bullying scenario by a new employee, in a small UK sales office, illustrates the different roles individuals take in a bullying scenario in which a newcomer is quickly isolated and bullied. Weak leadership at the top of the group had created a vacuum into which a bully and henchman moved. Other employees were bystanders and outsiders.

> My job description was a mish-mash of working in different departments. I was supposed to be MD's assistant but he already had an assistant. He never came out of his office and sat playing on his computer. There was his secretary who they called the sick–ret-ary because she was always off sick a lot. There was the woman in the accounts department who ran all the books and was privy to everything. She had this thing about locking everything—locking cupboards, locking drawers. She knew everything and had the MD's

ear; she had a lot of power and influence. Then there was this woman who was the despatch manager who was friendly with the woman in accounts, she was a very strong personality. There was a harmless chap in sales administration and there was the sales manager who had a foul temper. He wasn't there very much of the time, thank goodness. He used to slam doors and swear a lot.

There was a chap in the despatch department who these women (from accounts and the despatches manager) used to run down. He would tremble most of the time and seemed close to having a breakdown because his work was always being criticised. Then there was a guy in the warehouse who never came out. He kept himself to himself and even had his lunch and tea there. It was such a small place. It was claustrophobic. Nobody got on with each other, it was unhealthy. There was no teamwork.

I would walk into the room and they [the two women] would shut up straight away and press their lips together. There was a terrible atmosphere when I appeared. I think they did it to other people but they had either become immune to it, or kept themselves to themselves, or kept out of the way. The chap in the sales office had been there a number of years and he kept his head down and that's how he survived. I tried to find an ally in the secretary but she used to go home at lunchtimes. I didn't have any support from my boss because he was such a weak man. He let these two women walk right over him.

I would ask how to do something. They [the two woman] said they didn't know, but they obviously did know. I was so nervous. I lost confidence. I was getting to a stage where I was frightened to do anything. I was getting panic attacks. I lasted six weeks. One day the MD was so abrupt and asked me to do something I just broke down and said I have to go home and I just ran out of the building. The doctor signed me off for two weeks. I was off for weeks and then I got a letter saying—you've only just started and you've had too much time off so you are fired.

As bullying intensifies, group members become increasingly isolated from each other and victims become excluded from work activities (White, 1998). On the surface the group lacks cohesion and fragments (White, 2007). Individuals seem unable to help themselves or, if they do, their attempts at constructive change are thwarted. Even individuals who are not targets but who witness bullying, suffer negative consequences comparable to direct victims (Low, Radhakrisnan, Schneider, & Rounds, 2007).

Exclusion from groups

When victims try to make sense of what has happened to them, they conceptualise their experiences of being bullied in terms of group conflict which has been resolved through rejection and expulsion of a victim (Strandmark & Hallberg, 2007). Victims identify bullying behaviour in terms of isolation and exclusion by the group (Archer, 1999).

In a study of the evolution of an unstructured work group, from the start of a project through to its end, an individual was singled out and denigrated in a gradual process of collective victimisation (Salamon & Maitlis, 2010). A repeated pattern of aggression became an integral part of the relationship between the target and group. The target was criticised for the various behaviours but then expected to act these out on behalf of the members, as victimisation appeared to become "institutionalised" within the group (Salamon & Maitlis, 2010).

Amongst school children, bullying is taken to be justifiable when an outsider is perceived as a threat to the group, but unjustifiable when someone from outside a group presents no threat to the group identity (Ojala & Nesdale, 2004). If new arrivals are perceived as a threat to the preservation of group activities or norms, the more the threat increases so does the likelihood of exclusion (Archer, 1999). Archer (1999) gives an example of how a young line manager, with only a few years experience in the Fire Service, was "crucified" by his colleagues because they felt it was an affront to their dignity that such a "junior" was put in charge of them.

Other employees, more established in work, may also become victims. For example, those who feel motivated to improve routines and procedures claim they are often viewed as threatening by colleagues and superiors (Strandmark & Hallberg, 2007). With differing norms and values, power struggles develop. Slander and insults are used by the bully/bullies to alter group members' perceptions of the victim (Strandmark & Hallberg, 2007). If the conflicts remain unsolved, the power struggles are transformed into systemic bullying, with victims being stigmatised as deviant persons. The bullying behaviour gradually escalates and becomes more distressing for the victim who feels rejected and resentful. After leaving work, victims are often informed, by former work colleagues, that the bullying is still ongoing but in other forms and with others involved (Strandmark & Hallberg, 2007).

Individuals who are excluded from the workgroup are often outsiders who differ from the rest of the group (Thylefors, 1987). The choice of victim may be from a group which is especially susceptible, for example, ethnic or religious minority, the disabled, newcomers, or a marginal insider such as the boss's son (Gold, 2010). Some ethnic employees felt they were outsiders because their religious beliefs prevented them from joining in weekly out-of-hours socialising which involved alcohol (Fevre, Lewis, Robinson & Jones, 2011). These employees understood the traditions of the company but felt that managers did not suggest or encourage alternative team events. This led to a sense of social isolation and exclusion.

In an organisation with a high percentage of male employees, training in team bonding was usually arranged for weekends and often at outdoor pursuit centres. Some of the staff could not attend as they had other commitments. The women, in particular, felt excluded. Even when they joined in some did not have the physic or stamina to complete the tasks. Instead of creating bonds within the team, the activities generated fissures and further anxieties in the group, leading potentially to further bullying in a department where bullying was already rife.

Some victims become excluded because they are outdated and prioritise, or stick to, their own ways of doing things rather than adjusting to a group consensus. Such individuals are at risk of becoming scapegoats for the group (Thylefors, 1987).

A scapegoat is an individual on whom blame is placed for the wrongdoings of others. This term, whilst describing a common dynamic in human relations today, derives from an ancient practice described in the Hebrew Bible (Leviticus 16:21–27). On the Day of the Atonement, two goats were chosen, one to carry the iniquities and transgressions of the people away into the barren wilderness (the scapegoat), the second to be killed as a victim or sacrificial sin offering for the community.

The bullying of a targeted individual by a group may represent a scapegoating process in which the collective scapegoating of an individual by a group is a means of venting its shared frustration (Agervold, 2007; Brodsky, 1976; Thylefors, 1987). A scapegoat can bring unity back to a group that is threatened by its own anxieties or its own violence (Thylefors, 1987). Yet for the targeted individual, the focus of systematic and probing aggression is likely to have severe consequences (Aquino & Thau, 2009).

Scapegoating may also arise in homogeneous groups where employees are often of similar age, gender, and social background and also have the same norms, values, and education. Members may develop "group-think" and avoid raising difficult questions about conflict. The groups can be maintained because members act as one against a common enemy such as an outsider or newcomer (Strandmark & Hallberg, 2007). Girard (2010) suggests that when members of a group imitate each other they become too similar and then have to find a means of dealing with "contagious similarity". As a group becomes increasingly "pure", the mechanism that reintroduces difference into a situation, in which everyone has come to resemble everyone else, is sacrifice. Hence the need for a scapegoat. Yet a scapegoat only remains effective as long as members of the group believe in its guilt. When the scapegoat leaves and the group seems to have been purged of the "impure elements" which corrupted it, the relief is short-lived and mimetic rivalry returns (Girard, 2010).

A very successful car sales rep refused to adapt to new, more aggressive marketing tactics and prescriptive reporting procedures imposed by top management. Over time his lack of group conformity and intransigence isolated him from his colleagues and antagonised management. The case went to a tribunal during which the evidence given against him was vague. One colleague became very confused and contradictory in his statements. The outcome of a very costly court case was that the previously successful sales rep lost his job. His colleagues later admitted that the hearing had been a traumatic experience.

It appeared the rep had become a scapegoat for the group. The anxieties relating to the adoption of the new procedures were displaced onto the sales representative rather than being collectively articulated to top management and duly addressed. This displacement freed the members to conform, perhaps reluctantly, to the new demands and expectations made on them from "above".

Although projection of anxieties onto the scapegoat may be an unconscious defence, there is a great deal of evidence to show that the process of scapegoating in our organisations today derives a considerable proportion of its momentum from conscious and deliberate attempts to evade responsibility (Gold, 2010).

Inter-group bullying

Within the workplace there may be misunderstanding and feuds between teams or between departments. These often occur where there are extremes of management. Excessive controls, monitoring, and targets may get in the way of focussing on the primary task. Collaboration with others necessary for the effective use of resources and care for clients becomes secondary to the achievement of the targets.

For example, Fevre, Lewis, Robinson, and Jones (2011) report that in a hospital, a pressure cooker-environment had been created in which the tensions between clinicians and administrators/managers seemed to be a fact of life. Tempers were frayed, insults traded, and intimidation practiced. Some clinical professionals felt managers did not understand clinical needs. Some administrators and managers felt that clinical professionals had too much control. One administrator, with responsibility for reducing waiting times, ended up in a slanging match in a hospital corridor with a senior consultant as to which patients could be seen and the times of those appointments.

Bullying also occurs between groups where there is a lack of clear direction and focus from senior managers which results in poor communication across the organisation, and/or feuding between teams and considerable inefficiency.

For example, in an organisation with a laissez-faire style of management (see Chapter Four for a description), there was conflict between two departments. One employee said,

> There was a falling out between our department [finances] and marketing and so we don't have much to do with them. Two of us are going to a talk, by the marketing department, for our customers and we are going to see if what they are saying about the organisation is the same as us. They don't come to us anymore and ask. It'll be interesting to see what slant they put on things—everything is rosy here etc. We have to be more straightforward and realistic. They don't know us. We shall be in the audience to ask questions.

Sometimes individuals from one group are bullied by individuals from another group. The motives for this may be well hidden within the complex dynamics between the two teams and only come to light when someone from outside of the organisation, such as a researcher or organisational consultant, investigates the conflict.

For example, a line manager of a small team bullied the receptionist of another team. In an attempt to stop the bullying, staff duties were rotated so that there were different employees on the reception desk. However this failed to stop the bullying. Different personality types were recruited to the post of receptionist but still the bullying continued. In spite of collective collaboration, the bully continued to pick on the stress points of the different receptionists. Later, the line manager revealed that she had wanted her own receptionist and was aggrieved that she was not allowed to have one.

The motive for this bullying may have been rooted in envy and jealousy; however, there was a lack of recognition for the value of the work of this employee by her manager and within the organisation as a whole. She had very little support in a particularly challenging role.

Summary of the research review

Employees are vulnerable to being bullied when entering into a group for the first time. They often have to prove that they can "fit in" whilst adjusting to the norms and values of the majority. Responses of their colleagues to them may determine how well they can integrate and contribute to the successful working of the group. Bullying and scapegoating are more likely to occur where there are noticeable differences between the newcomer and the group, where there is rigidity of thinking by the individual and/or the group, and inflexibility in the integration process through, for example, outdated initiations.

Within bullying scenarios group members take on a variety of roles. Some of these are active, such as the role of henchman. Most members are bystanders. Colleagues are often reluctant to defend the victim and their opinions are often influenced by the bully. As the group dynamics evolve, perceptions of the victim or scapegoat generally become fixed in projective gridlock (see Chapter One) and victims become increasingly isolated from the group.

Scapegoating and bullying of individuals are a means by which group norms, identity, and unity can be preserved. By scapegoating a specific individual, the group is then more able to function in an apparently more cohesive way. The worries of the group are handed over to the scapegoat, who bears them on behalf of the other members. Unless scapegoats have an inner resilience, they will be sent "into the wilderness", an exit which is only a temporary solution to the group's problems. The next newcomer or existing member who most deviates from the group norms and values is likely to be selected as the new scapegoat.

An alternative scenario develops when a group member is being bullied by an individual from outside the group. The group may try to work collectively to defend that individual but these efforts may fail due to the deeply hidden motives of the bully and the dysfunctional nature of the organisation's culture and weak leadership.

Psychodynamic theories of groups

Introduction

As we have seen in the research review, there are times when a group appears to take on a life of its own and has its own identity. It is as if a group mind exists which can be taken to be as real as an individual's mind (Stapley, 2006). The notion of a collective unconscious is known as "group-as-a-whole". The unconscious life of groups is taken to be different from, but related to, the unconscious life of its individual members. In this way of thinking about groups, underlying problems with the group can be addressed (Obholzer & Roberts, 1994).

When joining a group we establish contact with its emotional life. The group gradually becomes part of our identity and we become part of its identity. In this integration process, however, we also lose some of our individual distinctiveness. This loss is particularly noticeable amongst groups and gangs of children and adolescents. Individuals can find anonymity and, within a gang, children can do things that they may not otherwise contemplate doing by themselves, for example, living out their aggressive impulses (Waddell, 2007). However, membership often comes at a price. If an individual lacks resilience and has weakened boundaries, a group can wipe out an individual's capacity for independent thought and judgment (Waddell, 2007).

Within the working environment, similar dynamics can be noted. Small groups, in particular, have little or no private space and projections can feel very intense, making some individuals feel vulnerable (Carr, 2009).

Within larger groups it is possible to observe, often fleetingly, defences used in similar ways to those used by individuals to defend against anxieties. For example, divisions or splits in large groups, equivalent to an individual's intrapsychic splitting, may only stabilise when one part of the group has gained control over the whole group. In large groups fragmentation and splitting occurs so frequently and swiftly, it is often difficult to observe and follow (Gould, Stapley, & Stein, 2001). Sometimes groups may split in two, with one team developing characteristics which are opposite in character to those of another team. For example, in one organisation a group acquired a reputation for quiet and constructive work whilst another group was notoriously aggressive and difficult (Menzies Lyth, 1989). Menzies Lyth suggests that the quiet group may have been projecting its unconscious and unacknowledged anti-task attitudes and hostility on to the second group, thereby freeing members to engage with the task in hand.

As the dynamics of large groups in organisations are often fluctuating and diffuse, much of our knowledge of the unconscious life of groups come from group relations conferences. Unlike traditional conferences, which have speakers and debates on specific topics, group relations conferences are gatherings of individuals who meet with the primary aim of studying the evolving group dynamics of which they are a part. Roles are not fixed. There are no hierarchies, targets, or customers to please. Free from many of the constraints of organisational life, participants can begin to understand what happens when their internal worlds meet. They can experience, feel, and engage first hand with struggles within themselves and within a group setting. Issues of race and gender can be discussed openly. Scapegoating and bullying can be seen to be happening in real time rather than ignored until contentious and difficult to resolve. Participants become aware of changes between old and new identities, both of themselves and of the constantly re-forming group (Halton, 2010).

Individuals and groups

Valency

As the research on bullying shows, joining a group can prove to be an overwhelming experience for some individuals, particularly when they have difficulty in fitting in or are perceived by group members to be a threat. The term used to describe the "fit" of an individual into a group is valency, a concept taken from chemistry where it denotes the power of the combination of atoms. When applied to group dynamics, valency refers to an individual's capacity for using spontaneous and instinctive emotional responses towards other individuals and the establishment of a pattern of behaviour (Obholzer & Miller, 2004). Those individuals who have little difficulty in joining and integrating themselves into groups can be said to have high valency. Others who struggle to fit may have low valency.

For example, Oade (2009) describes how an academic decided to leave a university, an environment to which he was well suited, to take up the offer of a job in an oil company. Soon after starting his new role, he quickly found that his ways of working were not popular with colleagues. His strengths—a methodical, thoughtful, quality-conscious style—were routinely characterised by his colleagues as weaknesses, slow, unimaginative, and unpersuasive. He lost credibility with the group. A colleague began bullying him. Instead of standing up for himself he allowed the bullying to continue until he was publicly humiliated in front of colleagues. Eventually he decided to return to the academic world where his skills were, once more, appreciated.

Even when, on the surface, group members may appear to have similar feelings and beliefs as our own, we may still get very anxious. It may be difficult to understand the origin of these feelings. Sometimes our anxieties may relate to our patterns of early attachments with our mothers, fathers, or carers. Ambivalent feelings may be raised, such as love and hate, or relief and despair. There may be other early influences, such as bonding with siblings. These, in particular, may impact on our choice of roles within a group. Sibling relationships can have a profound impact upon our sense of "self" and our interactions with others as well as subsequently shaping our roles in organisational life (Kane, 2011; Lister, 2001). These early relationships can affect our choice of how we take up our roles as well as our sense of personal authority. For example, when a new employee joins a group, this event may arouse memories, in established employees, of how they felt as children when a new sibling arrived in the family. The early childhood struggles for the attention of the parents, and possible disappointments, may in adult life again trigger feelings of displacement and loss. Established employees may, at this time of change and adjustment, regress to early defences such as splitting and project their anxieties on to others, thereby replicating, or echoing, sibling rivalries and struggles of their early years. Anxieties about these early relationships may continue to affect working relationships for many years.

For example, a woman professor who had been a disappointment to her parents because she was not a boy and had not received the educational opportunities to which her brothers had been privileged, picked on and bullied a new female lecturer. By singling out and bullying one of the few females in the department she may, at an unconscious level, have been mirroring her own childhood feelings of rejection within her own family through her behaviour towards the lecturer.

Ongoing family conflict can also be played out in the workplace, as illustrated by the relationship between a head teacher and new young teacher. The head teacher often said to the teacher "You are just like my daughter". It was well known in the school that the head had a difficult relationship with her daughter and constantly denigrated her. Within the school she continued projecting her anxieties about her daughter on to the new teacher. From the teacher's perspective, there was no chance of fitting into the school whilst an unhappy home relationship was being replicated in the workplace. The young teacher moved to another school.

When employees are asked to describe how, and why, they are drawn to particular types of work or institutions, factors such as financial reward, the kudos of working for a particular company, or the challenges and rewards of working in a service sector appear uppermost in their minds. Yet, at a deeper level, they may be drawn towards certain workplaces, or groups, by unconscious desires to meet deeper needs. These organisations and groups may help them to suppress sensations and emotions which are too difficult for them to bear (Morgan-Jones, 2010). An employee may then use the group to express and legitimise those emotions on his/her behalf.

One victim of bullying, whilst telling her story, often repeated the expression "I love my work, I really love my work". It seemed she had to convince herself of this fact. However, her valency for the requirements of the job was low. In taking on the role and sticking with it even though she had been bullied, she may have been trying to work through deeper issues regarding relationships from her past.

Transitional objects and transitional space

When making the transition from home life to nursery school, or kindergarten, children are often encouraged to take their favourite toy such as a teddy bear or fluffy creature to school to help them to adjust to their new environment. A child's sense of self may be comforted, supported, and strengthened by the presence of these transitional objects.

Transitional objects are also used by children in their play to help them discover and comprehend the outside world. For example, a child returning home from school may use the toy to act out scenes from the school day. Through play, some of the anxieties arising in the adjustment process can be worked through. Yet play requires space, both psychic and intersubjective. When a carer is sensitive to a child's need for space, the child can reflect on, and play, with his/her experiences in imaginative and creative ways, thereby developing a better understanding of the world. However, when parents and carers are very needy themselves, a child's space may be restricted by their demanding presence and their own needs to dominate and control. The child then lacks the transitional space needed to reflect on new situations and to avoid conflict with others.

Transitional space is an intersubjective space, an area that exists as a resting place for the individual engaged in the perpetual task of keeping inner and outer reality separate yet interrelated. It is an area of reality testing. When work groups are undergoing change, they are often in a state of not knowing precisely what the task is and they need space to play, to be imaginative and creative. Transitional space and objects can be seen as enabling groups of employees to operate through change (Gould, Stapley, & Stein, 2001).

In an organisation which had undergone rapid change, there were considerable differences in appearance between an office in which there was no bullying and one where bullying was rife. Where there was no evidence of bullying, employees had pictures of their families and colourful mugs on their desks and fluffy toys balanced on their computers. These objects, symbols of security and familiarity, occupied their personal space and acted as transitional objects for the staff in a context of rapid change and relocation to a new site.

In another team where the leader was overtly bullying his staff, desks were bereft of personal items. Ownership of space and the presence of personal objects was discouraged and interpersonal space was constantly interrupted by group members. One team member said, "You haven't got any private time. Your phone calls are listened in to and you can hear other people. Staff management is very difficult". Space for senior managers to read reports and reflect was at a premium. In this team frustrations and tensions easily built, making it more difficult for the staff to engage effectively with each other and their work.

When leaders crowd out "space" by their strength and aggressive presence, they weaken their teams (Bing, 2012). Lack of team space can lower the quality of decision-making because the leader is insulated from divergent points of view that might add helpful insights or information. The group dynamic can develop a rigid adherence to a stated purpose as represented and advanced by the leader, rather than authentic engagement with and between team members which is deepened by rich dialogue. The learning and growth needed for an organisation to rise to the challenges of external stakeholders is stymied.

In bullying scenarios, psychic and intersubjective spaces, as shown in Chapters One and Two, are often occupied by fixed perceptions and projective gridlock. Space for groups to engage with others, in healthy ways, are limited.

Shame

We all need to feel that we are valued for who we are and what we can offer to a group in the roles we take up in the workplace. The way in which our contribution is perceived and received affects our relationships with others and our ability to be effectively and efficiently productive in our work tasks. Just as young children need carers to nurture them so that they can grow and develop, likewise employees hope their work groups will provide them with favourable emotional responses and, in Winnicott's terms, a suitable holding environment (Stapley, 2006). When group members perceive an organisation's holding environment to be "good enough" and have basic trust in it, employees can help each other to feel valued and to work effectively with each other.

However, where an individual cannot offer something of value, particular to him/herself, that individual loses a sense of identity, develops a lack of self-esteem, and the potential for shame develops (Honneth, 1995). Shame is an emotional response to an awareness of the differences between expectations of the self and what is witnessed by an "other". It often follows from a violation of normative expectations, real or imaginary, and comes from the experience of not being, or doing, what you or the other person wants or expects, particularly when one's accomplishments, abilities, and qualities are made to feel inferior or, worse, despicable, especially when success has been expected (Campbell, Coldicott, & Kinsella, 1994). When an individual feels shame there is a struggle for recognition and the opening up of an opportunity for others to denigrate and insult (Honneth, 1995).

For example, a hotel receptionist, with many years' experience in different hotel chains, started a new job with the expectation that he would be treated with respect and given the opportunity to fulfil his role. He had not anticipated that his line manager would deliberately tamper with a computer program to create errors and make him look foolish. He was blamed and humiliated in front of other staff. It took him some time to realise what was happening, particularly as the actions of his line manager seemed illogical. These actions not only affected the new employee's standing with other hotel employees but also impacted on the profitability of the business.

When we are robbed of opportunities to attribute value to our own abilities and to bring something of positive significance to the working group we feel a discontinuity, or gulf, between ourselves and others. We become strangers to each other. There is an inner experience of wanting to hide, the feeling of falling, of the ground opening up and swallowing us (Flynn, 2001).

The following quotation will resonate with those readers who are, or have been, victims of workplace bullying:

> In the gaps and clumsy steps in human intercourse, in the misunderstandings, the misperceptions, and misjudgements, in the blank mocking eyes where empathy should be, in the look of disgust where a smile was anticipated, in the loneliness and disappointment of inarticulate desire that cannot be communicated because the words cannot be found, in the terrible hopeless absence when human connection fails, and in the empty yet rage-filled desolation of abuse—there in these holes and missing bits lies shame. Shame is where we fail. (Mollon, 2002, p. xi)

Mollon (2002) goes on to describe how in shame we fall out of the dance, that choreography of the human theatre. In the depth of shame, where our connection with others should be, there seems to be a hole, which Grotstein (1990) refers to as the black hole of non-meaning. It is a space where reality cannot be grasped. We return to the topic of black holes in Chapter Four.

But how does shame work? Where there is shame there is a fragmentation within the psyche and the splitting which goes beyond that of the paranoid-schizoid form of splitting into 'good and "bad" (Asser, 2004). It is a severe form of projective identification in which splitting and fragmentation take place with such ferocity that "good" and "bad" are "cut into" minute pieces and become indistinguishable before they are expelled. The target who receives the projections must be possessed, controlled, and labelled to ensure those projections remain externalised. Any signs of independent life in the target are crushed either by subtly undermining him/her, or through overt aggression.

Shame and guilt

In the dynamics of projective identification, as described in Chapter One, an individual, such as a bully, strives to find and to induce in the other the embodiment of his/her projected anxieties. If the target refuses to collude he/she may feel guilty for not being that which is demanded by the bully. However, if the target of the projections succumbs, that individual will feel shame and inferiority and is then guilty of self-betrayal. As shame intensifies, the individual loses empathy with him/herself and without the soothing words, or touch of another, hatred of the self may grow without limits (Mollon, 2002).

When a group is fragmented, with many members taking the role of bystander, it is difficult for a victim of bullying to find support and avoid feeling shame and guilt for his/her apparent mistakes and faults. The only confirmation available is one of failure, and this is from the bully.

It is not easy to entangle guilt from shame (Jacoby, 1996). Shame is generally to do with feelings of weakness and a failure to do what is expected, whereas guilt is a response to strength and power. When, for example, a victim is faced with having to move out of a masochistic role, to take a more aggressive or even sadistic stance, he/she is likely to feel guilty. This is not the role he/she had been "taught" and internalised in childhood. The omnipotent parent "reappears", unconsciously and subconsciously. Guilt is associated with the dread of punishment and retribution (Rycroft, 1995). The victim relives those feelings of not being good enough—failing to do what is "right" in the eyes of his/her parents and fears an inevitable punishment.

Defences against shame

Bullies fear that their own shame may be exposed. The potential for shame may be defended against with a range of defences such as confusion, envy and jealousy, and arrogance. Confusion in the form of inconsistency, displays of superiority, contempt for others, and arrogance are characteristics that we so often find in bullies. Confusion arises when what has been lost in excessive projective identification is replaced by excessive introjection. There is a fusion of ego and object. Good or bad aspects of the self can be identified with good or bad aspects of the object, and good or bad aspects of the object can be identified with good or bad aspects of the self (Eigen, 1996). There can be a myriad of permutations. When the introjections cannot be assembled in a coherent way, the result is confusion. Confusion may initially ward off feelings of vulnerability and shame. However, as shame reflects a sense of being disconnected, misunderstood, or excluded, then other defences such as envy and jealousy, with their characteristics of splitting, may follow.

The defence of arrogance, for example, works in a perverse way. It acts as a mask that hides an uneasy fear, yet constantly exposes it because the wearer of the mask needs to see that which he/she is afraid of in the other (Long, 2008). The arrogant need others to be shamed lest their own contempt is turned inward (Long, 2008). The following example shows that when changes occur which are unpredicted and difficult to manage, an individual who is fearful of her own shame, suddenly feels that the situation is out of control and starts to project anxieties on to others. Shame occurs when we feel we are placed out of the context within which we wish to be interpreted (Schneider, 1997).

A teacher who felt ashamed of aspects of her family background, moved into a different social strata and became successful in her career. However, her choice of top-quality designer clothing and boasts of social contacts seemed excessive and were out of keeping with the lifestyle of other teachers. When she gained an appointment of head teacher in an élite educational institution, her desire for grandeur was further unleashed. She chose very expensive décor for the classrooms and yet the basic materials were not ordered. When radical changes had to be made to the teaching arrangements by events outside of her control, she struggled to cope. As new members of staff were taken on, she bullied them through excessive monitoring and undermining them behind their backs. (Dominance masks the fear of weakness, and the certainty found in monitoring and measuring others masks the fear of not knowing.) When those teachers left she began bullying established staff. Eventually her mask slipped.

Group dynamics

Bion's basic assumptions

A standard classification of groups, from a psychodynamic perspective, is Bion's basic assumptions (Bion, 1961). Bion postulated that every group operates at two levels. First, there is the work group which has come together for some specific and agreed purpose, or task. Second, at an unconscious level, the group is held together by shared assumptions about the group and the members' contribution to it. Although on the surface a work group may be behaving rationally in pursuit of tasks, its members are, at the same time, combined together in one of three primitive shared assumptions: "basic assumption dependency", "fight and flight", and "pairing" (Bion, 1961).

In the first categorisation, basic dependency mode, there appears to be dependency of group members on a seemingly omnipotent, or omniscient leader, often a person, or even a doctrine. The group behaves as if it expects to be fed and nurtured by the leader. Members feel united through feelings of inadequacy, immaturity, and incompetence (Gould, Stapley & Stein, 2001). They use a range of defences such as idealisation, projected omnipotence, denial, envy, and greed. This type of basic assumption can be found in bullying scenarios, for example, where members fall into subservience to an autocratic leader.

In the second categorisation, fight and flight mode, a group behaves as if its purpose is to identify an external enemy or threat, from which it has either to attack or to flee. Members may project their desire for fight, or flight, on to someone to lead them. Over time, they may become disappointed with their leader, particularly if he/she fails to live up to their expectations and then they undermine him/her. Groups in this mode may also invent fantasy enemies in some other departments or organisations, and direct their energy and resources into competition or into scapegoating members (Stacey, 2007). For example, a lack of direction and coordination from the leadership at the top of an organisation resulted in teams becoming distant from each other. In fleeing into their own spaces, the teams developed their own norms and values. Group-think became prevalent and misunderstandings developed between teams, creating the potential for bullying.

The third categorisation, pairing mode, illustrates how a group can be focussed on two members who are expected to produce solutions to the group's problems. There is an expectation that a pair, such as a CEO and managing director, or team leader and line manager, will relieve the employees' anxieties. However, this pairing can prove destructive, as solutions are projected away from group ownership into the idealised couple. There are few opportunities for members to deal with difficulties and challenges as they arise. They are less likely to take responsibility for themselves and their actions.

Bion's three basic assumptions are useful for identifying patterns of behaviour within groups in organisations and are a good starting point in thinking about how bullying may be arising in some parts of an organisation but not in others. However, most working groups are complex and evolving, a mix of categories rather than clearly distinctive ones (Obholzer, 2003). Groups also shift from stable work groups, characterised by design and clear shared intention, to disintegrative dynamics (Gould, Stapley & Stein, 2001).

Basic assumptions: Oneness and Me-ness

Two further basic assumptions were added to Bion's original classification. Turquet (1974) contributed the basic assumption "Oneness", in which a group comes together to join in a powerful union with some omnipotent force. This enables members to surrender themselves with some kind of safe passivity; members seem lost in an oceanic feeling of unity (Stacey, 2007).

Carr (2009) described this basic assumption in a large study group at a group relationships conference:

> It was totally silent, not a chair scraped, no one coughed, lit a cigarette, or spoke. It was as if the group had become like the Marie Celeste on the sea of dynamic—fully in order but devoid of human life. It was not sinking, but neither was it going anywhere. There was a pervasive sense of comfortable well being. On a warm day in a crowded (and in those days) smoke filled room, people were lethargic: the members were dozing after lunch and the consultants either could not find a way to intervene or had joined the membership. After a long silence a voice rumbled from the back row. "I haven't the slightest idea what is going on". It was Pierre Turquet speaking. (Carr, 2009, p. 262)

This comment from Turquet helped the group to shift out of the comfortable world they had inhabited and establish a dialogue.

The basic assumption "Me-ness", which is about dependency on oneself and one's own resources was added by Lawrence (Lawrence, Bain, & Gould, 1996). This assumption was drawn up in response to turbulent changes in society, especially the way individuals are increasingly driven into their own inner realities in order to exclude and deny the perceived disturbing realities from outside. When an external environment is not predictable, or dependable, dependency has to come from within the individual. This assumption has been compared to Steiner's (1993) psychic retreats. Steiner (1993) describes how patients in the clinical setting withdraw behind a powerful system of defences which serve as a protective armour, or hiding place, from which they appear unreachable to the analyst. Patients emerge with great caution, like snails coming out of their shells, and retreat once more if the experience leads to pain or anxiety.

In a clinical setting or a group relations conference there is time to observe individuals and groups, but in an organisational context we may only gain glimpses of a basic assumption "in action". The following is an example of basic assumption Me-ness.

In a large organisation, in which bullying was breaking out, HR staff spent time and effort in setting up a conference call so that employees in different localities could participate in a discussion on new strategies. A few employees gathered around a table, other participants, some only a short walking distance away, chose to stay in their offices and "participate" from afar, whilst others were in distant locations. The technology was slow and failed to connect all of the members. Those present in the room were very quiet, almost passive. Few spoke and the HR managers rapidly concluded the session. Rather than engaging in a fruitful discussion, the "participants" seemed satisfied that the technology was a substitute for their efforts. The HR staff and the technology were taking responsibility for everything. Members of this group seemed to have retreated within themselves, reliant on unreliable technology to bring about communication on their behalf.

As we have seen above, research shows that in bullying scenarios it is possible to find examples of most of these types of basic assumptions, in particular, flight and fight and Me-ness (White, 2007). The group dynamics of bullying scenarios are particularly complex, far more so than where there is no, or little evidence, of bullying. As shown in the research review, bystanders tend to isolate themselves from others, retreating into their own inner resources for survival, there being little nurturing or recognition available from the group. Often bystanders may only emerge "out of their shells", change roles, and become defenders of victims, when the victim of bullying announces he/she is leaving.

On the surface of groups in which there is bullying there is a fragmentation of the group giving rise to isolation of individuals from each other and a fragility to the group dynamics. Beneath the surface, however, there is collusion of submission and helplessness which unconsciously prevents group members from being able to engage with each other to make positive changes. This sort of impasse most closely matches Hopper's basic assumption (White, 2007).

Hopper's basic assumption

Hopper (2003) claimed the title "the fourth basic assumption" with his theory of incohesion: aggregation/massification—aggregation and massification being described as the bipolar states of incohesion. Aggregation can be likened to a handful of gravel or a set of billiard balls (Hopper, 2003). Where aggregation occurs in groups, members distance themselves from their own feelings and those of others. The group has too much individuality for members to engage with each other in positive ways and the fragmented nature of the group, like that of basic assumption me-ness, generates ignorance and misunderstanding of social norms. Characteristics of groups displaying aggregation are sarcasm, mindlessness, a capacity for violent action, and sadistic scapegoating (Hopper, 2003).

Massification, on the other hand, seems to bring the group together. However, the appearance of solidarity is an illusion and is highly dependent on the maintenance of fantasy. It can be likened to a handful of warm, wet sponges or a lump of dough (Hopper, 2003).

In an organisational context, massification can be seen in the form of collusions. The term collusion comes from the Latin *colludere* ("to play with") but there is also "collusion in the modern sense; to keep up false appearance … to the injury of another person" (*Oxford Latin Dictionary*). The game of mutual self-deception is played with two or more individuals, often at a conscious level but also unconsciously and subconsciously; each player plays the other's game although they may not necessarily be fully aware of doing so (Laing, 1969a). In workplace collusions, there is often non-conscious collaboration aimed at either a mutual satisfaction of hidden needs, or a covering up of something that needs to be hidden (Shruijer, 2009). For example, diversity may be suppressed to maintain an illusion of harmony, or confrontation avoided to hide the fear of rejection or powerlessness. Deep group collusions both maintain illusions and disguise internal delusions. They are a psycho-merger.

A further complication is that the two states—aggregation and massification—are not static, but in a state of flux. In the same way that traumatised people who are overwhelmed by their fear of annihilation are caught in incessant motion, without the possibility of resolution, so incohesive social systems oscillate incessantly between states of aggregation and states of massification (Hopper, 2003). These oscillations show motion and process but no dynamic dialectical movement: "me—not me". There is an absence of the tension between sameness and difference. The healthy intrapsychic and intersubjective rhythms, as described in Chapters One and Two, are not available to foster recognition of group members for each other. Positive engagement with each other, in mutuality and trust, is stymied. The group dynamics are incohesive and in a state of social paralysis, or social stasis. Any movement is that of repetition compulsion (see Chapter Two). Nothing can be resolved, as new dynamics cannot be created. Where group dynamics become stuck and impasses develop, such as in bullying scenarios, further bullying appears to be an attempt to release the stuckness, but these efforts are futile because of the lack of recognition of the other (White, 2007).

Scapegoating and bullying

As explained in the research review, a scapegoat is someone chosen to carry the sins on behalf of the group "into the wilderness". The scapegoat is kept alive by the group but after being expelled its fate is irrelevant. Scapegoating is partly the result of group efforts to foster or maintain integration. Rather than engaging and working through anxieties generated with the group, these are projected onto certain individuals. These employees may be on the boundary of the group, interfacing with clients or external stakeholders, or they may have a lower valency than the rest of the group. The group may produce a scapegoat at a time of transition, such as in a merger. The scapegoated individual acts as a temporary container of anxieties whilst the changes take place.

Scapegoating can also be a consequence of the specific provocations, deviant behaviours, or ineptitude of scapegoated individuals (Gold, 2010). The group may not have the resources to cope with that individual. The most effective scapegoating occurs when the dynamics not only meet the needs of the group but also some of the needs of the victim, for example, an individual's tendency to be outspoken, or rebellious (Gold, 2010). The scapegoat may also have certain attributes, such as honesty, which are desired and envied by the group.

The other goat, in the Leviticus account, is sacrificed by, and within the group, as a sacrificial sin offering. I suggest that this second goat can be likened to a victim of bullying. Victims are humiliated, and often psychologically destroyed, their fates being of little interest to the group members, except when they concern their own survival.

The following examples of bullying and scapegoating are taken from two contrasting organisations: a rapidly changing administrative company; and two slowly evolving libraries, an old one and a new one, under the direction of the same manager. Theories outlined above are used to illustrate the group dynamics.

Bullying and scapegoating in teams A and B in an administrative company

The team leader of team A was new and unfamiliar with the ways of working in the organisation. His valency level was low. Top management had very high expectations of him. These expectations gave rise to the potential for shame, particularly when the team's targets began to slip. The leader constantly tested his staff by suddenly changing his orders. The inconsistency in his demands generated confusion and anxiety amongst the team. He overtly bullied the most vulnerable members of the team, those who had a lower valency than others. By denigrating his staff, claiming that they were stuck in their ways and that his ways were superior, the displays of arrogance may have been a defence against potential shame—failure to reach the set targets.

Over time, team members became increasingly isolated from each other. There was a lack of group cohesion, with staff denying recognition to each other. Members were concerned primarily about their own survival. Victims had no assistance to resolve conflicts. This group dynamic fits the basic assumption, Me-ness. The surface dynamics match Hopper's (2003) description of aggregation. At deeper levels, however, members showed fantasies of escapism, feelings of entrapment, idealisation, and denial which prevented them from engaging with the reality of their situation. These fantasies seemed, in part, to echo projections from the leader. For example, he fantasised about the team's project and idealised his role. There was an unconscious and subconscious collusion of subservience by the team, creating an illusion of solidarity held together by fantasy. In Hopper's (2003) terms this would be an example of massification.

In contrast, the dynamics in team B were less complex. Team B's leader provided more containment and working through of anxieties than the leader of team A. Rather than group fragmentation, there was greater engagement with reality and group cohesiveness. One member of the group had obligations, from time to time, to another department. This dual responsibility was onerous and was made more challenging when the leader and colleagues accused him of not "pulling his weight". He was made to feel guilty that he was not always available when the team needed him; he felt scapegoated. Outwardly he appeared sufficiently confident in his abilities, and got personal kudos from his two roles, but he was ashamed of letting the team down. His valency levels for the group were often low. The extra workload was damaging his physical health and he wondered how much longer he could continue to cope with the burdens placed on him.

The key difference between team A and team B was in recognition within the group. The victims of bullying were easily disposed of, whereas the scapegoat had value to his team. He was better able to endure his "heavy load", albeit in the short term, than the victims in team A.

Bullying and scapegoating in the libraries

There was a vacuum in leadership of the two libraries, an old one and a new one. The director was a distant figure, preferring to work with external stakeholders rather than engage with operational difficulties. She distanced herself from the ongoing bullying and scapegoating by attributing stress to the personality of the individuals.

In the old library, Ms. M had taken on many of the day-to-day responsibilities for management of the staff even though this was outside her official remit. With no clear mandate, problems arose. She was not always kept up-to-date with information by the director and this made her look foolish in front of her colleagues. One of her tasks was to discipline staff but she had not been granted the formal authority to do so. When she reprimanded one of the team members, colleagues objected and began to bully her. Snide comments were made about her behind her back, staff refused to speak to her, and there was a lot of gossip.

Although Ms. M was determined to be successful in her role, she seemed constantly worried about what others thought of her and tended to internalise her anxieties. No help was forthcoming from the director or from the group.

In the new library, Mrs. T, a scapegoat, had also taken on more than her allotted share of responsibilities. Her working boundaries, at the front of the library, were not clear. Colleagues considered her to be very reliable, but accused her of "playing the martyr". Complaints from customers about untidiness, noise, and general disorder in the library were directed to, and blamed on, Mrs. T. She admitted to "getting flak" from colleagues and agreed with her colleagues that she was the most stressed member of the team.

The main difference between the dynamics in the new library and those in the old were the levels of containment and the capacity for working through anxieties. A senior member of staff from the new library stepped, unofficially, into a management role and offered help and recognition to some of the staff. However, he did little to acknowledge Mrs. T's difficulties. The director also appeared oblivious to the strains this employee was experiencing. Rather than introjecting the projections from the group, which Ms. M appeared to do, Mrs. T set boundaries for herself. She was aware of her role as a carrier of stress on behalf of the group and was more able to engage with reality. Knowing that she was nearing retirement age and would be leaving within a year, she was able to continue as a scapegoat.

Summary of the psychodynamic theories

From psychodynamic theory on groups, a picture emerges of a complex interplay of the unconscious lives of individuals and of groups. Groups tend to take on an identity of their own. Although individuals can find security within a group, membership can bring a loss of individual thought. For those individuals with low levels of resilience and weakened boundaries from childhood, the challenges of joining new groups can, at times, be overwhelming.

Arrival into a group is a crucial time in determining whether bullying will arise. Our capacity to fit—or valency—within groups depends on many factors. Early relationships with mothers and carers may, years later, affect our feelings about how we relate to others and impact on our vulnerability when joining a new group. Sibling relationships in childhood may influence our choice of roles in the workplace and may also be a determining factor in whether we welcome or resent newcomers. Decisions on employment and even careers may, in fact, be governed less by rational decisions and more by deeper inner needs which we are unable to recognise and acknowledge.

When changes take place in groups, transitional space helps in providing for reflection and sense-making. Some form of continuity, such as that given by transitional objects, helps to keep a sense of personal and group identity in challenging times.

When we are unable to offer something of value to a group, or when our efforts and skills are rejected, we may feel ashamed. A struggle for recognition begins. Where there is a lack of empathy from others, gaps open up and "black holes" form where connections are no longer being made. Here the potential for bullying is considerable. When a bully feels potential shame, he/she may try to defend against these feelings through confusion, arrogance, or envy and jealousy. He/she has to get rid of his/her anxieties and find a container for them. That container, the victim, has to be controlled and monitored. If the victim is unable to find help within the group, and this is unlikely given the fragmented and stuck nature of the group dynamics, he/she may be unable to find empathy for him/herself and becomes guilty of self-betrayal.

As shown in the research review, those trapped within a typical bullying scenario struggle to gain a positive resolution. The group dynamics are characterised by a fragmentation on the surface and unconscious and subconscious collusions beneath. This type of dynamics fits the description of Hopper's fourth basic assumption. Members retreat into themselves and tend to depend on their own inner resources for survival. As the collusions of subservience are so deep, they restrict members' ability to make changes to improve the health of the group. Further bullying is inevitable as attempts are made to break the impasses and create something new. This is futile, as there is no resolution to the ruptures, just a repetition of old patterns of behaviour.

Transitional space and/or transitional objects are needed to help the group break the impasses and move forward. Change can come from small steps to transform the culture and release the stuckness, as seen in the case study in Chapter Five. Organisational consultants, trained in psychodynamic ways of working, can also assist in this process by offering their ability to provide containment, to work through anxieties, and to analyse the deeper issues which are restricting healthy group interactions. Victims can get support through counselling and psychotherapy to help them alleviate the impasses in the relationships and reconcile them with their own past experiences.

The subtle differences between bullying and scapegoating were illustrated with case studies. In bullying scenarios the group dynamics were more complex and fragmented than where there was scapegoating. Group members were more concerned with self-survival rather than collaboration. The unconscious and subconscious collusions in the bullying groups gave a stuckness to the group dynamics and the fate of the victims within the group was deemed irrelevant. Scapegoating groups offered more recognition and containment of anxieties for members than was found in the bullying scenarios. The scapegoats were judged, by the group, in absolute terms. The individuals played a distinctive role on behalf of the group. Although they were blamed for the "sins" of the group and had to hold to these until the time was right for them to be expelled, they were aware of their roles, the burden they were carrying, and their inevitable fate. They had a greater sense of reality than the victims of bullying.

Questions and answers

How do the deeper group dynamics foster bullying?

Survival mode

When the culture of the organisation is characterised by fear, poor communication, or excessive controls, employees become primarily concerned with their own survival rather than engaging with each other. As personal agendas come to the fore, the group fragments and energy resources are drained away. The fate of a victim is of little relevance. These groups may initially be operating in basic assumption Me-ness or fight and flight. As the bullying dynamics evolve and escalate, the deeper dynamics can be likened to Hopper's fourth basic assumption, described above.

Turning a blind eye

The research review shows that most witnesses of bullying tend to be passive rather than active. They are often bystanders. Passivity facilitates bullying in two ways: first, it gives a message to bullies that their actions are acceptable; second, when targets of bullying are struggling to cope, there is no one to help them.

Impasses

When problems arise, as they inevitably do, there is insufficient containment and working through of anxieties within these groups. Members fall into subservience, beaten down by a culture of bullying, and helpless to improve the dynamics, as they are fragmented on the surface but, beneath, are stuck in unconscious and subconscious collusions. Further bullying is an attempt to release the stuckness. With help, for example, from an organisational consultant offering some containment of anxieties, members can begin to release the impasses.

Why do some individuals become stuck in their roles within the group?

A lack of reflective space

Beyond the practical everyday obligations of financial commitments, family responsibilities, or lack of alternative employment and other factors which bind employees to their current situation, individuals may be unable, or unwilling, to reflect on why they have chosen a particular job or role. They may lack the psychic space for reflection and be completely unaware of how their deeper needs, perhaps pertaining to childhood, are being met within groups which they have chosen to join.

Perversity

If employees' childhood homes were ones of constant conflict, or emotionally cold, they may perversely feel "at home" in workplaces which are conflict-ridden, or where empathy is lacking. In persevering in their search for recognition within these unhealthy organisations, they are continually likely to be scapegoated or bullied, or to become bullies. Rather like children who cling desperately to an abusive parent, victims may also be too frightened to move on but also too frightened stay. They remain with a dysfunctional working group, repeating the same mistakes from the past, that is, repetition compulsion, in a futile attempt to find some resolution.

Victims are stuck in a no-win situation until they can begin to explore their feelings instead of accepting the projections of others as their reality. Containment and working through of anxieties can be provided either by counselling or by psychotherapy.

Boiled frogs

Some victims stay in organisations even though either they, or the organisation, have changed and their levels of valency have declined considerably. They may not feel valued, they may be abused, and yet they remain. Charles Handy (1989) describes individuals who are unaware of a changing environment and lack an ability to respond to changes as being like "boiled frogs". If you put a frog in a pan of cold water it will not react if the water is heated up slowly and gradually and will allow itself to be boiled alive.

They feel too ashamed to try to move

When employees have had a start in life which denied them the opportunity to develop self-confidence and self-esteem, various defences may be triggered when they enter a new working environment. Some victims idealise the group as a defence against anxiety so that when a gap opens between expectations and reality, they may be shocked. Shame and guilt arise. They may be too ashamed and not confident enough to move to another organisation or team.

When does scapegoating become bullying?

Anxiety levels rise

For a scapegoat to become a victim, the group dynamics have to change. There needs to be a trigger, for example, an increase in anxiety levels due to a takeover or a restructuring of the organisation. If group members become more concerned about self-survival than about the group, the dynamics fragment. With little, or no, support from colleagues, an already burdened scapegoat would be vulnerable to attacks by group members who cope by projecting their anxieties on to others.

Loss of containment and internalisation of anxieties

The scapegoat has value to the group as he/she carries "the sins" of the group on behalf of the members. The scapegoats in the case studies seemed to be aware of their roles, and accepted them in the knowledge that they would probably be leaving the team. They were able to set boundaries for themselves. However, a scapegoat could become a victim if he/she were to internalise the anxieties and lose that sense of reality.

HR managers reading this may wonder why it is important to know the difference between bullying and scapegoating. When faced with an employee who is very stressed, as were the scapegoats in the examples above, it would be possible to gain an impression that they were being bullied. However, no bullies were to be found.

If incorrectly diagnosed, much time, effort, and expense could be wasted in a blame game, inquiries, disciplinary procedures, etc.

A scapegoat, given some support, such as a clearer job description and recognition from management for his/her value and contribution, could begin to release the stuckness in the group dynamics and help the group to function in a more effective way. He/she tends to have a greater sense of reality than a victim, being more able to contain and work through the projections. In the example given above, the director of the libraries saw stress in terms of the personality of the individuals, rather than as a systemic issue. If she had been encouraged to take a more proactive role and had familiarised herself with the work of her staff, many of the scapegoating and bullying issues could have been easily resolved.

How can individuals work together to improve group dynamics?

> We know that people show up in a new company wanting to engage. Very few people think, "I'm going to do as little as humanly possible and be as destructive as I can". They start off thinking this is a shining new opportunity and then the job they do, the leader they get, the environment they're in either translates that optimism into having a great time and doing a great job or not quite so much. For an organisation that's around about 10% in terms of productivity [according to research by Gallup]. (Arkin, 2010, p. 21)

Use transitional objects and transitional space

These can help in the resolution of bullying. For example, within a department in an organisation, two teams had been in conflict, and not communicating with each other, for some time. In an attempt to resolve the impasse, the assistant manager of the department provided a drinks dispenser for the teams to share. One of the team members said,

"It was one of the best things we have ever done. Staff had to come out of their offices and just in doing that and carrying drinks past each other we got some social interaction. It was a very cheap and very effective way of bringing the teams together."

Group relations training

Whatever the nature of workplace teams, whether stable and enduring for years or transitory and coming together to work on short-term projects, there are underlying unconscious dynamics. Group relations training can be a cost-effective way of understanding the deeper dynamics of groups, as the experiences gained have a long-lasting impact on learning. It is through seeing and feeling the deeper dynamics of groups, watching how roles change, how groups split, and how stuckness can be released, that employees learn to recognise key features of unconscious and subconscious dynamics, that is, how conflicts arise and can be diffused.

Recruiting for diversity, not just to tick a box but to create a healthier team

In groups which are too homogeneous, or too harmonious, mimetic rivalry may arise. Raising contentious issues can be problematic with groups which have developed strong "group-think". Recruitment of "difference" can help to redress the balance. However, consideration also needs to be given to valency. If an employee is recruited who is very different from the rest of the group, a scapegoating or bullying dynamic may develop as the group attempts to defend itself against the anxiety this provokes. When considering valency, an awareness of bias in HR management is helpful. In a survey of biases held by HR professionals in terms of diversity in the workplace, a particular bias showed prejudice against overweight women (Syedain, 2012).

What personal biases of the HR manager are being "worked through" in the appointment process?

Acknowledge history—both personal and collective

Transitional objects such as personal items, for example, photos of an employee's family, can help individuals to feel more secure at work.

Rather than the past being wiped out in change, objects relating to the group's history can help to give a sense of continuity.

The emperor is wearing no clothes

Courage needs to be cultivated if individuals are to feel that they can speak out. It is the little actions or gestures, the social first aid, that can be most effective in creating positive engagement with others. Often it just takes one person to say the "emperor is wearing no clothes" and others will join in to say, "this is not appropriate behaviour, stop it".

Transitional space

Transitional space, a space to reflect and play with experiences of change, is needed if healthier intrapsychic and intersubjective rhythms necessary for creative responses are to be found. When stress levels are high, teams tend to retreat into their own spaces, but this creates fissures throughout an organisation.

In an attempt to bring different departments and specialists together to learn about each other's work and to foster improved levels of compassionate care, Schwartz Rounds are being introduced in some UK hospitals. Schwartz Rounds support the carer/patent relationship by providing space to reflect on the cost and impact of caring (Wren, 2012). All staff in a hospital are invited to meetings, lasting an hour, once a month. Before the meetings a group of staff discuss, with a skilled facilitator, difficult emotional and social issues that arise when caring for patients. At the meeting the group gives a brief summary of a patient's case history. Then panellists take it in turns to describe their involvement in the case and, in particular, how it made them feel and what sort of challenges it raised for them. The discussion is opened up for participants to ask questions, share experiences, and reflect on the challenges of care. The Rounds are designed to be a safe and confidential environment.

Schwartz Rounds have been found to create a sense of community, support, and comfort for the staff and to allow for new and important conversations to take place about vital aspects of clinical and organisational experience (Wren, 2012).

Holding environments

When an employee is upset about his/her dealings either with clients or with colleagues, problems are best nipped in the bud. By listening closely to a problem, raising questions about perceptions and feelings about what the employee thinks ought to be done, a manager may find the root causes of the difficulties. These may relate to experiences in previous work groups. By offering alternative ways of seeing the problem and proposing another meeting, the manager has, for the time being, contained the employee's anxieties, which is preferable to these being "spilt" into the group or left to fester within the psyche of the worried employee.

How can HR managers identify groups which are at risk of developing into bullying and scapegoating scenarios?

Have you noticed a sudden downturn in productivity, staff complaining of health problems and becoming withdrawn? Has the focus on the primary task been lost? Are personal issues coming to the fore and creating a struggle for survival? Is pettiness taking over from constructive conversations?

Which groups lack diversity? Mimetic rivalry may arise when members are too similar in gender, age, experience, or qualifications, providing the potential for scapegoating and bullying.

When groups are primarily focussed on ticking boxes, they are unlikely to be able to reflect on their practices or create space to find creative solutions to problems. Frustrations will build and bullying erupt.

If a team is boasting about its achievements, rather than being swept up in the celebrations, take a reality check. Are the employees realistic about their achievements or in a fantasy land? In reality testing we go back, again and again, to test our beliefs, our perceptions, our assessment of what we can achieve (Lear, 2000).

Where there is a desire for a "pristine" organisation, one in which everything is ultra-politically correct, the negative aspects will go underground and emerge at weak points in the structure of the organisation, such as in teams where there is a particular lack of recognition and containment. What are those teams holding on behalf of the organisation? For example, staff in a student services department in a university received very little recognition for their often challenging work.

The department was under-resourced, partly because the budget was not being used in an effective way. Top management did not want to acknowledge that there were students at the university who needed help. By doing so they would also have had to admit that not everything was perfect. The lack of recognition for the staff was a key contributing factor to the long-term bullying within this department.

Where a victim or bully has been removed and no action has been taken to facilitate change in the group dynamics, the unconscious dynamics may not have altered. Another victim will be chosen, or possibly another bully will emerge, even if those individuals initially show no tendency to become victims or bullies. These roles will re-emerge to meet the needs of the group for containment of anxieties.

If questions are not asked, stories are then made up by employees and gossip becomes the discourse of the day. Employees find themselves in a fantasy land of confusion and inconsistency, ideal for creating bullying scenarios. Ask questions on behalf of the group. What is stopping the group from moving forward? What role is the victim, or bully, performing on behalf of the group to release the stuck dynamics? What are the underlying stress factors? Why is the energy of the group being diverted into bullying instead of being used in the primary task? Is that task clear? Who are the containers of anxiety? There are no quick fixes but solutions cannot be found until someone takes the initiative and gives recognition to teams that are struggling to cope with organisational pressures.

CHAPTER FOUR

Organisations

Introduction

This chapter deviates from the format of the previous chapters to include an extra section, at the beginning, on contextualising bullying. This addition is a description of some of the social, technological, and political contexts in which workplace bullying has taken place in the past and is occurring today. As organisations are not islands cut off from their surroundings but entities which constantly interact across their boundaries with external stakeholders and other influences, the assumption is made that we can better understand the dynamic nature of bullying in our organisations when we acknowledge and understand these evolving contexts.

This additional section is followed by a review of the research on bullying from an organisational perspective. The review begins with explanations of the structural and cultural factors which generate bullying and is followed by descriptions of styles of leadership known to foster dysfunctional employee relationships. A description is give of cyber-bullying, taken mainly from research in schools. Models of bullying, illustrating its dynamic nature, are outlined. Theoretical findings are illustrated with examples from research and from anecdotal evidence collated over many years.

The third part of the chapter presents psychodynamic theories that are key to our understanding of the organisational aspects of bullying. Concepts of boundaries and containment, social defences, loss and mourning, are examined together with an introduction to the concept of the vacuum as the site of conflict. Finally, there is the question and answer section which brings together theories of bullying and psychoanalysis from a pragmatic standpoint. The questions are as follows:

When does leadership become bullying?
How does bullying become institutionalised?
Why does bullying occur in some parts of an organisation but not in others?
How can HR managers promote well-being and engagement based on a psychodynamic perspective of workplace bullying?

Contextualising bullying

Bullying in the workplace tends to be viewed as a fairly recent phenomenon, with statistical records dating back to the 1980s. Yet historical data suggests otherwise. Historical archives show that bullying has occurred in workplaces throughout the ages. For example, documentary evidence from the late medieval era indicates that bullying was common in the UK city of York in relations between the élite in the corporation (mayor and city council), the citizens, and the workers in the lower ranks of society. The city was organised into guilds—small groups of men involved in making craft products such as nails, fabrics, stained glass, and roof tiles, or in merchandising products such as clothes, wine, and groceries. The corporation, and dominating guild masters, controlled the labour supply, wages, product price, and quality and quantities of production in addition to establishing strict standards of behaviour for York's residents. Apprentices were required by their masters to work a minimum four-year apprenticeship had few rights or, practically speaking, none at all, and effectively no remuneration for their labours. Journeymen, having served their apprenticeships, worked for low pay and sometimes still lived within the households of their masters. They were workers with an occupation but since they were not fully-fledged members of the guild they did not hold citizenship in the city. While not as vulnerable as apprentices, journeymen were nevertheless not immune to bad treatment (Davidson & White, 2013).

Working life in York in that era was thus set against a background of considerable power differentials between groups—the Crown, city corporation, the Church, guild masters, and all the others. Civic records of the time present a pervasive fear of instability (Davidson & White, 2013). Emanating from the top of the establishment was a general nervousness about disorder amongst the inhabitants and about misbehaviour or rebellion against rules. Harsh punishments, sometimes involving incarçeration in jail, were meted out to offenders for the most petty of crimes. In an era characterised by political turbulence, climate change, plagues, and feuds, working life was often fragile and fraught.

The lives of many workers, however, deteriorated further during the Industrial Revolution, when draconian factory conditions were imposed on them. As is well known, these early factories went much further in turning men, women, and often children into automatons labouring in filthy, poorly lit, and dangerous environments. Worse than in the late Middle Ages, the lives of workers would be regimented, short, and brutish. For example, in the Farfield woollen mill in Cumbria, UK in 1815, management edicts about employees' behaviour were clearly set out on a board on the factory wall. Fines were given for various misdemeanours, such as talking to other workers, stopping machinery during cleaning, spilling oil, or dropping bobbins on the factory floor. The employers could dismiss workers on the spot; employees had to give four weeks' notice. Of course not all of these controls can be attributed to bullying. Yet excessive management controls, through which employees had few rights, fostered the likely exploitation of workers.

Much has changed since those dismal times. Whilst the trajectory has not been one of constant progress, it seems correct, as Elias (1982) suggests, that there has been historic progress in societies in which the more "animalistic" human activities are progressively converted into self-restraint and invested with feelings of shame. This civilising process has involved a change of human conduct and sentiment which, at least since the early years of the Industrial Revolution, has tended to take place in quite a specific direction and has happened in a largely unplanned manner. However, old familiar stories of job insecurity or long hours for little pay still abound in sweatshops and industrial sites around the world.

In the UK, the deaths of Chinese workers gathering cockles (shellfish) in February, 2004, on the mudflats of Morecambe Bay in the north of England brought to light immigrant workers living below the eyes of the law in virtual slavery, seemingly with no rights and no respect from their bosses. Their working conditions appeared little different from those of the apprentices in the late medieval era or, even worse, factory workers of the early Industrial Revolution.

In contrast to the slow incremental change of working life from past eras, today many employees are affected by rapid change, globalisation, vastly increased communication and competition, and greater demands for goods and services. Slow incremental change has been replaced by constant movement, a movement which Bauman (2003) describes as "liquid modernity". This implies that reality is not solid but moves like a liquid and cannot keep its shape. Boundaries between stakeholders, customers, financiers, markets, governments, and labour supply have become blurred.

> An unprecedented fluidity, fragility and in-built transience (the famed "flexibility") mark all sorts of social bonds which but a few dozen years ago, combined into a durable, reliable framework inside which a web of human interactions could be securely woven. They affect particularly and perhaps most seminally, employment and professional relations. (Bauman, 2003, p. 91)

Hierarchies and chains of command today are less structured than in the past. Formal collective working practices have been replaced by a privatisation of human problems (Bauman, 2003). The "psychological contract", a term coined by Chris Agyris in the 1960s to describe the employer-employee relationship, is generally no longer about fair wages for a fair day's pay or a linear relationship, but has become complex and increasingly difficult to manage as authority, boundaries, and roles are often shifting, ambiguous, and contested. The increased complexity is accompanied by difficulties in finding coherence, consistency, and continuity.

In "fluid" working environments, much is expected from employees, including managers, in terms of cooperation with others in teams and networks in order to meet the challenges of new product and service development. Employees at every level of organisations are being asked to assume more authority and accountability and to take on a greater variety of tasks involving collaboration and engagement with others. The interface between the outside and inside of the organisation is no longer the domain of the management board or of sales representatives. The need for greater cooperation, flexibility, adaptability, and appreciation of diversity in our "liquid" organisations demands high levels of trust and good communication skills.

Much employee interaction takes place electronically. Use of technology, particularly social media, facilitates rapid, frequent, direct communication with few boundaries. The nature of this communication, albeit rapid and responsive, creates a distance and loss of face-to-face connectivity. Taking clues from body language and the sharing of cultural norms and expectations in face-to-face meetings, is becoming less common, particularly within institutions working globally. Difficulties can arise when employees have little or no chance to meet, are working across time zones, and using languages other than their "mother tongue". Technological communication can create an illusory feeling of being connected and in touch with people, without the experience of being fully engaged with a situation, individuals, or a team (Cardona, 2003). There is the potential for avoiding genuine dialogue and a masking of emotions. In the matrix between the real world and the electronic world, validity of the self, what it is to be human, brings incoherence for those who may already feel vulnerable. Boundaries are easily crossed, for example, between work and personal life, creating conflicts of interests. Communication can be easily monitored; the manager might be looking in and tracking the location of employees. When the workplace situation becomes complex and structures fall apart, personality comes to the fore (Thylefors, 1987).

The character and culture of group life is becoming ever more crucial to the success of private and public organisations operating domestically or worldwide. If organisations are to survive in highly competitive environments, the capacity for connectedness has to be developed in creative ways.

As organisational life has become more flexible and "liquid", our capacity to attribute meaning to our working lives is increasingly being challenged. In taking up fluid roles, employees have to try to find identity for themselves. Increasingly, individual success is self-determined but also increasingly more dependent on cooperation with other employees. With a rising interest in finding personal meaning in work this may result in an over-identification with work, particularly if employees are uncertain about their own identities. They will tend to try to keep up an appearance and create an image which fits their working context. When keeping up an image becomes of paramount importance, individuals may cover their actions by masking their behaviour. They may be seduced into believing that the images of themselves and of others are real. For example, by giving a considerable degree of freedom of decision- making to employee Nick Leeson, Barings Bank found to their cost that he could mask his activities by being allowed to supervise himself. Likewise, at Enron debts were hidden in "packaging", and the revenue provided by their power companies was gradually run down, in the creation of an unsustainable fantasy (Stein, 2011).

Within our present era there has been an emergence of values of greed, consumerism, acquisition, and exploitation (Hoggett, 1992). Individual pleasure, rather than working for the common good, acknowledges reality but also denies it, and creates a societal state which turns a blind eye and establishes abusive cycles which are difficult to break (Long, 2002). Bullying is one of those abusive cycles.

Although employees are increasingly expected to be engaged in their work, show initiative, and be innovative, controls are increasingly measurable and outputs quantifiable. Auditable practices tend to be treated as tick-box games to mask the reality of professional life (McGivern & Ferlie, 2007). Strategic horizons appear to be shifting closer to the here and now and planning for the future appears problematic. In the recourse to statistical evidence, there is no time and space to question what is right or wrong or to reflect: we have to act now (Žižek, 2008). However, if we are to know who we are, we need to be in a moral space. This is a space in which questions arise about what is good or bad, what is worth doing and what not, what has meaning and importance for us and what is trivial and secondary (Taylor, 2004).

In an era of excessive targets and expectations, false images, and 24/7 contact with others, HR rhetoric has stepped in to attempt to ease the burden. The HR mantra that "people are our greatest asset" displays the need to take care of employees and to ensure that they are fit; the actions associated with this may be a means of making the employee more "knowable" but also more controllable. Mantras on health and well-being may become split-off from reality in a move to value human capital as a commercial imperative in order to maximise output. Likewise, rhetoric in the form of political correctness also supports our sense of ourselves as easily damaged, requiring protection and continuous shoring up by others. It fosters the fantasy of an ideal community of respect, a belief that we could speak in simple ways to each other and be accepting and open (Eisold, 2009).

In spite of the use of technology to speed up communication and attempts by HR managers to provide "squeaky clean" working environments intended to meet all employees' needs, compared with 2007 managers are working longer hours, are more likely to go to work whilst sick, and are increasingly suffering from stress and depression (Worrell & Cooper, 2012). The complexity of organisational life today has brought its own problems in terms of exploitation of labour, chiefly emotional labour. Ninety-two per cent of a thousand managers questioned reported their organisation had been restructured in the past year, whilst almost half had seen compulsory redundancies.

Bauman (2004) suggests that in the capitalist drive for "more" there is waste, not just waste which goes into "landfill sites" but also wasted lives. I suggest that he could also be talking about the wasted lives created through bullying.

With the introduction of numerous employment laws, policies, and procedures, health and safety requirements, and a decline in harsh physical labour over the past fifty years, it would be cosy to assume that working life is so much more civilised than in past eras. Yet the fluidity of boundaries and identities, and increased interaction, challenge workplace identities and feelings of security in new ways. The constant recourse to measurements and controls, with little time and space for reflection, also impacts on where, how, and why bullying scenarios develop. The following research review illustrates how the changes in organisational life, outlined above, seep under the skin of organisations to provide fertile breeding grounds for bullying.

Research review

Culture and structure: institutionalising bullying through rhetoric, cliques, traditions, and structural fractures

Two main concepts—organisational climate and culture—are used in the research on bullying to describe the nature of organisational contexts. These are closely related and appear to be used almost interchangeably.

The term organisational climate relates to the understanding and perceptions of organisational practices and procedures that are shared among members of an organisation (Schneider, 1975). It is a product of member interaction and collective perceptions of autonomy, trust, cohesiveness, support, recognition, innovation, and fairness, which both reflects prevalent norms and is a major influence on shaping behaviour (Moran & Volkwein, 1992). Likewise, culture implies a shared experience between members in which "values" and assumptions are created, adapted, and constrained in such a way that both reflects and is influenced by an organisation's structural and dynamic dimensions (Kondra & Hurst, 2009). Examples of cultural aspects of organisations include buildings, logos, policies and written procedures, rules, norms and values, rewards and sanctions, rhetoric, stories, rituals and myths. Organisational culture arises not just from how subsystems relate to each other but also from how they relate to the whole organisation and how the whole organisation relates to its external environment.

> In talking about culture we are really talking about a process of reality construction that allows people to see and understand particular events, actions, objects, utterances, or situations in distinctive ways. These patterns of understanding help us to cope with the situation being encountered and also provide a basis for making our own behaviour sensible and meaningful. (Morgan, 1997, p. 138)

How bullying becomes institutionalised

Examples of how bullying becomes institutionalised within cultures are shown in the research chiefly through rhetoric, traditions, and cliques.

Rhetoric

Rhetoric can seep into deep levels within an organisation to foster bullying in quite subtle ways (Liefooghe & Mackenzie Davey, 2010). Even HR measures to tackle bullying, such as policies, procedures, and support systems, can by their very nature subvert the discourse of bullying. For example, in drawing up an anti-bullying policy, management have the right to define what is, and is not, bullying. This can limit discussions on the legitimate use of power. Management rhetoric can also be used to both produce and confirm employees as victims who are damaged and therefore in need of protection and of a range of experts to "rescue" them (Liefooghe & Mackenzie Davey, 2010). These actions reinforce the perception that bullying is an issue for individuals rather than a systemic one.

HR departments may go out of their way to tick all the boxes to manage bullying effectively, yet at the same time ignore the cultural and structural problems which can generate much of the bullying in the first place. For example, a logistics company, which could be described as a "model employer" in terms of having policies, training, and interventions to tackle bullying, had a culture in which employees no longer believed they would be treated with respect (Fevre & Lewis, 2012). These employees felt they could not rely on colleagues to treat them fairly, more work would be demanded from them than was humanly possible, and they could be dismissed without reason.

In management's desire to control, and to make known what is happening in the organisation, it can seem that everything that moves is measured. Even processes such as 360 degree feedback, which on the surface sorts out the caring, people-orientated managers from the ruthless and manipulative, may, in fact, do exactly the opposite (Clutterbuck, 2011). Honesty of colleagues tends be related to how genuinely open the manager is to critical feedback. Therefore, the managers who are good at the work may score lower than managers who bully, as employees want to avoid the aggression that comes from being honest. After a while, employees tend to see the behaviour of dysfunctional and divisive managers as "normal" (Clutterbuck, 2011).

Conventional solutions tend not to prevent bullying or effectively manage it because they do not address the problems at source, as the culture that produces policies and procedures dictates how they are put into operation (Fevre & Lewis, 2012).

A new employee in an HR department said,

> We have a buddy system. When someone comes in we get allocated a buddy. Me and my buddy hated each other from day one. I was afraid to ask her things and it shouldn't be like that. You should be able to say—where are the loos? On the first day I sat with my legs crossed all day, I was too scared to ask.

Procedures, however well-intentioned, cannot be effective if there is a culture of fear and loss of voice. Bullying can become institutionalised through fear of not being listened to and the consequences of speaking out (Liefooghe & Mackenzie Davey, 2003).

A police officer said,

> Bullying is institutionalised through silence. It's institutionalised fear. You don't speak out because you think about your pension.

When communication is top-down, with little acknowledgement of who is receiving it or why, a lack of trust and cynicism develops (White, 2007).

The CEO of a large UK organisation thumped his fist on the table and yelled at his audience,

> I will not have bullying here!

One of his employees said,

> A stress survey came out this week. The most stressful thing was getting the email in the first place because it was paying lip service to the idea. It wasn't even trying to evaluate whether there were high levels in a scientific way. They just asked the team leaders to find out if anyone was stressed that day. As a result of the survey, the board immediately issued an edict telling us not to work such long hours. The next day they announced yet more staff cuts.

Much effort went into collating statistics in this organisation but little attention was given to their accuracy or relevance. For example, a survey on harassment carried out by a group of consultants contained a basic mathematical error which inflated the statistics on harassment levels. The results generated much stress amongst the women employees and disbelief from some of the men. One group of women were so anxious that they moved their workstations so they could sit together for protection.

A new employee, within days of starting her job, came face to face with the challenges of working in a culture where top-down communication style was pervasive and restrictive. She said,

> I had to go to an induction. They were trying to tell me things quickly but I found it too much to take in all at the same time. I had no idea what they were talking about. One of the girls burst into tears but no one sat her down and said this is how this works etc. She didn't have a clue. They need to have a set timescale for induction. Here it is a bit of if and when.

Traditions

Traditions of rituals and initiations can provide a valuable link with the past and help an organisation to keep a strong identity. However, when used in a rigid way, with little thought to their relevance and respect for employees, they can create opportunities for bullying. An intimidating use of discipline and humiliating initiation rites, which would be unacceptable in other organisations, had been institutionalised within the Fire Service culture (Archer, 1999). Much emphasis was placed on maintaining traditions through justifications such as "we've always done it like this". Those fire-fighters who became officers and managers under the traditional hierarchical structures and had experienced bullying behaviour themselves, either directly or indirectly, tended to take it as the norm. Their familiarity with power abuse may prevent its destructive outcomes from being properly recognised or identified (Archer, 1999).

Cliques

As shown in Chapter Three, groups can take on a life and identity of their own and defences, common in individuals, come into play. A collective unconscious can develop. Employees may do things which they would not normally consider by themselves, including working out their aggression on others.

In a hospital, informal alliances, of small groups of individuals, formed a vital role in bullying (Hutchinson, Vickers, Jackson, & Wilkes, 2010). These alliances were comprised of groups of employees who had considerable influence over daily working practices, such as rites of passage and membership. The thoughts, actions, and behaviour of the nurses increasingly came under the influence of relentless attention to rules and strict adherence to discipline and obedience established within the culture of the cliques. Adherence to the "rules" fostered a "non-thinking, robotic mode" and acquiescence to ritual forms of humiliation, which were often conducted in front of patients or other colleagues. Members of the cliques learnt to accept unfair workload allocation and demeaning work, so much so that it became normalised and part of everyday practice. Being kept under high levels of surveillance and control silenced the nurses' resistance and limited the opportunity for change (Hutchinson, Vickers, Jackson, & Wilkes, 2010).

Structural fractures

Bullying occurs where there are fractures in an organisation's structure (White, 2007). Structures can clash, like tectonic plates of the earth's crust moving against each other. For example, bullying occurs where structural systems are not working for the benefit of employees or the organisation as a whole; or where roles are not clearly defined and boundaries are contested; or where demands exceed basic resources.

Pay, performance, and reviews

Tensions rise and frustrations build where systems are changed without careful thought to the consequences, such as the creation of divisions between staff which generate feelings of unjust treatment by "the organisation". For example, the lack of opportunity for negotiation, appraisal, and accompanying performance-related pay in a financial institution, were viewed as unfair, particularly when managers were often under pressure to increase staff performance, reduce overtime, and cut costs to meet their targets (Liefooghe & Mackenzie Davey, 2003).

> If your overtime's cut because your manager's got to make his targets, they say, you know, 10% reduction in overtime. So he's telling you there's no overtime but your customers are saying "I need this and need it now". You're then getting effectively getting bullied in two directions. (Liefooghe & Mackenzie Davey, 2003, p. 227)

One of the main clashes which gave rise to bullying in a civil service organisation was the imposition of a team-based structure on top of an outdated pay and promotion system; the systems worked against each other (White, 2007). Team leaders needed to keep expertise within their teams, but the only way that employees could gain a pay rise and promotion was to move to other areas; traditionally staff had moved every few years. One team leader got exceptionally angry when he heard that staff were leaving his team, especially when he had provided specific training for them. He said,

> There is no way of adding extra value, no bonuses and the only incentive is the next promotion which is usually out of the team. Career development is in the hands of the staff, therefore there is no continuity within the team.

Changes to retention and promotion procedures were gradually being introduced but over time. Jobs were upgraded within teams but only when posts became vacant. An employee said,

> People's commitment is to themselves first, because they aren't getting the reward or recognition that they deserve so they put themselves first. We have lost a key member of our team today. He is so valuable it is quite unbelievable. They are upgrading his post when he leaves. Why couldn't they have upgraded him and we could have kept him.

In another organisation, an appraisal system was being slowly rolled out but was taking time to implement. Some of the managers had not had the information they needed from HR to implement their team's personal development reviews. This led to staff feeling insecure. One member of staff said,

> I didn't get my review and someone from HR said if it wasn't done by 1st June then she didn't know whether I would have a job. It was up to my boss to do the review but he didn't know what the position would be but he would get his secretary to look into it on 2nd June. I have been here six months and he hadn't had any complaints. I went back to HR and asked what was going on and they were all blaming each other. It should have been a transparent process. My boss and I just cobble something together in ten minutes based on the little he knew about what I had been doing.

Within two Belgian organisations, one from the textile industry and one from financial services, feelings of job insecurity led to frustration, and generated competition and suspicion (De Cuyer, Baillien, & De Witte, 2009). Some workers lashed out at co-workers as an attempt to exercise a degree of control.

Job demands/workload/resources

Research findings show a complex interplay between job demands, workload, and resources. High job demands increase the likelihood of employees being bullied over time, whereas high job resources seem to prevent the future occurrence of workplace bullying (Baillen, Neyens, De Witte, & De Cuyer, 2009).

Employees in an HR department complained of job demands which seemed to have little purpose. One employee said,

> We've been on initiative overload for about five years and people are fed up with it. We have had so many changes recently. They don't seem to run their course before the next lot and you don't see the benefits before the next lot are introduced. You feel frustrated because you don't feel you've achieving anything.

A colleague added,

> There is this constant feeding of the machine. It wants this information and that information but it doesn't know why it wants it, but it has to have a lot of it all of the time. It is hungry for information but there is little output from it.

Job demands can contribute to bullying when they are so energy-depleting they result in psychological strain and burnout (Baillien, Rodriguez-Muñoz, Van den Broeck, & De Witte, 2011). On the other hand, job resources contribute to workers' optimal functioning, for example, levels of engagement with work. The researchers suggest employees with high job demands and low job resources may violate working norms and colleagues may bully each other because of the pressures of work. For example, in a department where bullying had been breaking out over a period of ten years, time-wasting and under-use of resources were the key frustrations which gave rise to colleagues bullying each other (White, 2007).

An employee said,

> There was a review of the department. It was a trauma. I remember there was a lot of ill feeling, There was a push from the director to work in a certain way but we couldn't envisage how it was going to work, it was very idealistic. It was you know the practicalities—we have no space. In practice how is it going to work? It felt like we would have more pressures added to us. To be honest the review hasn't changed anything really. HR have just mentioned there may be another review. I can't go through that again. You are hunting around for every available space, sharing desks, sharing rooms. We need more space. There is the feeling we are not valued by the rest of the institution.

Perceptions of job demands, workload, and resources between employees who are bullied and those who are not have been found to differ. Targets and observers of bullying had higher perceptions of job demands and lower perceptions of control and support resources, compared to other employees (Tuckey, Dollard, Hosking, & Winefield, 2009). Higher levels of dissatisfaction were found amongst the bullied than the non-bullied in relation to the level of responsibility, work control, recognition of work, and promotional prospects (O'Moore & Lynch, 2007). Tuckey Dollard, Hosking, and Winefield (2009) compared front-line police officers who were bullied to those who were not bullied, in terms of three factors: job control, support resources, and job demands. Those who had been exposed to bullying, reported lower levels of job control, for example, the freedom to make decisions and ability to control when, and how, activities are performed. They also reported having lower support resources, for example, less help with solving complex tasks and a lack of emotional support from others in threatening situations. Their job demands were perceived to be higher than those who were not bullied. In comparison, workers who faced high demands but had high levels of control and support were less likely to experience bullying.

Particularly vulnerable are those who experience reductions in resources which then impact on their ability to carry out their basic tasks. For example, a sales company's petrol allowances were cut to a standard amount for all reps, irrespective of where they worked. For one rep in a rural area, with clients sometimes hundreds of miles apart, the reduced allowance was only sufficient for visiting two clients a month instead of her usual round of about ten per week. She was informed that if she went over her allowance the amount would be docked from her pay. The imposition of the new rules undermined her effectiveness. She felt ashamed that her targets could no longer be reached. This made her more vulnerable to being bullied by her aggressive manager.

The lack of support to carry out tasks in hand can become a focus of frustration and anger for staff when they perceive that resources are available but not being used for the benefit of the organisation and the customers. Staff in one organisation complained about the lack of transparency regarding budgets. The financial resources for taking on new staff were available but managers were very slow to recruit. Existing staff often had to take on extra responsibilities outside of their remit in order to cover for vacancies. Much of the bullying within this department occurred around vacuums, where staff had left and had not been replaced (White, 2007).

One employee said,

> There is money sitting in the budget. People leave and they are not replaced, or they are only replaced ages afterwards even though they know someone is leaving. One member of staff left. They knew she was leaving but no one prepared a job description so when she did leave there was a huge vacuum for someone else. Colleagues get lumbered and there is huge stress for someone trying to do two jobs. Why weren't they ready straight away to get something moving? They eventually said they would get someone to do a few extra hours but not before someone is really suffering from stress, so it feels that the wheels are turning slowly and people get damaged on the way.

When individuals experience high job demands and low resources, they have the potential to become annoying targets (Baillien, Rodriguez-Muñoz, Van den Broek, & De Witte, 2011). A bully who felt unsupported and under-resourced targeted another employee who had similar challenges. The target said,

> I'm really struggling here, I'm trying to do an almost full-time job in part-time hours. I'm the lowest paid for what I do. I have anxiety when it is not just the client who has the issue. It is when that client's issues could possibly affect others who are around and that's when it gets quite stressful for me. I have to take lots of different roles and I have to think—hold on I shouldn't have this responsibility.

Resources, in terms of support within an organisation, play a key role in helping victims to resolve bullying for themselves and whilst support from family and friends can help victims to maintain their positions for a while, it does not necessarily help them find a resolution (White, 1998).

For example, an engineer, who was not far from retirement and contented with a job he had been doing for many, many years, suddenly had his area of responsibility almost doubled. This involved a lot of travelling. He gave it a try but was exhausted by the work and felt that he did not have the physical stamina for the increased workload. Managers refused to compromise. The employee felt bullied by his managers and by the system. He had worked for the company all his life, never had time off, and always been loyal employee. With considerable sadness, he went on long-term sick leave.

A supportive social climate within a group, or department, may primarily depend on empowering employees and fair leadership. This conclusion has been supported by studies showing the importance of transformational leadership to prevent conflicts within groups (Kotlyar & Karakowsky, 2006; Skogstad, Torsheim, & Einarsen, 2011).

Role conflict

Einarsen (1999) suggests that incompatible demands and expectations around roles, tasks, and responsibilities may act as a precursor to conflict and to poor worker relationships.

One case study involved a hairdresser in a salon owned by a company which prided itself on staff development. The cultural expectations were that staff might better themselves by seeking promotion either within the company, which often involved moving to another city, or moving out of the organisation and working for other hairdressers. Although the employee had been on numerous courses and risen to the position of assistant manager, she wanted to stay at that level and continue to live near her family. She refused to apply to move to a different location, or travel out of the area to another salon. The boss got very frustrated and angry with her intransigence. An unpleasant and unfriendly atmosphere developed between the two of them. Expectations on both sides had been thwarted. Colleagues lost respect for her. She developed health problems which affected her ability to work. She had much time off sick and now plans to leave the hairdressing profession completely.

Role conflicts may also arise when there are variations in management styles within a team or within a department. For example, an autocratic leader at the top of a department had a deputy who, in comparison had a laissez-faire style of management. This created confusion and potential for bullying. One of the staff said,

> I feel that I get direction from my team leader but don't from my line manager. He tends to bend with the wind and is not strong enough character to say, 'this is it, this is the way we should be going'. There's a strong character at the top and weaker character beneath, there's a danger then that you just become a yes man and then you are just all over the place.

Role conflict and role ambiguity can escalate when handled badly, with the weaker party trapped in the target position, whereas the more powerful partly is most likely to become a perpetrator (Baillen, Rodriguez-Muñoz, Van de Broeck, & De Witte, 2011). For example, role conflict arises when top management fails to give adequate support for middle or line managers who are expected to implement change programmes (Branch, Ramsay, & Barker, 2007). The power and authorisation of middle managers in introducing changes can then be perceived as illegitimate by subordinates who show their disrespect through upward bullying.

> A middle manager recounted a situation in which staff came as a group to meetings as if preparing a concerted an attack on him. He said, "It's not only about undermining me, it's about undermining systems". (Branch, Ramsay, & Barker, 2007, p. 13)

Upwards bullying may be one of the few ways by which dissatisfaction with organisational issues can be voiced by staff (Liefooghe & Mackenzie Davey, 2001).

Leadership and management styles

The terms "leadership" and "management" are used more or less synonymously in the research on workplace bullying. However, there are differences. Essentially, leadership sets the future and direction of an organisation. The aim of leadership is to maximise the human potential of an organisation (Western, 2008). The word "management" has two derivations: first, from the Italian word "*maneggiare*", which implies taking charge and directing, particularly in the context of war; a second derivation is from the French word "*ménager*", or careful housekeeper, giving a gentler and a nurturing interpretation of the role. The concept of manager seems to have kept this dual character (Mant, 1977). It is possible to be engaged with management without being a manager, as management is intrinsic to human agency. For example, organising a dinner party or getting oneself to the gym involves management. However, to be a manager is to be institutionally empowered to determine and/or regulate certain aspects of the action of others.

Throughout the history of the research on bullying, links have been found between bullying and leadership and management. For example, the most important factors in predicting bullying appear to be the lack of constructive leadership, the lack of possibilities to monitor and control work tasks, and, in particular, a high level of role conflict (Einarsen, Raknes, & Matthiesen, 1994). The main causes of bullying are related to the organisation of work and the quality of leadership behaviour (Leymann, 1996). More recent research has found that unfair and unsupportive leadership practices and the presence of role conflict significantly predicate the overall incidence of bullying (Hauge, Einarsen, Knardahl, Lau, Notelers, & Skogstad, 2011). In the UK, about eighty per cent of perpetrators of bullying include managers compared with fifty per cent in Scandinavia (Rayner, Hoel, & Cooper, 2002). In a survey of 4,000 British employees, just over two thirds of incidents of bullying were blamed on managers, supervisors, or employers (Fevre & Lewis, 2012).

Autocratic leadership

Workplace bullying is commonly associated, in terms of the nature of control, with the extremes of leadership—autocratic and laissez-faire. A large-scale study of psychosocial issues at work in the UK found autocratic leadership was the strongest predictor of observed bullying, followed by laissez-faire leadership (Hoel, Glasø, Hetland, Cooper, & Einarsen, 2010). Ninety per cent of respondents who had been bullied reported that the leadership in their organisation was autocratic (O'Moore & Lynch, 2007).

This domineering, controlling, intrusive, and often petty style of leadership is not one which engenders trust or respect amongst employees. Where the use of force by managers or leaders is motivated by self-interest, narcissism, or self-aggrandisement rather than by the perceived interest of the organisation, such behaviour is more likely to be seen as illegitimate and an abuse of power by those at the receiving end, as well as by observers (Ashford, 1994). Destructive leaders foster helplessness and despair amongst subordinates and, by the close control of the workforce, curb initiatives (Ashford, 1994).

Differences in perceptions of bullying have been found between those who are bullied and observers of bullying. The witnesses tend to associate bullying with autocratic or tyrannical leaders' behaviour, whereas targets relate bullying more to unpredictable styles of leadership, where punishment is meted out or delivered on the leader's own terms, independent of the behaviour of a subordinate (Hoel, Glasø, Hetland, Cooper, & Einarsen, 2010).

A survey of blue-collar workers from a Danish manufacturing company showed that nine out of ten employees who had been bullied felt that they only received negative feedback from management, and they were also far more likely than other employees to report receiving insufficient information from their immediate superiors (Agervold & Mikkleson, 2004). Levels of bullying were compared in different departments and it was found that in a department with the most bullying, the manager's style was rated as the most significant factor, whereas in the department with a moderate degree of bullying, role clarity was rated as being more significant (Agervold & Mikkleson, 2004). Employees in the department with most bullying reported more mental fatigue/burnout than employees in other departments.

In another study, psychological distress was found to be worse when supervisors perpetrated the aggression rather than co-workers, or outside aggressors such as customers (Hershcovis & Barling, 2010). Supervisor aggression also impacted on workplace attitudes such as job satisfaction, commitment, and intention to quit, and was related to lower levels of performance (Hershcovis & Barling, 2010).

Various explanations are given for the links between autocratic styles of leadership and bullying. First, leaders may move out of their fields of competence, feel insecure, and, therefore, compensate through denigrating others. Managers may resort to bullying behaviours because they have exceeded their skill level and competency during downsizing and structural change (Sheenhan, 1999). From a questionnaire to employees in an institution of higher education in the UK, Lewis (1999) found the two most prominent features of bullying were a lack of professionally trained middle and senior managers, and a power imbalance between managers and lecturers. Managers who are failing to manage their own pressures and stress in particularly stressful circumstances may revert to, or fall into, autocratic or even tyrannical styles of leadership, so much so that involvement with staff and constructive criticism may be replaced by rage, shouting, and other threatening and incomprehensible behaviours (Hoel & Salin, 2003). These negative and aggressive acts may appear "out of the blue", catching employees off guard by their unpredictability, thus making it difficult for them to protect and defend themselves (Hoel, Glasø, Hetland, Cooper, & Einarsen, 2010).

Second, an authoritarian style of leadership or management may create a climate of fear where there is no room for criticism and where complaining may be considered futile (Hoel & Salin, 2003). A lack of respect and trust in the leader-subordinate relationship may increase the need for emotions to be regulated through repressing, or faking them, thus in the long term having a detrimental effect on recipients, such as reduced job satisfaction, health problems, and increased intention to leave (Glasø, Ekerholt, Barman, & Einarsen, 2006).

Third, in a review of the research on bullying and destructive leadership, Ferris, Zinko, Brouer, Buckley, and Harvey (2007), propose conceptualising bullying by leaders as a form of organisational politics. A leader may employ bullying behaviour as a strategic attempt to influence others in order to maximise personal and/or organisational objectives. During organisational change, for example, in restructuring, there may be higher levels of internal competition for jobs, thereby motivating a bully to eliminate "competitors" (Salin, 2003). In organisations where there is a focus on short-term improvements in productivity, targets may work harder to comply with a bully's demands. Increased productivity may also come from members of the audience as they attempt to avoid becoming targets. Some targeted employees may decide to leave and their positions may be filled by others seen to be more qualified (Ferris, Zinko, Brouer, Buckley, & Harvey, 2007).

For example, a teacher nearing retirement and set in his ways was bullied by a newly appointed head teacher. The aggressive approach used by the head teacher appeared to have the aim of getting rid of the older teacher to make much-needed radical changes to the school. The teacher could not cope with the demands made on him. He left the school and was replaced by a much younger and lower-paid teacher. This had two benefits. First, funds were released from a very tight school budget, as the new teacher was cheaper to employ. Second, the young teacher was malleable and quickly adjusted to the new ways of working. The initial changes to the school were positive but as soon as results began to improve, the head teacher focussed on gaining his next promotion. However, the abrasive and narcissistic style of the head teacher had impacted on other staff. Initially they increased their commitment and workload but soon became cynical and stressed. After the head teacher left the school its reputation went into decline. Deeper issues within the school community had been glossed over and had not been addressed. The changes had been unsustainable.

Laissez-faire leadership

At the opposite end of the spectrum to autocratic leadership is laissez-faire leadership. In this style of leadership, leaders exert a minimum effort to get required work done combined with a minimum of concern for subordinates. It is a passive form of leadership which violates the legitimate interest of the organisation by, for example, wasting employees' time as well as creating problems for subordinates when their legitimate leadership expectations continually fail to be met (Assland, Skogstad, & Einarsen, 2008). Employees can feel that their organisation is drifting and that no one cares for them. Then they struggle to survive. Leaders who lead in a laissez-faire manner tend not to intervene until problems are either brought to their attention or become so serious that action can no longer be avoided. One employee said,

> We had the CEO's statement recently and it was a proposal, I think. There was little vision. Management are too slow to catch a cold. They couldn't organise a 'whatsit' in a brewery. They have all these bits of paper that say that they can do this or the other. They haven't got the push, or they are scared to put their heads above the parapet, or the bureaucracy is so bad that it doesn't allow them to do such things. I get so frustrated, I'm angry. I'm sure they feel if they make a decision that they would go up in smoke. I do feel that they would self-combust; there is all talk and no action. If my boss sits on the fence much longer, he'll get blown off.

Chaotic workplaces depress citizenship and bullies feel free to intimate and belittle others at will, whereas in coherent, well-organised workplaces there is little evidence of interpersonal conflict (Hodson, Roscigno, & Lopez, 2006). Weak and indistinct leadership contributes to workplace conflicts going unresolved and can eventually escalate into bullying (Strandmark & Hallberg, 2007). An abdication of leadership provides fertile ground for bullying between peers or colleagues due to managers' ignorance. This results in a failure to recognise incidents of bullying and to intervene (Hoel & Salin, 2003).

When decisions are inappropriately left to the group, or when leaders' absences give rise to operational and cooperational problems, foundations may be formed for group conflicts and peer bullying, hence acting as antecedents to bullying (Hoel, Glasø, Hetland, Cooper, & Einarsen, 2010). Within situations with a laissez-faire leadership by an immediate superior, there is a relatively strong association with elevated levels of role conflicts as well as role ambiguity (Skogstad, Einarsen, Torsheim, Assland, & Hetland, 2007). In an organisation where top managers operate a laissez-faire style, more bullying was found to occur in teams where the leaders mimicked this style of leadership than where there were more structured management styles (White, 2007). Staff in one department where bullying was rife said,

> Things sit around for ages, there is frustration with that. Decisions don't get made and you muddle on as best as you can really.
>
> Our proposal for more staff has sat on his [the team leader's] desk for six months and nothing has happened and another year slips by and at the end of the day it is the clients who lose out. They are the people who we are meant to be serving and that is very frustrating and it puts pressure on us of course. It is very, very frustrating.
>
> There is no feeling there is a person we all look up to and every time we have a meeting it is so unbelievably tedious and people resent having to go because it is a complete waste of time, so any attempt to make us into a more cohesive group doesn't seem to work because of the lack of dynamic leadership.

Cyberbullying

Just as research into traditional bullying in schools began many years before research into workplace bullying, so our understanding of cyber-bullying, at the time of writing, is gained mainly from research with children.

There is evidence that children involved in traditional bullying also partake in cyberbullying. Thirty per cent of traditional victims were cyber victims and had similar psychological profiles to traditional victims of bullying, while eighty-five per cent of victims knew the bully (Gorvig, 2011). The low levels of popularity and low self-concept of traditional victims were also found for chat victims. Likewise over-protective behaviour on the part of cyber-victims' parents was observed. Most cyberbullying was carried out by one, or a few, students, usually from the same year group as the victims (Smith, Mahdavi, Cravalho, Fisher, Russell, & Tippett, 2008). Sixty per cent of cyberbullies were traditional bullies (Gorvig, 2011).

Chat in chat rooms is seen to represent an important medium in the everyday life of adolescents. Forty per cent of chatters reported that their chat friends were just as important as their real school friends (Katzer, Fethenhauer, & Belschack, 2009). Prevalence rates for bullying in internet chat rooms are comparable with those for bullying in school. Twenty-eight per cent of victimised chatters reported always falling victim to the same bullies.

There are, however, numerous differences between cyberbullying and traditional bullying. There are few time boundaries, audience numbers can be greater, and there is greater opportunity for anonymity. In traditional bullying, once victims get home from school they are away from the bullying until the next day. With cyberbullying, the victim may continue to receive electronic messages irrespective of his/her location. Cyberbullying can reach particularly large audiences outside a peer group, compared with the small groups that are the usual audience in traditional bullying (Slojne & Smith, 2008). On social networking sites the audience can be infinite. In cyberbullying, a comment, or video clip, can be accessed more than once, resulting in repeated bullying. Online postings have a permanent quality, with information being copied on to other sites. The victim is left wondering from where in the world the attacker is coming (Lipton, 2011).

The type of media which raised most concerns amongst adolescents was the picture/video clip. This most obviously public form of cyberbullying can show the victim in some embarrassing or hurtful situation. It can potentially reach a large audience and be viewed by the victim too (Slojne & Smith, 2008). The fear of not knowing who had seen the picture/clip was also given as a reason for this type of bullying having a more damaging impact than emails and text messaging (Slojne & Smith, 2008).

The person carrying out the bullying may be less aware, or even unaware, of the consequence of his/her actions. Without direct feedback there are few opportunities to show empathy with the victim, or remorse for his/her actions. There is also less opportunity for bystander intervention (Slojne & Smith, 2008). The internet is a comparatively cheap and quick way for an abuser to harass victims and its impact is immediate, unlike traditional bullying in which the response-time may vary. The technology can be used to seek revenge, as its viral nature makes it easier to be cruel online (Patchin & Hindurja, 2012). In "Second Life", a space where participants can create their own identities, environments, occupations, and pastimes, the term used for cyberbullying is "grieving".

In traditional bullying the victim usually knows the identity of the bully whereas in internet chat rooms participants are able to "talk" anonymously with the interaction partners without revealing their true identity or real physical characteristics. Thus, it is possible for chatters to create a whole new identity (Katzer, Fetchenhauer, & Belschak, 2009).

Teenagers find social networking sites give a heightened emotional intensity; digital life is the "place for hope", the place where something new will come to the participants. The emotional charge can be high. There is evidence that the anonymity of chat rooms may help victims to abandon their negative self-images, such as their unpopularity or social rejection by other pupils, and put themselves into more assertive roles. This may help to break the vicious circle of victimisation if they experience themselves as being more integrated into a group. In school their presence at the edge of the playground, or sitting alone at a school desk, draws attention to their isolation (Katzer, Fetchenhauer, & Belschak, 2009). Within cyberspace there are few rules and no norms. It is easier to escape from life and not be a perpetual target.

Victims of cyberbullying, just like some traditional victims, can provoke attacks by bullies. For example, victims reported visiting high-risk locations such as right-wing extremist, pornographic, or hooligan chat rooms (Katzer, Fetchenhauer, & Belschak, 2009). This may indicate that victims often place themselves in situations in which victimisation is more likely. Victims of traditional bullying also visited these sites.

Some victims develop false identities as a disguise and then use the sites to discuss their personal problems with others, using the sites as a confessional to get rid of their personal angst and unhappiness. However their openness may signal to the chat room visitor "I am weak", "I am an easy target" and could therefore invite victimisation. When individuals live part of their lives in virtual places such as "Second Life", computer games, and social networking sites, vexed relationships can develop between what is true in the real world and what is true in simulation (Turkle, 2011). It seems ironic that an avatar, who appears in a bodily form possibly nothing like the participant, seems to be most accepting of the participant's truest self (Turkle, 2011).

Just as fights can develop in the playground, chat rooms and social networking sites are also scenes of conflict. Fights can escalate for no apparent reason but, unlike fisticuffs in the playground, there is no physical presence and no feedback from an individual's body language to exert a moderating force. There is no barrier to expressions of rage (Turkle, 2011). Laws drawn up for the real world often do not translate well when applied to cyberspace (Lipton, 2011). This raises challenges not just for schools in terms of supervision and monitoring but also for workplaces, where the use of social networking as a means of communicating with staff is on the increase.

Models of the organisational dynamics of bullying

There are few simple cause and effect relationships in bullying, as one cause does not always lead to the same effect; however not many models capture the systemic and dynamic nature of bullying. Patterns of escalating conflict from Neidl (1996), Kelly (1999), and White (2007) are outlined in Chapter Two but these primarily focus on individuals, rather than on the contexts which give rise to bullying. Here I shall outline details of a few key models which focus on organisational issues: chiefly those of Rayner, Hoel, and Cooper (2002); Salin (2003); systemic models from research into bullying in schools; and the contextualisation theory of workplace bullying (White, 2007).

The majority of workplace bullying researchers use quantitative techniques and, from time to time, use analogies to give "life" to their statistics. A UNISON (2009) survey found twenty-two per cent of witnesses of bullying left their jobs and seventy per cent felt stressed by contact with bullying at work. There is a ripple effect of bullying from targets to witnesses (Rayner, Hoel, & Cooper, 2002). These ripples extend to home and social life too and these, in turn, can be reflected back to impact on working life.

A model frequently referred to in the research is that of Salin (2003). For bullying to occur, three factors must be in place: enabling conditions, motivating factors, and triggers (Salin, 2003). Enabling factors provide fertile conditions for bullying but are not sufficient to explain how it starts. For example, due to low levels of employment within an area, employees may be particularly dependent on a particular type of work or workplace for their livelihood, and ruthless managers, or bullies, can abuse this dependency (Crawford, 1999). The second factor involves motivating structures and processes. For example, high levels of internal competition for posts can take precedence over the need for effective team collaboration. When employees identify very closely with an organisation, and get a buzz from doing so, bullies can blend their identities with an organisation and let their monomania run wild (Crawford, 1999). The third requirement for bullying to take place is a trigger. Triggers include a variety of change factors within the workplace, for example, the introduction of new structures, policies, and procedures (Salin, 2003).

Another model with three antecedents suggests that workplace bullying is the product of three tracks or pathways: an individual's inability to cope with frustration; the consequence of escalating interpersonal conflicts; and destructive team and organisational cultures (Baillen, Neyens, De Witte, & De Cuyper, 2009). An ecological model extends this further to include the microsystem of the bully and target, the mesosystems of the immediate workgroup, including the manager, the exosystem of the organisation, and the macrosystem, society (Johnson, 2011).

Causes of bullying are to be found in the relationship and interaction between the individual and his/her ways of relating to the surroundings, the workgroup as a whole, the organisation and its structure, and the overall togetherness (Thylefors, 1987). Although Thylefors (1987) is recognised in the research for her contribution to understanding scapegoating, her advocacy for a systemic conceptualisation of bullying seems to have been marginalised in the dominant milieu of psychological and statistical analysis.

Many school bullying researchers, however, have adopted systemic models of bullying and victimisation. Atlas and Pepler's (1998) model is based on the assumption that bullying behaviour is an interaction that occurs between individuals and unfolds within a social ecological context. Bullying is taken to be influenced by the individual characteristics of the bully and the victim, the dyadic interactional processes between them, the presence of peers and teachers, and the school context in which bullying behaviour unfolds. Systemic intervention practiced in schools focuses on bullies and victims but also incorporates peers, teachers, school administrators, and parents (Craig, Pepler, & Atlas, 2000).

Life in the workplace tends to be more complex than life in schools and more challenging to observe. Little research has been carried out to show how bullying scenarios develop in workplace contexts. One such study, however, indicates that bullying occurs around vacuums of support and where there is accumulation of the most negative aspects of an organisation's culture, for example, poor communication and "thinking in boxes". These factors create organisational "black holes" into which bullies and victims are drawn (White, 2010).

Few models give guidelines to HR managers interested in the systemic links between individuals, groups, and organisational contexts. One of these is the contextualisation theory of workplace bullying (White, 2007). It is designed to identify areas in organisations which are at risk of developing bullying scenarios. This theory is based on Honneth's (1995) three patterns of recognition: rights, community value, and love.

The contextualisation theory

Employees have the right to basic respect to enable them to carry out their tasks without being unduly hindered. Where we find bullying, rights are often denied. For example, denying employees their holiday entitlements; doubling an employee's area of responsibility without consultation, thereby generating overload and stress; creating unnecessary delays in replacing staff with no indication of when the employment vacuum will be filled; and ignoring health and safety obligations regarding psychological health. When rights are denied, self-respect is lost (Honneth, 1995).

Community value is about connectedness and collaboration between and within groups as well as across an organisation. When employees are valued within an organisation and recognised by other employees for their contributions, they have pride in their collective accomplishments. However, when an individual, or group of employees, feels they have nothing of value to offer, there is potential for a loss of self-esteem. Misunderstandings between employees are inevitable, potentially resulting in scapegoating and bullying. An extreme form of the loss of self-esteem in an individual is social death (Honneth, 1995). This is an apt description of the fate of some victims of workplace bullying.

Love, the third pattern of recognition, relates to basic self-confidence which, according to Honneth (1995), is about having a capacity to express needs and desire without fear of being abandoned. When bullying arises, management often turn a "blind eye". Team members and even HR staff and union representatives shy away from engaging with the challenges and resort to disciplinary procedures as a quick fix and temporary containment for their anxieties. However, these procedures can provoke further anxiety for those involved. In the long term costs could be high. Courage is needed if difficult conversations are to take place.

If bullying is to be prevented, rights need to be in place, and employees recognised for their contributions and given a "voice". Bullying is most likely to occur in organisations when these three patterns of recognition are missing (White, 2007).

Summary of the research review

We may assume that bullying has occurred in workplaces throughout time. No organisation, whether large and corporate or publicly owned, or a small start-up or family business, seems immune to bullying. New eras bring new challenges and the present era of rapid change, globalisation, fluidity of boundaries and roles, and increased electronic communication provides different contexts in which bullying can arise.

The research review presents bullying as a manifestation of a complex interplay of organisational factors including leadership styles, culture, and structural fractures.

Bullying becomes institutionalised when negative patterns of behaviour become normalised through rhetoric, traditions, and cliques. Management rhetoric can mask reality. It can close down the voices of employees, particularly those from further down the hierarchy, and curtail the opportunities for raising questions, particularly when these involve emotional issues. Outbreaks of bullying tend to be ignored until they get out of hand and then are dealt with on an individualistic basis. A rigid adherence to outmoded ways of working allows bullying behaviour to continue on the grounds that "this is the way things have always been done". Organisational cliques, often detached from the norms and values of the rest of an organisation, foster environments in which bullying behaviour becomes institutionalised within groups.

Management systems may fail to work for the benefit of all employees, particularly when legitimate rights are not being met and where individuals feel they are unable to make a valued contribution due to a lack of resources or lack support from colleagues. In these situations tensions rise and frustrations build, creating the potential for bullying. Poor access to resources, combined with high workplace demands, drain employees' energy and weaken the position of individuals and groups, making it more likely that bullies or victims will emerge.

The most prevalent leadership styles associated with bullying are autocratic and laissez-faire. These represent the extremes of organisational control. Autocratic leadership, characterised by domineering and overtly controlling styles, is intrusive and often petty. "Top-down heavy" communication gives little space for employees' voices to be heard. Feelings of fear, helplessness, and subservience are generated and trust and respect are lacking. With little recognition for employees, pressures build. These result in an explosion of bullying on to the surface around structural fractures and concentrations of the most negative aspects of an organisation's culture. Laissez-faire leadership, on the other hand, is characterised by a lack of care and concern for employees and the organisation as a whole. It fosters role conflict and ambiguity, group fragmentation, confusion, and chaos. Much time is wasted. The general lack of direction and support, inefficiency, and poor use of resources generates frustration and conflict between individuals and groups. Both these styles of leadership show a lack of recognition for employees' legitimate rights and the genuine long-term interests of the organisation. The financial benefit of having effective employee engagement with work seems to be misunderstood.

The increasing use of technology means that employees can be accessible 24/7. With few boundaries in place, and no observers as witnesses, managers can relatively easily get rid of their angst on to subordinates. The instantaneous nature of this form of communication can result in vicious attacks. It can be assumed from the research on cyberbullying in schools that adults who are bullies or victims in real life will probably take on those roles in cyberspace too. Provocative victims, as described in Chapter Two, will possibly also be risk-takers in their use of technology, thus furthering their vulnerability. One of the most difficult aspects of managing cyberbullying in organisations is the detachment created by the technology.

> "Being alone can start to seem like a precondition for being together because it is easier to communicate if you can focus, without interruption, on your screen". (Turkle, 2011, p. 155)

As the home increasingly becomes the office, cyberspace may seem preferable to day-to-day and face-to-face interactions with colleagues. With increasing social isolation from colleagues, there is the potential for a loss of social skills, in particular empathy, and for a rise in levels of bullying. With few boundaries in place, from ethical codes or the law, cyberfights amongst colleagues are as probable as they are amongst children online. Realms of fantasy and reality can easily become blurred.

HR managers are not helped in their tasks of tackling bullying by the scarcity of models portraying the systemic nature of bullying. Restricted by the research community's preference for measuring organisational life with statistical programmes and dissecting events rather than making connections, it is research into bullying in schools which gives insights into how bullying arises from an interplay of systemic factors and how a broad range of actions can be used to prevent and effectively manage bullying. More models, such as White's (2010) vacuums and black holes model are needed to capture the interrelated and deeper dynamics underlying bullying scenarios. Researchers also need to consider the needs of HR professionals and tailor their research to providing models, such as the contextualisation theory of workplace bullying (White, 2007), which can be of practical use.

Psychodynamic theories

Through a psychodynamic understanding of the workplace we can begin to appreciate how cultural and structural aspects of organisational life, outlined above, become embedded to such an extent that individuals feel powerless to improve their working environments and create healthier relationships. We can also begin to appreciate how the extremes of leadership create deep insecurities for employees.

From a psychodynamic perspective an organisation is understood to have an unconscious life of its own. Like individuals, organisations develop defences against difficult emotions which are too threatening or too painful to acknowledge (Obholzer & Roberts, 1994). These emotions may arise as a response to external threats, such as competitors increasing their market share or entering the market with new rival products; or they may arise from government pressures to achieve new targets or change structures. Alternatively, they may be triggered by social, economic, or technological changes. Heightened emotional states may also be generated from within organisations by conflicts between management and employees or between groups and individuals fighting for resources, as described in the research review above.

A range of defences such as denial, fantasy, splitting, and envy can be used collectively by employees. These defences operate at such deep levels it is often difficult for employees to appreciate their complexity and origins. The emotional state of an organisation forms much of its cultural identity, just as emotions help to form the character of an individual (Long, 2008).

In illustrating the deeper aspects of organisational dynamics which give rise to bullying, we revisit the concepts of projection, splitting, love and hate, and the life and death instinct introduced in Chapter One, and the concept of collusion from Chapter Three. Additional theories include: the concept of social defences, which is key to understanding how bullying becomes institutionalised; loss and mourning; and vacuums in organisations which are spaces in which bullying becomes established.

Boundaries in organisations

As described in Chapter One, at the individual level, boundaries are those unseen, immeasurable limits which separate us from others. They enable us to afford ourselves some protection from the experiences and feelings expressed by others and yet also allow us to engage with, and be influenced by, others. Boundaries help us to find our identity and help us to focus on our work without being flooded by anxieties.

Boundaries of organisations operate in similar ways. The boundary of an organisation contributes to its sense of identity, for example, in terms of its USP (unique selling point) and its market positioning both with customers and competitors. If a boundary is either too rigid or too open, organisations have difficulties in relating to the outside world. When an organisation has very firm boundaries the impetus for change is low. However, when boundaries of an organisation are too open, employees, particularly leaders and managers, are buffeted by demands from external stakeholders and the organisation may struggle to keep a clear identity and focus on the task in hand. Permeable boundaries allow for a steady two-way flow of communication, enabling the development of a clear "corporate" image and recognition of the external "other" by, for example, a competitor.

Organisations also have internal boundaries. Obvious ones are formed by buildings and departments. Identity badges form boundaries between permanent employees, visitors and those providing outsourced activities such as provision of food and the disposal of waste.

When organisations are very structured, and roles clearly defined, both external and internal organisational boundaries are easy to recognise. Employees also have a clearer picture in their minds about the identity of the organisation. Armstrong (2005) calls this "the organisation-in-the-mind". "Organisation-in-the-mind" is a term given to an individual's perception of how organisational activities and relations are organised, structured, and connected (Armstrong, 2005). In clearly bounded organisations with traditional structures, employees are more likely to have consensus about the primary tasks as well as the norms, values, and ethical standing of their organisation. However, as organisations are taking on flatter, more lateral designs and are no longer bounded and containable within a traditional vertical form, there is a loss of tightly differentiated roles and responsibilities. Boundaries of tasks are contested. The psychological contract has become increasingly complex. Expectations of an employee and outputs inevitably become based on matters of individual competence, flair, and the ability to take on tasks (Armstrong, 2005).

As boundaries tend to be constantly shifting, they have become interfaces of places and time, moments of contact between different parts and processes of complex systems. With an increasing fluidity of boundaries, relationships have been likened to sibling relationships rather than ones with clear authority and structures; hence they can be difficult to manage, both for the individual employee and the leader. When roles are not clear, and boundaries are constantly contested, employees' anxiety levels may rise. Some individuals, such as potential bullies and victims, find it difficult to cope with these situations. Potential bullies are vulnerable to taking the defensive measure of projecting their anxieties on to others in a malicious way.

Containment

As we have seen through the research on workplace bullying, when anger, confusion, despair, fear, and anxiety rush to the surface, normal working life is swept aside, leaving employees unable to focus rationally and to engage with reality. When they are confronted with work-related situations that they find disturbing, upsetting, or anxiety-provoking, employees may seek out containers for their anxieties. Bullies, for example, select vulnerable individuals as their containers, often because there is little containment offered within the organisation or within a group. Yet, in a climate of constant change, mergers, and restructuring, organisations are no longer able to provide clear boundaries and sufficient containment within a hierarchical structure of stable roles. Increasingly a leader's or manager's own capacity to contain and work through anxieties has become an essential element for stability and growth. This capacity involves more than containing and working through anxieties generated within him/herself and includes those emanating from within the group and from within the culture and structure of the organisation. A manager's ability to be psychologically present has increasingly become a key ingredient to the functioning, development, and stability of staff (Cardona, 2003). The challenge for managers is to be able to create new frames for containment in which, through interaction with others, an idea of, and a feel for, the enterprise of the organisation can be developed which both grounds, and recovers, the exchange and enactment of thought (James & Huffington, 2004).

As organisational structures are becoming flatter it is not just managers who need to provide containment. Rather than locating the capacity for containment in any one single person or even in management alone, an organisation needs enough individuals carrying roles that could be classified as "containment leaders" (Lohmar & Lazar, 2006). They do not need to be in prominent leadership positions but may be any team member who is capable of providing an anxiety-binding function.

Individuals offering containment need to be competent, have the ability to show empathy, and be able to set boundaries for themselves, otherwise their own energy will be drained. Containment means helping others to make sense of their experiences, using self-reflection as a source of information about others, orientating others towards work task requirements, and interpreting anxiety-arousing situations. For example, a manager finds time to support an employee who is upset; an employee shares his/her fears about redundancies with another colleague; spaces are created in which a group of employees are able to confront what makes them anxious so they are better able to make choices about how to proceed. Learning to manage anxiety is part of the maturing process of individuals (Boydell, 2005).

When sources of anxiety are deep and inaccessible, the psychoanalytically oriented consultant can bring about insights through taking up a listening position on the boundary between conscious and unconscious meanings, working simultaneously with problems at both levels (Obholzer & Roberts, 1994)

When successful, containment is marked by a shifting of the task, through the conscious intervention of a member or leader (Kahn, 2001). On an unconscious level, employees who become containers are capable of dealing with tension, aggression, and anxiety in a calming and integrating way, as well as repeatedly providing "reality checks" for the group as a whole (Lohmar & Lazar, 2006).

Often problems cannot be solved immediately and there is a need for reflection on the essence of the problems at hand, allowing them just to exist, just to be there. To get to this space involves a suspension of conscious control over thought which French and Simpson (2001) call negative capability. Negative capability, a term taken from the poet John Keats, involves a capacity for containment; it is the capacity to live with, and to tolerate, ambiguity and paradox, to stay in the place of uncertainty in order to allow for the emergence of new thoughts or perceptions.

In bullying scenarios this space and capacity is absent. Within the individuals involved there is a lack of psychic space. Between them intersubjective space becomes stuck. There are impasses in group dynamics and an inability within an organisation's management style or culture to make space and time for new ideas to emerge. Efforts to create new relationships or new ideas, products, services, structures, and cultures are thwarted. Instead there is repetition compulsion, the need to go over and over the past instead of moving forward.

We return to the topic of boundaries and containment throughout this chapter, as they are a cornerstone to understanding the deeper dynamics of organisational life and are particularly important for appreciating how bullying scenarios develop.

Social defences

Social defences are helpful concepts for understanding how bullying becomes institutionalised. As explained in Chapter One, individuals defend themselves against anxiety-provoking situations, for example, through defences such as denial, splitting, projection, displacement, and regression. These defences also come into play at deep levels within organisations and are known as social defences.

Social defences arise over time when members of an organisation collude, unconsciously or subconsciously, in response to organisational anxiety-provoking challenges. The most common defence mechanisms to organisational change include repression (blocking out unpleasant experiences), regression (resorting to previous actions that felt safe), projection (projecting unwanted or unacknowledged feelings on to others), reaction formation (excessively manifesting feelings opposite to the threatening one), and denial (Vince & Broussine, 1996).

Menzies Lyth (1970), in her research to find new ways of working in a hospital, first discovered the presence of social defences when she noted that nursing tasks themselves invoked deep and primitive anxieties within the staff. The closer and more concentrated a relationship between the patient and the nurse, the more the nurse was likely to experience the impact of anxiety. As these anxieties could be potentially overwhelming, nurses defended against them through various means, for example, professional detachment, denial of feelings, and depersonalisation of the patients through defining them by numbers and ailments. To prevent staff becoming too attached to longer-term patients, nurses were moved around the hospital from department to department. A rigid, and ritual, use of tasks was also used as a means of containing anxieties. Sometimes these defences appeared excessive, for example, waking patients to give them their sleeping tablets. Few attempts were made to help the nurses confront anxiety-evoking experiences and develop a capacity to tolerate and deal more effectively with anxieties (Menzies Lyth, 1970).

Although social defences may alleviate anxieties, they may also exacerbate them (Menzies Lyth, 1970). With advances in clinical procedures in the years that have passed since Menzies Lyth's study, it could be expected that training for nurses would include an awareness of excessive use of social defences and of the impact of these on patient care. However, Pitterman (2005) found that evidence-based practice (EBP) in the health service in Australia is creating a fantasy world of certainty. This world is framed in the rhetoric of rationality, practicality, and technology: the EBP discourse is a possible defence against uncertainty and ambiguity in an era of unpredictability and rapid change. As such it is usurping other discourses, particularly those emanating from non-rationalist paradigms related to the role of emotion and relationships in the clinical encounter (Pitterman, 2005). In an attempt to protect this fantasy world, psychic defences of denial, splitting, projective identification, and scapegoating are mobilised.

The clinician, as if robbed by an envious attack, loses the dignity of professional integrity, creativity, subjective understanding and emotional intelligence. These characteristics constitute the right to engage with humanity and create meaning, understanding and healing through connection (Pitterman, 2005).

Recent reports on the failures of Mid-Staffordshire hospital in the UK further illustrate Pitterman's concerns for the loss of humanity within the health care sector. The lack of compassion for patients shown by some staff, the inability of employees to listen to relatives concerned about the treatment of their loved ones, and reports of the excessive use of targets to the detriment of patient care and a range of other systemic failures, show how, at a deep level, structures and systems can create social defences which detach employees from their primary task.

Another example of social defences arising from the demands for change, in particular the demands by stakeholders for a target driven culture, is from higher education. A loss, for example, of dependency or economic stability has been defended against by a pathological demand for checking and the development of a system which endlessly collects data and sets targets in order to control an object (professional academia) which is deemed untrustworthy (Cummins, 2002). Yet these attempts to collect data are not in order to know, but in order to produce a "certificate of comfort" to reassure those at the top of the organisation and other stakeholders. Universities may have become collusively caught up in the desire to produce comfort, a reassurance that all is well (Cummins, 2002).

Some employees try to defend against their anxieties by finding some containment within cliques or by mimicking others. A feeling of belonging may offer some security and yet this may come at a price. For example, engineers in Java unwittingly mirrored their boss's bad behaviour by regularly interrupting each other, acting impatiently and abrasively, fidgeting, and running late (Goldman, 2008). They seemed unable to focus on pending projects and multitasked to the point of absurdity, and this dysfunctional behaviour morphed into a toxic division-wide phenomena. By being tempted to conform excessively with the perceived demands of the organisation, an employee may stop being able to differentiate between his personal and moral values and what he/she thinks is valued by the organisation (Krantz & Smilansky, 2006). Furthermore, if incentivised through overidentification with rewards and targets, the potential arises for the corruption of roles, boundaries, and values.

> Just as individual defences immerse the individual in a world of neurotic make-believe detached from reality, so too do organisational defences immerse their members in collective delusions in which they pursue chimerical projects or run blindly away from nonexistent threats, while disregarding real problems and opportunities. (Gabriel & Carr, 2002, p. 357)

It is often difficult to identify the deeper issues holding back progress. The accompanying persecutory feelings associated with change can get misattributed and ways of working can become distorted (Armstrong, 2002). These ways of working can become so integrated within the culture and structure of an organisation that the sources of anxiety, particularly when they originate from within an organisation, become masked by the defensive responses. For example, an organisation which was a brand leader for many years began to lose its competitive edge with the arrival of new competitors into the market. Perhaps paralysed by fear of the success of their new rivals, or shame that they were no longer in the top rank, management appeared to go into a collective state of denial. (On an individual level, denial inhibits psychic integration and when anxiety cannot be engaged with and becomes too great, there is a risk of regressing to primitive defences such as splitting.) Within the organisation splits appeared to develop throughout the culture and structures, with employees becoming increasingly disconnected from each other. These defences interfered with employees' sense of reality and judgement, potentially leading to confusion and errors. Further distancing from reality could exasperate anxiety levels, hence giving the potential for bullying to arise, as individuals were unable to engage with their own anxieties and those being generated within the organisation. A loss of confidence would create an inevitable further loss in competitive positioning.

> Like the individual neurotic, the organisation then finds itself at the centre of a vicious circle. Just as a neurotic's personal self delusions deepen the suffering for which they ostensibly offer consolation, likewise corporate delusions merely reinforce the malaise of the organisation. (Gabriel & Carr, 2002, p. 357)

Once aroused, unconscious paranoid mechanisms can readily take over. They can distort or magnify the real reasons for anxiety. For example, managers may mobilise social defences to meet needs in a crisis situation by splitting off their own passive, hopeless, fearful, and critical aspects of themselves and projecting them into a specific group of employees (Gale, 2007). This enables the managers to feel task orientated, hopeful, and trusting towards their bosses, boards, and shareholders. The group of employees is then perceived as failing and, in extreme cases, may be forced to fail on behalf of the managers.

An alternative scenario may develop when employees try to preserve the belief that they are "good" and others, such as senior managers, or geographically separated groups and minorities, are "bad" (James & Huffington, 2004). These defensive strategies may provide sufficient containment of anxieties for work to be possible by the "good" group, but may detract from overall resources and energy available for others within the organisation.

Sometimes changes are so radical that even the social defence systems used by employees fall apart. For example, when routines have been dismantled employees may feel helpless, in part, from the loss of capacity to contain primitive emotional states (Krantz, 2001). When bombarded by constant change, employees may become weary and detached from their work and each other (Obhlozer, 2003). For example, a combination of high demands from managers, low levels of support, and poor resources, resulted in staff of a hospital's outpatients department complaining of feeling tired and having low energy levels. Bullying had been breaking out amongst the group for some time. Within the waiting room there was the usual provision of services for patients such as a drinks dispenser, but prominently placed in the centre of the room was a particularly large display of batteries which were available for purchase by the patients for hearing aids and other devices. It was almost as if, at an unconscious level, the nurses may have been trying to engage with their lack of energy and tiredness by providing batteries (a source of energy) in the "heart" of the department, there being little opportunity provided to engage with their deeper needs within the structures of the hospital.

It is, however, within virtual teams which rely primarily on electronic communication that identifying and managing the under-the-surface dynamics is particularly difficult. This form of communication, as described in the research review, is devoid of body language and facial expressions. It is more vulnerable to unconscious distortions. Rather than the introjection of authority and the roles found in traditional organisations, networks of this nature are essentially self-organising and loosely managed. They form temporary "containers" for the task in hand. Employees may project fantasies on to the network and then gain affiliation to the network through their fantasies. Given the often temporary nature of the work and the fleeting nature of engagement with others, employees may develop illusions about what has been achieved through the contacts and outputs. Opportunities for developing trust, mutuality, and interdependence are then particularly limited. The potential for cyberbullying, however, could be considerable.

Loss and mourning

Organisations always have to deal with the tension of maintaining the status quo and an often putative need for change (Carr, 2004). Change, by its very nature, involves a loss of something or someone. Much of the day-to-day loss in organisations is associated with temporary disruptions, for example, moving office, changes in routines and procedures, and loss of the camaraderie of colleagues when structures are altered. More radical experiences of loss occur in mergers and takeovers where there is often a temporary loss of cultural meanings until new cultures become established. Employees may be lost to redundancy, move on, or retire. In extreme cases, the loss may be the failure of a business and the death of an organisation, such as Lehman Brothers or Woolworths.

Whether unconscious or conscious, our attachments to working life provide us with a sense of security and when they are removed or changed, for example, when new technology is implemented, the organisation is restructured, or new business processes are established, anxiety levels rise. In new, unpredictable environments there may be feelings of deep sadness for what has been lost and a profound sense of helplessness as traditions are abandoned and familiar practices discarded.

Employees' experiences of loss during times of change have been likened to those experienced by infants at the loss of the primary carer (Grady & Grady, 2013). Grady and Grady (2008) draw on the observations by Spitz and Wolf (1946) of institutionalised infants in Romania. Over half the children had experienced inadequate mothering and separation during the Second World War and showed symptoms of anaclitic depression. When the infants had been separated from their mothers for between one and two weeks they would stop crying and become increasingly passive, resisting contact, refusing to eat, and failing to respond to external stimulation. They had an extremely weak sense of identity and a reduced sensitivity to pain. There was insufficient energy within their nervous systems to connect the neural structures and some of these children turned to self-harming. Bowlby (1968) lists similar attachment behaviours resulting from separation and/or loss of the primary carer.

In the workplace, loss of attachments generates instability in the lives of employees, a decrease in morale and productivity, and increased absenteeism (Grady & Grady, 2013). These characteristics are very similar to those reported by researchers into workplace bullying. This implies that the dynamics of loss that occur in organisational change could play a key role in the establishment of bullying scenarios, particularly where there is a rush to implement change and the impact of change on employees is ignored.

> Too often newly appointed managers take the attitude of discarding the past and focussing on the future. They may do this for several reasons. They don't want to be associated with the mistakes of the past. They want to be seen as bringers of hope, as new brooms. Perhaps unconsciously, they want to help their systems to overcome the pain or guilt of past mistakes. But some acknowledgement of the past is required to move on, lest unfinished business remains and festers. (Chapman & Long, 2008, p. 45)

The dynamic of loss can permeate an organisation at deep levels. Underlying patterns of loss may linger beneath the surface, creating an impasse to the group dynamics. For example, in one large organisation much change had been endured by employees in terms of a relocation and restructuring. In the opinion of some employees, top management failed to acknowledge the impact of these changes on stress levels (White, 2007). An underlying dynamic of loss had formed within the organisation and this resonated with other losses. In one team, the team leader, who had experienced a recent personal loss, projected his feelings of loss on to his staff. Each team member appeared stuck in his/her own pocket of potential loss. This triggered a stuckness within the group dynamics. The leader, who operated an open door policy, and was highly respected by colleagues and thoughtful towards his staff, became increasingly frustrated and angry that his team were unable to reach their targets. HR staff became concerned that his anger could turn into bullying. Without the intervention of a skilled consultant, knowledgeable about the deeper aspects of organisational life, the dynamic of loss could have continued to create serious problems for this team.

When dealing with loss, associated with downsizing and restructuring, there is a tendency to repeatedly try to solve problems by regarding those who are being lost as less than human, 'dead wood' to be disposed of (Stein, 2008). Colleagues who are left behind may defend against their possible guilt by viewing those who have left with contempt and mistrust.

> One withdraws identification and compassion from them. Instead of something akin to "There but for the grace of G-d go I", they might say "He/she/they must have done *something* to get fired". (Stein, 2008, p. 305)

A group of employees vulnerable to being made redundant, or bullied, are those who are unable to let go of old ways of working and to change to new working practices. They may cling to memories of a previous role in nostalgic and idealised ways. Yet the myths fomented by nostalgia, like most myths, are wish-fulfilling self delusions, partial satisfactions in the realm of fantasies of real desire (Gabriel, 1993).

Employees who are able to let go of loss have ambivalent feelings, a balance between love and hate, whereas those who are locked into nostalgia may be unable to acknowledge their hateful feelings towards loss. Their balance of love and hate goes awry. They cannot acknowledge the reality of loss, are unable to complete the mourning process and so become melancholic. The melancholic displays something else beside that which is lacking in mourning—an extraordinary diminution in his self-regard, an impoverishment of his ego on a grand scale; he/she has lost self-respect (Gay, 1989). In mourning it is the world that has become poor and empty; in melancholia it is the ego itself (Freud, 1917).

Melancholia is like an open wound emptying the ego until it is completely impoverished (Gay, 1989). From an intrapsychic perspective deadness returns. From an intersubjective perspective the melancholic, who cannot separate from the lost object/work rituals/colleagues/places, constantly seeks that which was lost. This search for the lost other may be displaced on to objects, or other employees, in an unhealthy and obsessive way resulting in harassment and bullying.

For healthy growth to take place in organisations during times of change, employees need to be free to mourn collectively and managers need to acknowledge the efforts required in adapting to new ways. Yet this is not easy, even in the most well-considered change programmes. Finding space to mourn is particularly difficult in mergers and acquisitions when familiar systems are threatened, suspended, and often abandoned. In this process, organisations are often rebranded to give a new corporate identity, value statements are re-written, and policies and procedures redrafted.

In mergers the ideal scenario is the formation of a symbiotic relationship, but the reality is that containment often becomes contested, with one organisation viewed as the container and the other the contained (De Gooijer, 2009). As a result of the possible fear of annihilation from the other organisation, splitting and projection can set in and a rigid view of the other organisation, or leaders or groups, quickly becomes established and entrenched. This is an organisational form of projective gridlock, as described in Chapter Two. If a merger, like an interpersonal relationship, is imbued with too much anxiety it may either become parasitic or dominated by hostility, and when one organisation is devalued it could be restructured out of existence soon after the merger (De Gooijer, 2009).

In a merger of three organisations, an underlying pattern of stuckness developed (Knight, 2008). These organisations had very different cultures and even four years after the merger there was an impasse in the new organisation. This stuckness was in the form of learned helplessness brought about through a lack of clarity between actions and outcomes, a decrease in incentives, inability to learn, and anxiety in the form of confusion and frustration. The pervading cultural dynamic which was being vicariously shared between colleagues and new employees was: "You are helpless and cannot effect change, so why bother to try". These employees had fallen into a subservience from which they could not escape, a dysfunctional spiral of helplessness (Knight, 2008). This pattern is similar to the interpersonal dynamics of domination and submission described in Chapter Two.

In acquisitions it is clear who dominates. Yet to avoid splitting, repetition compulsion, and withdrawal of engagement, there needs to be an acknowledgement of the loss, or potential loss. For healing to take place there needs to be an acceptance of loss and the need to mourn, recognition that one may have harmed others, and a wish to make reparation. This is possible. An example of a successful acquisition is that of a Dutch company acquired by a French organisation. Much attention was given to food and drink served at meal times, with the CEO insisting that Dutch preferences were honoured. These included serving milk instead of wine at lunchtimes. These cultural traditions were maintained until the takeover was well established. In further attempts to neutralise rather than polarise differences, all meetings were conducted in English. Attempts to acknowledge differences, to recognise the other, led to the first of many successful takeovers in which "recognition of the other" became an established hallmark of the company under the leadership of that particular CEO.

Food and drink also proved to be a means of offering sustenance in the mourning process in a company whose ending was forecast and planned (Kahn, 2012). It could be assumed that when a closure date for an organisation is given, mourning for the loss would be acknowledged. However, Kahn (2012), in her study of a "dying" financial institution, found an evasion of grief. Coping mechanisms used by the staff included manic jolliness and excessive celebrations with food, feasting, even gorging. The jolliest of all employees, the head of the department, played the happiest and wittiest of roles to defend both the team and herself from the vicissitudes of her own leadership role and the roles of her team members. Kahn (2012) suggests that this manic, or pathological, reparation could be based on denial of depressive feelings, or, in the case of the leader, a compulsion to eliminate depressive anxiety and avoid coming to terms with the impending loss. The use of food and drink in this way could also be interpreted as a symbolic way of providing "life" to employees in a time of loss and the impending "death" of the organisation; perchance an enlivening of the death instinct.

Vacuums

There is an adage "Nature abhors a vacuum". It is generally acknowledged in the discourse on politics that where there is a power vacuum, there will be conflict. For example, when the dictator of a country suddenly dies there are concerns about who will succeed and often there is a fight amongst potential leaders to take that vacant seat. This can lead to civil unrest. Likewise in city gangs, the arrest of a gang leader does not necessarily mean that the gang disbands. It is more likely that conflict will break out between gang members as they assert their authority to take the top role.

Vacuums are also sites of conflict in organisations. They can occur anywhere, not just at the top. They are spaces, void of matter, where something has been lost or taken away, for example, where vacancies are left unfilled, or resources are withheld from employees or where individuals are undermined. Vacuums are characterised by a lack of recognition (White, 2007).

HR managers who believe that bullying is just about a clash of personalities and not part of a much bigger picture, often move victims or, more rarely, a bully, to another area of the organisation. However, if the culture, structural issues, and group dynamics which created a vacuum in the first place are not changed, and if support is withheld from the replacement, a new victim or new bully will probably emerge. Bullying will recur. Much will depend on whether the new employee has "a good enough mother within" (see Chapter One), adequate personal boundaries, and the capability to contain and work through anxieties generated within him/herself, within the group, and within the organisation.

Organisational conflicts often move from a point of origin to another part of the system to be released. For example, senior managers may attribute "the problem" to middle management who, in turn, experience themselves as victims of forces outside their control or understanding. Unresolved and hidden conflicts appear to be exported horizontally to other groups, as in inter-departmental struggles, or vertically upwards through idealisation of leadership, followed later by his/her denigration, or, more frequently, downwards, thus leading to front-line, endemic, micro-conflicts (Brunning & Perini, 2010).

For example, two executives may suppress differences between them to avoid a damaging a shaky relationship, only to find middle management unwittingly enacting their fight (Bing & Sullivan, 2009). They may be projecting their anxieties on to middle managers, but, at the same time, they are creating a vacuum of support for their colleagues. As shown in Chapter Three, where there is a vacuum of leadership within a team, bullying can break out wherever there are structural fractures. Anxieties may appear to move throughout a team, like molten magma under pressure, to fractures in the structure where, for example, staff struggle with limited resources, little support, and high job demands. The frustrations explode at that point as bullying.

Where vacuums form in organisations, potential victims, who need to reach out to others for recognition, move into these spaces. They are attracted both by the space and, initially, by the attention they get from a bully. Potential bullies, on the other hand, are fearful of these spaces because of the lack of boundaries and containment. They feel at an unconscious and subconscious level that they are falling into a void, particularly when others crumble into subservience.

Next to vacuums there appears to be a concentration of the most negative aspects of an organisation's culture (White, 2007). These concentrations act like cosmic black holes, regions in space where gravity is so strong that whatever enters it will be split in two, split again and again, and eventually mangled in a cosmic whirlpool. Cosmic black holes are where the fabric of time and space is warped, curving back on itself and taking the exit doors with it.

As we have seen in Chapter Three, where there is bullying, the group dynamics fragment on the surface, but beneath, at unconscious and subconscious levels, there are collusions of subservience. Unable to gain recognition from within the group, bullies and victims "fall" into the black hole; the bully desperately trying to find some boundaries and the victim trying to reach an "other". As bullying develops, the projections from bullies become fixed and gridlocked (see Chapter One) and it is increasingly difficult for targets to escape. Entangled in a black hole of cultural negativity, bullies and victims engage as false selves (see Chapter Two). They lose a sense of reality as psychic space, the space needed for reflective thought and for the movement of ideas, becomes stuck in a rigidity of past stories. Effective engagement with work becomes increasingly difficult without the necessary support to set boundaries, reduce the vacuums, and change the culture within that part of an organisation. If no support is forthcoming, the bully and victim find themselves in a dance of death (see Chapter Two). The bully and the victim return to the psychic state of deadness from whence they came.

And yet not all is lost. Vacuums are not always spaces of destruction. They can provide space for creating new and healthier relationships, for new ideas to emerge, new structures and processes, and even new products. Much depends on effective cultural change, acknowledgement of loss, and recognition of the other. The case study in Chapter Five illustrates how these changes can be successful.

Summary of psychodynamic theories

Psychodynamic theories of boundaries, containment, social defences, loss, and vacuums give deep insights into understanding how change impacts on the deeper dynamics of organisational life to create bullying scenarios.

Bullying is likely to arise where an organisation's boundaries are excessively open or too closed. Where boundaries are too open to external influences, an organisation may not be able to keep a consistent identity. Employees are less likely to have a shared and cohesive picture of the "organisation in the mind". There is likely to be disruption, inconsistency, and stress for employees. Where boundaries are too closed, the organisation may not be able to change sufficiently to adapt to demands of the external environment, such as stakeholders.

The inflexibility may generate frustrations amongst employees, leading to a build-up of tension and conflict. However, where boundaries have a healthy balance and are permeable, there is less potential for bullying to develop.

Over time, as organisations have become flatter in structure and virtual networks have evolved, organisational boundaries have also become more contested. Individuals who have weaker personal boundaries due to childhood experiences or trauma may feel particularly insecure in these organisations.

As shown in the research review, when bullying becomes institutionalised through, for example, rhetoric, tradition, and cliques, bullying is particularly difficult to manage. Social defences can become so embedded within the culture and structures that employees may be unable to identify and appreciate what is happening, particularly when they use these defences to defend against their own anxieties. Colluding in denial or through excessive routines, monitoring, and target setting, can further entrench the more negative cultural aspects of organisational life. Space for reflection, containment, and working through of anxieties is restricted around black holes and fractures. Incongruities between pay and performance and disparities between resources and demands give rise to frustrations, anger, and the potential for bullying.

Whenever change takes place in organisations, something is lost. This is the nature of change. Some employees, however, are very attached to places and routines. Potential victims and potential bullies may find these changes, and loss of attachments, particularly difficult to endure. This may be due to the reactivating of a loss from childhood, traumatic events in life, or an inability or fear of letting go of objects and individuals. Repetition compulsion (see Chapter Two) is the default position. Other employees defend against the anxiety of constant change through becoming emotionally detached from their work. An increasing use of social media for communication, and the networked nature of organisational structures, further facilitates this detachment.

When employees cannot engage with the love and hate associated with loss, the past may be idealised as nostalgia. Some employees may show signs of melancholia, such as an impoverished ego or a false attachment to others to contain their anxieties. The challenges of coping with loss are particularly acute in mergers and acquisitions. In mergers containment may be contested, leading to a reduced capacity for containment and working through of anxieties within groups and for individuals as well as for an increased potential for bullying. In acquisitions there is potential for splitting into "good" and "bad", with the predatory organisation being perceived as the "bad guys". Patterns of splitting may permeate the culture of the organisation as well as the psyche of individuals.

Grady and Grady (2013) make an important link between the nature of loss experienced by individuals and loss in organisational life. Their reports of outcomes of low productivity, decline in morale, and high absenteeism, are very similar to those where bullying occurs. From this link it could be argued that bullying is essentially about loss of attachments in times of change. Attempts made in bullying to enliven the potential psychic deadness (see Chapter One) may mask the need to mourn. Without recognition of the loss encountered, the organisation, as well as individuals, may get stuck in deep defences such as denial, which can generate further splitting and foster the group impasses characteristic of bullying scenarios.

Where vacuums occur in organisations, there can be opportunities for generating new thoughts, new procedures, and new policies. However, unless time and space are given for reflection and engagement with reality, efforts—however well-meaning—can be futile. Bullies and victims, drawn into vacuums, become entangled in their patterns of domination and submission, as shown in Chapter Two. They become trapped in organisational black holes, whirlpools of negative culture, and "dance" their way towards "death", as illustrated on the front cover of this book.

The Danse Macabre is a 21st century version of the medieval woodcuts which portray death in the form of skeletons or decaying bodies, often with a scythe in hand, luring all whatever their status. Death is portrayed as leading, dominating and determining the rhythm of the dance. Trapped in a spiral, a victim's fate is no longer in his/her own hands. Dialogues are futile. The end game is death (White & Davidson, 2011).

Questions and answers

When does leadership become bullying?

A lack of the ability to contain and work through anxieties

There are many occasions when stresses can become excessive and a wide variety of situations could provoke a leader into bullying.

However, a leader only bullies when he/she is unable to contain and work through anxieties from different sources, for example, from within him/herself, those generated within the organisation, and those from across the external boundaries of the organisation. When a leader lacks resilience there is a regression to the primitive defence of splitting in his/her psyche into "good" and "bad". The leader keeps the feelings of goodness for him/herself and projects feelings of badness on to others. Boundaries are tested to find a suitable container. When a target introjects the projections, and becomes a victim, that individual is perceived, for example, as being unreliable or a failure. These perceptions reflect the unconscious thoughts of the leader. They become fixed in projective gridlock.

The leader's primary concern is self-survival

The above research review indicates that bullying is most likely to occur when leaders show extremes of control, either over-controlling, characteristic of an autocratic style, or lacking focus, as in a laissez-faire style.

When self-survival is of uppermost concern to a leader, he/she is likely to be either over- controlling or effectively absent. In an autocratic style of leadership there is often only space for the voice of the leader. With a lack of recognition for others, pressures build within an organisation, particularly where there is little opportunity to work through issues of dispute and potential conflicts. Anxieties are then pushed under the surface to re-emerge again elsewhere. For example, they may emerge at weak structural points, or where boundaries are contested, or in concentrations of the most negative aspects of an organisation's culture. They also emerge where there is a lack of containment and working through of anxieties available from managers and other colleagues, particularly around vacuums of support.

A laissez-faire style of leadership in an organisation shows itself as of lack of a clear corporate identity and direction. This lack of leadership may produce different cultures in parts of an organisation and the adoption of different leadership styles from those at the top. Teams may develop different values from each other. Although the senior managers may not necessarily bully their colleagues directly, they effectively show they do not care for them or even for the organisation's future. With a lack of clear direction, employees are not able to gain "an organisation in the mind" which is shared with others. This results in misunderstandings, chaos, confusion, and a build-up of frustrations at not being able to instigate effective change. Energy is dissipated rather than harnessed, making working life unnecessarily anxiety-provoking and providing a suitable context in which colleagues bully each other.

Excessive expectations

Leaders may potentially turn into bullies if too much is expected of them, especially if they are idolised as messiahs. Messianic leaders can build dynamic cultures, but these are unsustainable over long periods (Western, 2008). Employees may become submissive to the leader's every whim (see Chapter Three—basic assumption Dependency). Employees may initially perceive a leader as being very, very good and continue this idealisation for a period of time. If boundaries are not set for the leader, he/she may humiliate the employees, diminishing the value of their contribution to the workplace. A pattern of domination and submission (see Chapter Two) could be set up, with individuals being pulled into bullying dynamics.

Hypocrisy

The US company Enron had a statement of vision and values, comprising four principles: respect, integrity, communication, and excellence. However, the real core values were that immoral, illegitimate, and illegal activities were tolerated, if not downright encouraged (Stein, 2011). The splitting of reality from rhetoric by top management in any organisation can foster a climate in which further splitting can be mirrored throughout an organisation, providing a fertile environment for bullying.

Lack of time and space for reflection

In rapidly changing environmental conditions, time targets have risen up the working agenda. In a rush to find quick fixes and provide the next "sound bite", there is little time and space for reflection. The lack of psychic space—psychic deadness—is a key feature of bullies (see Chapter One). Leaders in particular need to possess negative capability, that ability to reflect and live with uncertainty and ambiguity, if they wish to foster healthy organisations. When space and time are not available there is a lack of empathy, black holes may develop, and vulnerable individuals find themselves pulled into a dance of death (see Chapter Two and above). Reflexive ways of thinking, and learning, are needed to generate creative solutions to bullying.

Inflexibility

Rigidity of thinking is common in bullying scenarios. Inflexibility is seen as splitting, projective gridlock, and impasses in groups (see Chapter Three). It is an indication that there is a lack of healthy intrapsychic and intersubjective rhythms.

In our increasingly "fluid" organisations, one of the qualities needed by leaders is the ability to evolve with their environments, rather than getting stuck in outmoded ways (Burgoyne, 2011). Leaders need to be authentic, emotionally intelligent, sensitive, and less rational (Western, 2008). The rigidity and inflexibility of bullies does not fit with these requirements.

How does bullying become institutionalised?

According to the research review above, bullying becomes institutionalised through traditions and rituals, rhetoric and cliques. If we look behind these cultural issues we often find defences against anxiety, known as social defences. As shown in the examples above, these take many forms. Here are three key factors of particular relevance to organisations in our present era.

Measurements

In our rapidly changing organisations, managers and employees tend to cling on to "targets and statistics" as if they were transitional objects (see Chapter Three). This is particularly noticeable where few employees can provide "containment" (see above). Where there is lack of flexible thinking, target-setting may become so institutionalised that it creates an environment for bullying to flourish. For example, bank employees at the interface with customers were expected to update their area manager on the number of targets they had achieved on a twice, sometimes thrice, daily basis. This activity not only cut into their time with customers, thus taking them away from their primary task, but also pushed them into "encouraging" customers to take products and services which may not have been suitable for their needs or ability to pay in order to reach the bank's prescribed targets.

It appeared that a culture of greed, unethical practices, huge bonuses, and the object-focused nature of the banking sector at the time filtered down the hierarchy. The target culture became a defence against anxieties. For line managers in particular, the pressure to get results from their staff was great. It fostered an environment in which bullying was easily institutionalised.

This product-selling marketing strategy, in a customer-focussed business, has proved far too narrow. Rather than a "product sell"-focussed strategy, other organisations, such as Cable and Wireless Worldwide (Meech, 2011) have opted for a broader way of working—a "solution sell" approach.

In excessively target-focussed organisations, those aspects of organisational life which are not easy to measure, such as compassion, care, common sense (implying an ability to reflect), can be easily brushed to one side. Yet it is these qualities that help to "oil" the workings of any organisation. They foster engagement with colleagues and clients.

Cliques

As explained above, bullying may also become institutionalised through cliques. These are most likely to form where there is a lack of clear leadership and direction. If employees cannot find the recognition they need from within an institution, they seek it within a working group. The group may then develop its own informal rules and regulations. Individuals "buy in" to these groups as an attempt to lessen their own anxieties and use the group as a social defence against anxiety. Membership of cliques restricts thought and the ability to reflect and question the moral and ethical values which are being eschewed by the individual and the organisation. Rather than a collaborative approach to problem solving, employees tend to be forced towards a particular stance which they may not agree with, but to which they feel they have to comply, as shown in the example of bank staff above. Cliques tend to have a "group-think" of their own in which bullying behaviour may be normalised. These groups tend to get stuck in their ways as there is little space for opening up discussions, exposing the culture to new ideas, and providing other options. Although these groups may appear cohesive from afar, on closer inspection, they are likely to fit the descriptions of Hopper's fourth basic assumption (see Chapter Three).

Traditions

Traditions and rituals are changing rapidly, with increasing use of electronic communication. However, even new patterns of behaviour can quickly become established as the norm. In traditional working environments there are distinctive patterns of behaviour dictated by political correctness, office rules, and normal social etiquette. However, when individuals are separated from others, working in different locations or from home, they can start to take on new identities; shy employees may become flirtatious, quiet people noisy, and bullies become beneficiaries of any disorder (Kirwan-Taylor, 2010). With the lack of clear boundaries, some individuals are very vulnerable to becoming bullies. These individuals bully through exploiting the technology for their own ends. This can prove difficult to control. As soon as one portal is shut down, another one opens up.

Why does bullying occur in some parts of an organisation but not in others?

The potential for bullying may exist in many organisations and throughout a workplace but will only emerge if the conditions are favourable. Areas at risk of developing bullying are where:

- there is a mismatch between structural factors, for example, between pay and performance or between job demands and resources
- there is a concentration of the most negative aspects of an organisation's culture, for example, poor communication and a lack of transparency over budgets
- a team leader or manager offers little containment and working through of anxieties
- boundaries are unclear and roles ambiguous
- employees are not valued and or recognised by management
- loss is not acknowledged as part of change processes.

How can HR managers promote well-being and engagement based on a psychodynamic perspective of workplace bullying?

Bullying scenarios are complex, messy, energy draining, and a waste of resources. When faced with complexity of this nature, HR managers may feel overwhelmed. Increasingly policies and procedures are being shown to have a limited use and even act as temporary containers for the anxieties of HR managers rather than guides for effective change. However, as illustrated in the case study in Chapter Five, a wide range of measures can be taken to make organisations into healthier environments.

Traditionally the management of bullying scenarios has been through focusing on the individuals. Large organisations often provide access to EAPs (employee assistance programmes), one-to-one counselling, psychotherapy, and mediation in interpersonal disputes. These have a valuable place in tackling bullying. However, as this chapter has shown, bullying is a manifestation of the interactions between individuals, interpersonal relationships, group dynamics, and organisational contexts. All these need to be addressed. An individualistic approach only deals with one part of a bigger picture. Much more can be done to identify the root causes and find more creative and multi-pronged approaches.

An appreciation of unconscious processes

To successfully prevent, manage, and resolve bullying issues, there needs to be an acceptance that there are deeper issues in organisations than those which are measurable and visible. Social defences operate at unconscious levels within organisations, for example, denial, splitting, regression, and displacement.

HR managers may be too close to problems to recognise the underlying issues, especially the social defences. An organisational consultant trained in observing organisations can help to illuminate these issues. Alternatively, there are many courses such as those run by the Tavistock consultancy, OPUS, and the Institute of Psychoanalysis in London where employees can gain knowledge and expertise for themselves.

An awareness that change involves loss

Where leaders fail to appreciate the adjustments employees have to make in change programmes, not just to their working lives but sometimes to their personal lives too, the drive for change may take on an impetus of its own. There is a need to create space to mourn the passing of the old ways, otherwise some individuals may get stuck in nostalgia and even become melancholic. Emotional patterns of loss may permeate the organisation, giving rise to stuckness in group dynamics, outbreaks of bullying, and a fall in levels of productivity and engagement.

Simple gestures, such as acknowledging the history of an organisation, will help in anchoring the identity of the organisation, for example, displaying the portrait of a founder at the entrance to the headquarters.

Finding space and time

Managers and leaders need to be aware of how all the different aspects of "space" are managed. This includes personal space for reflection. By reflecting on their own behaviour with some help, for example, from a life coach, they may become more aware of their "default positions" and how they may be repeating mistakes from the past (see Chapter Two—repetition compulsion).

Rather than letting stress bottle up so that group dynamics become stuck and then explode as bullying, leaders need to be aware of their roles in managing the anxieties generated within their organisations, within the culture, within their departments, and within themselves. They need to be able to create their own space—both psychic and interpersonal—for reflection. In doing so they are better able to accept the need for dialogue and a continual exchange across all aspects of organisational space. An appreciation is needed of the underlying anxieties. As illustrated in this chapter, incidents of bullying are symptomatic of deeper issues which are not being addressed.

In their attempts to create a happy working environment, HR managers may try hard to please everyone. However, in attempting to satisfy employees' every need, they may mistakenly treat them as if they were needy children to be spoilt. An adult response to coping with the social defences is not to ignore anxiety but to work with it—to say "This is stressful and we need time and space to think about it".

Go beyond the platitudes of rhetoric

Although there is much talk in HR circles about engagement in work and with colleagues, this can only become a reality if there is an understanding of the deeper dynamics of engagement. Chapter Two gives in-depth insights into the interpersonal dynamics of mutuality and healthy interpersonal relationships which can form a theoretical foundation for effective action. Examples of how the intersubjective theories can be put into practice are given in the case study in Chapter Five.

CHAPTER FIVE

A case study

The aim in this chapter is to illustrate how some of the key theories of bullying from each of the four main chapters can be used to analyse a case study. This case study is an example of how an organisation, in which bullying was rife under the Former Owner, was transformed by New Management into a thriving enterprise, a market leader in its category, and a much healthier place to work.

The old ownership

The Former Owner of the organisation—a failing engineering company—had, for many years, taken every opportunity to show his contempt for the shop floor workers; for example, he regularly paraded around the factory wielding a cane with which he threatened to strike his staff. Workers were banned from the administrative offices and, in reinforcing the divide between production and administrative staff, he built a second storey especially to house these offices. This emphasised the upstairs–downstairs division. When he observed workers getting together, he regarded them with suspicion. The gathering of two or more workers on the shop floor was forbidden.

The factory machinery was obsolete, under-maintained, and liable to break down. Employees were often denied the basic tools to do their work. Production errors on the floor were routine and scrap rates high. The workers were constantly blamed for these failings.

The Former Owner made the most of any opportunity to show contempt for his employees. For example, from time to time he collected employees' work clothes and sent them to a local laundry. Upon their return, not only did he charge the cleaning cost to each employee, but he also added a mark-up that he put in his own pocket.

Even the administrative staff were not immune to his displays of omnipotence. On Friday evenings he met senior staff in the office area to play cards. If they failed to show up, or turned up and then won a game, these acts were described by staff as "a death wish". The exhibition of false "camaraderie" further split the production staff from the rest of the workforce.

In order to cope with day-to-day life, many of the shop floor workers developed defensive survival strategies such as avoiding eye contact with each other, keeping themselves to themselves, and refusing to cooperate with fellow employees for fear of being accused of conspiracy. The lack of trust was pervasive. If promises were made by the owner there was an expectation that they would be broken. When production schedules went wrong, individuals avoided accepting blame but accused others, even those they may have considered to be "friends". Workers developed their own techniques for keeping the machinery functional but they kept these to themselves—thereby insuring that they were indispensable to the company. Some workers became henchmen, spying on others and reporting back to the Former Owner.

As the workers had been treated in such a subservient manner and indoctrinated about their inferiority, they lacked the confidence to move to other places of employment. Some were frightened of being caught looking for work elsewhere and of the retribution that would inevitably follow from their boss. Others were so used to the abusive environment that they expected other workplaces to be like this one. They felt that even if they plucked up the courage to move on, they would find similar situations elsewhere. Some felt tied to their work because of family commitments in the area.

Unable to escape, and in survival mode, the employees found ways of maintaining some dignity through quiet non-cooperation. In resisting any form of change, they kept their good ideas to themselves, especially the ones which would improve productivity. They did the minimum amount of work. Mistakes were hidden and workers let others find them, thereby avoiding blame themselves. A blind eye was turned to any improper activities outside their areas of responsibility, such as sabotage. By leaving tools and other equipment in a bad shape, production problems were more likely to occur and to contribute to further high scrap rates and waste.

Although the abusive nature of the Former Owner constantly reminded the employees of his omnipotence and their subservience, there were occasions when the workers pulled together and showed their defiance. One of these was when employees asked for a water cooler to be installed on the factory floor. The Former Owner appeared next day with a broken cooler which, he proudly announced, he had picked up at the local dump. The employees took the cooler, and in their own time, stripped it down, cleaned and sterilised it, acquired replacement components, reassembled it, and put it into service.

New Management

Although the new owners had been aware, before they bought the business, that there had been little investment in technology and information systems for many years, they were stunned at the extent of the abusive treatment of the employees by the Former Owner and the dysfunctional nature of the culture. Bullying had become institutionalised through years of neglect, in terms of investment, lack of respect for the workforce, and a culture of fear.

The challenges facing the New Management were immense. After many years of verbal abuse from an autocratic boss, New Management knew employees would judge them by their actions, rather than their words. Yet there were so many priorities. Major changes were needed to the premises to provide a modern, efficient, and safe place to work, either by upgrading the existing factory or finding another site. Outdated and inadequate machinery and information systems needed replacing, both for the benefit of employees and customers, demonstrating long-term commitment to the business. Production strategies had to be refocussed on emerging products and markets. Of all the many priorities—structural, technological, and mechanical equipment which seemed essential almost without delay—New Management decided that the paramount and most daunting challenge was revolutionising the culture—"the way we get things done". Without cultural transformation no other improvements would enable the business to flourish and succeed.

Many of the immediate changes were small ones. For example, uncouth and offensive language was outlawed. Segregated spaces became more open and the upstairs–downstairs divide was broken down. The factory-office threshold was blurred by opening up the office area for use by the shop floor workers when they needed a quiet space and access to expertise for support. Planners and quality control personnel were placed on the shop floor rather than isolated from manufacturing. Separate toilets and kitchens for office and shop floor workers were abandoned and shared facilities made available. Employees were advised on how to leave these clean for other staff and how this was a sign of respect for others. The main doors between factory floor and offices were replaced with glass-panelled doors.

It took New Management many months to uncover the depth of the cultural malaise, as the fear of the employees was so acute. New Management needed to get employees talking openly. A safety committee was set up and recommendations implemented. An open door policy was instigated so that employees could get their concerns addressed on the spot, rather than hiding them away for others to find. New Management made it clear that they would not berate employees for making mistakes as long as they reported them immediately so that they could be rectified. They even complained if employees did not approach them about problems.

The organisational chart was turned upside down, thereby asserting that a primary purpose of almost every employee's task was to optimise the point of manufacture of production on the shop floor and emphasising that the "task" is more important than anyone's title or rank. With the aim of fostering respect, good ideas were celebrated, especially when they were the result of collaboration. Innovative ideas, that used to be punishable by the Former Owner with verbal threats or swipes from the cane, were turned into celebrations. Employees were openly applauded.

New Management gave employees a vision about plans for the next five years. This included adopting state of the art technologies in manufacturing and information systems throughout the company. At first, many employees were sceptical that this could be achieved and some said so. This lack of confidence in management was not encouraging but at least the workers, who for so long had feared expressing any initiative or opinion, had begun to find the courage to find their voice and that was regarded a mark of real progress.

Old ideas and habits had to be challenged. A commonality of interests had to be fostered and "buy-in" obtained from all employees for change to be effective. Complementary teams were formed, consisting of a range of viewpoints and technical, administrative, and entrepreneurial skills. These skills needed to be integrated for progress to be made in developing new products and entering new markets. However, in bringing together different perspectives, a clash of viewpoints and demands was inevitable. These clashes were accepted, encouraged, and even celebrated. To quote New Management: "Conflict is a natural part of the process of managing or living. Show me change and I'll show you conflict. Show me destructive conflict and I'll show you a dying workplace. Show me no conflict and I'll show you a dead workplace. Don't fear conflict. Make it constructive".

However, the newly released energies needed directing carefully as soon as they arose. The changes called for leadership by example and relentless teaching (described by New Management as missionary work) about the new ways of working—through trust and mutuality. There was a conviction that mutual respect and trust would come about gradually through small changes, as these would infiltrate the deeper aspects of organisational life. New Management worked on the premise of showing respect to their employees, valuing their input, and allowing them to express their views. There was an acceptance that the ideal resolution to conflict involves solutions that allow everyone to achieve all of their true objectives or, at least, address the complaints and suggestions. Variations in opinions and disputes were not feared but regarded as a chance for employees to learn from each other's differences and unique opportunities to obtain solutions and resolve issues to build mutual trust and respect for the first time. It was not easy, but that did not justify giving up. Compromise was viewed as a step in the right direction but not a final solution; and it meant that more work needed to be done.

Five years on, the organisation is a thriving and profitable company. There is respect and trust. Problems are advertised and shared. Those which arise on the shop floor are solved on the shop floor, rather than by office staff in a covey of élites. Managers go to the shop floor and ask workers to help them find solutions. The identity of everyone is embedded in the product because, according to New Management, "we all know that we are part of an integrated system that produces the product". There is excitement about the introduction of new technology and the challenge this brings in striving for higher productivity levels. Passion for work and efforts are celebrated, anger is decried. The employees "look forward to going to work".

"In our workplace our need is to nurture the interrelationships among different people and coordinate their full complement of separate, essential management and operational skills and needs. An essential skill in management is an awareness of interrelationships and interdependencies and everyone's sense of belonging to a scheme of things that is much larger than oneself or the sum of us all. And it allows us all to be fulfilled".

Analysis of the case study

The former company

The Former Owner displayed many of the characteristics of an autocratic and aggressive bully. First, his actions were irrational. He had a business to run but his main concern appeared to be the preservation of his own status. The impact of his bullying behaviour on the long-term financial success, or failure, of the company seemed irrelevant. Second, his behaviour indicated that his need for omnipotence and denigration of others was uppermost in his conscious and unconscious mind. Third, he wasted resources, both materially in terms of scrap on the factory floor and in the under-utilisation of employees' skills and ideas. Fourth, he fostered a culture of fear and showed a distinctive lack of trust and respect for others, including his immediate senior colleagues.

A key outcome of this style of autocratic management was "splitting" within the organisation. The factory was split off from the rest of the workforce; physically, in terms of location of the buildings, but shop floor workers were also isolated from, and refused access to, the facilities of the administrative staff. There were structural fractures, or splits, between job demands and the provision of resources to carry out the work. Bullying between employees emerged around these fractures, with employees blaming each other for errors and wastage.

The Former Owner's perception of the workers appeared fixed—they were mere objects to be used and abused. Fixed perceptions are a sign of projective gridlock. We may assume that he split his feelings into good and bad, kept the good feelings for himself and projected his "badness", for example, anxieties, anger, and rage, on to the workers. Their perceptions of him were also fixed. They viewed him as an object to be feared.

There were also splits within the group of workers. A few were henchmen, possibly identifying with the aggressor—the Former Owner—but most kept themselves to themselves. They were bystanders to each other. Recognition—that response from the other which makes meaningful the feelings, intentions, and actions of the self—was absent.

In this bullying scenario there are examples of the two paradoxes of recognition. First, there is the paradox of dependency and independency. The Former Owner was dependent on his shop floor workers "to come up with the goods" but he constantly denied his dependency on them by undermining them at every opportunity and through excessive controls and monitoring. When someone is controlled completely they cease to exist as a subject and become an object (Benjamin, 1988). The second paradox of recognition, the need to try to destroy the other to find reality, is shown in the lack of resistance to the Former Owner. No one stood up to him. No boundaries were set for him. His aggression had free reign to destroy whomever and whatever he chose, including his own organisation. He appeared unable to grasp the reality of his own destructiveness—hence the pending demise of the business before the "buy out" by New Management.

The workers were trapped like slaves. They had very few basic rights, not even the basic health and safety rights which many employees would take for granted. With a lack of rights it was difficult for them to carry out the tasks demanded of them. They lacked recognition both from the owner and from their colleagues and had effectively been robbed of any opportunity to feel that they could contribute to the success of the company and to the group, or be effectively engaged with their work and with each other. Even if the workers had tried to be defiant, they would have undoubtedly lost their jobs. These employees lacked a voice. There was only the voice of the Former Owner and his rhetoric ruled in a culture of fear. Within this organisation there was no transitional space for both Old Owner and workers to get in touch with a shared reality and engage with each other effectively.

When basic values and expectations are not being met, employees feel ashamed. Where there is shame, individuals find themselves in black holes of non-meaning, spaces where reality cannot be grasped; shame is where we fail (Mollon, 2002). There is no empathy.

We can surmise that the Former Owner could not acknowledge his own shame about the state of the company. Unconsciously, he had to seek out employees over whom he could manically triumph in order to hide his own vulnerability. In the projective identification dynamics of shame, any signs of independent life are crushed in subtly undermining or overtly aggressive ways. The object is only allowed to exist to the subject in so far as it coincides with what is projectively identified. Hence the workers could only exist as being inferior and as targets of denigration, insults, and the wrath of the Former Owner and his henchmen. Through his domination, the Former Owner could mask his fear of weakness and his potential shame.

The workers were trapped, fearful of moving on because of reprisals from the Former Owner but also fearful of finding similar situations elsewhere. They even felt that they did not have the right to leave. Escape was not an option as they feared the Former Owner would have prevented them from getting a job elsewhere. They had fallen into subservience. The group dynamics were typical of Hopper's fourth basic assumption. On the surface, the group was fragmented. There was a lack of recognition and a lack of empathy amongst workers for each other. Even the senior staff feared the Former Owner. At an unconscious and subconscious level there was a collusion of subservience which resulted in impasses. Attempts to release the stuckness and create something new were made through bullying by the Former Owner, through threats, and through colleagues bullying each other. They were all stuck in a pattern of repetition compulsion, forced to repeat the patterns of behaviour from the past and unable to create a new future. In a game of self-survival they continued to undermine each other.

Whatever the employees did, they would have failed to satisfy the demands made by the former owner. He was insatiable in his personal greed for recognition. They could not show initiative, neither were they supposed to work together, nor even meet, nor hold a conversation. They were "false selves", unable to find any form of authenticity. Those who take on a false self are traitors, not just to themselves but to each other. They cannot take the realness, aliveness, and autonomy of themselves and others for granted but have to become absorbed in contriving ways of trying to be real, keeping themselves alive (Laing, 1969b). These employees were caught in such a muddle, not knowing whether they were coming or going. Their efforts were often wasted, unproductive, and unprofitable.

This organisation was peppered with vacuums of support. The culture of fear fostered the development of black holes of negativity into which individuals were drawn. One of the few ways the workers could find to gain some recognition for themselves was through sabotaging the machinery and tools with which they had to work. Yet, in doing so, they undermined their own future employment, further adding to the cycle of domination and submission. They were unable to engage with reality and gradually moved towards the potential death of the organisation.

New Management

Under New Management spaces opened up. By allowing the workers access to other areas, besides the factory floor, the physical space became an intersubjective space, one in which dialogues could develop. The sharing of the toilet facilities and kitchens, and the removal of boundaries between the factory floor and administration, fostered movement of employees out of their confined areas. Boundaries which had been rigidly defined under the tight controls and monitoring by the Former Owner were broken down and communication improved. As employees were encouraged to talk to each other, permeable boundaries, rather than defensive ones, were established.

The constant monitoring of workers was replaced with transparency. New Management showed recognition to all the staff by rewriting the organisational chart. This was a visual portrayal of how all employees were valued, how their contributions were interrelated and interdependent. The workers could see that they were adding value and contributing to the company as a whole. These little changes began to facilitate the movement of the intrapsychic and intersubjective rhythms which had been stuck in projective gridlock and group impasses for many years.

The structural fractures between demands of the job and resources, which had generated friction and fear, were removed. Under New Management, if there was a problem with the machinery, workers were expected to report it, not just ignore it as they had done in the past. Turning a blind eye to faulty machinery and bad practice was decried by New Management. These changes also reduced the potential for shame. Mistakes, accidents, and problems now belonged to everyone. The blame game was replaced by effective reporting structures. Where there had been black holes—spaces where there was no empathy—recognition was fostered.

The culture of fear, so pervasive under the Former Owner, very slowly dissipated with the integration of the staff. The polarisation of powerful and helpless, and between active and passive, was broken down as New Management showed that they cared. However, there were no quick fixes. Cultural change is rarely straightforward and needs to be carefully managed. New Management were aware that as the old ways were replaced with the new, energies would be released and that these would generate anxieties which required both containment and working through. Clear boundaries had to be set on behaviour. Employees were told to respect each other, and were expected to be mature and well-balanced. This request may have seemed a tall order for workers who had been subjugated for so long. Yet they no longer had to waste their time putting on a "false self"; they could be true to themselves. The broken plates, referred to in Chapter Two, could meet on return. Reality could be discovered, rather than be imposed.

New Management introduced the concepts of mutuality and trust with the belief that "a healthy culture of mutual recognition can transform a rigid organisation into a thriving and self-sustaining one".

"Mutual recognition cannot be achieved through obedience, through identification with the other's power, or through repression" (Benjamin, 1988, p. 40). Mutuality is that ongoing, co-evolutionary process in which there is an acceptance of sameness and difference (Benjamin, 1988). There is a dialogue between the self and other, and acceptance of a constant tension and a continual exchange of influence. It does not mean that love and hate are synthesised so that love triumphs over hate. Rather it means that hate can be borne. There is a move towards the depressive position.

Transparent and participative structures and processes were adopted so that trusting relationships, essential for cooperation in "fluid" organisations, could foster the development of mutual loyalty and a commonly shared understanding of the key tasks, vision, and strategy. The changes, although not unwelcomed by the workers, were initially regarded with scepticism. Regression into the old ways and to the paranoid-schizoid position would have been inevitable from time to time in the early days. Yet progress had to be made in improving productivity and creating new products. Teams consisting of employees with complementary, but different skills, backgrounds, and values were set up. Factory workers and other staff were brought together. Given the old cultural splits within the organisation, there were inevitable differences in the way that employees talked to each other and acted towards each other. If the workers were to make a valuable contribution, they needed to feel that they could fit into the group and be accepted. There had to be some consideration of "valency". For the employees to value each other's different ways, there also needed to be transitional space for open dialogue. Sufficient containment and working through of anxieties was needed for difficult conversations to take place, for conflicts to be worked through. Courage—that willingness to stay open to difficult situations, rather than regressing into repetition compulsion and throwing away opportunities for change—had to be found.

According to Benjamin (1988), mutual harmonisation does not exclude discord but works through this with intrapsychic and intersubjective dialogues. There is an aliveness within these dialogues which allows for reality-testing, in which we go back again and again to test our beliefs, our perceptions, and our assessments of what we can achieve. Where there is mutuality, there is an engagement with the reality of others.

We may assume that, through an ongoing acceptance of sameness and difference, and a working through of intrapsychic and intersubjective rhythms, employees became better attuned to their new working environments, to the needs of their colleagues, and to their own needs. Congratulated by New Management for cooperation and collaboration, they were able to engage with each other and their work in effective and rewarding ways. They were no longer being led in a "dance of death" by the Former Owner, dragged down by psychic deadness, projective gridlock, rigid patterns of domination and submission, impasses in group dynamics, and black holes of non-meaning. The workers could create new meanings for themselves through collaboration with others. New products, new services, and a healthy balance sheet were attainable. Attunement, that pleasure of being with the other and sharing similar feelings, without demanding control, was possible.

The healthy co-evolution of this company is ongoing.

Conclusion

As shown in this case study, the fostering of mutual recognition is not about creating an end product, nor is it a utopia of peace and love, nor a happy-clappy environment. It cannot be ticked off on a checklist of targets. As explained in Chapter Two, mutuality involves a constant interplay of psychic and intersubjective rhythms.

The case study illustrates how a culture of fear can be transformed into a healthy working environment. Through small steps New Management gradually released the stuckness in the group dynamics. Fixed perceptions were broken down. The intrapsychic and intersubjective rhythms began to move, as impasses were released. New Management acknowledged that when adapting to change, and creating something new, disputes and conflict are inevitable. Workplace relationships, like other relationships, are demanding and challenging, but also rewarding. It is the way these relationships are handled that determines whether the outcome is fruitful or more work is required.

> The fate of a conflict—whether it will turn to antagonism or co-operation, to peace or war—depends therefore on how it is managed and what structures enable it to be worked through. (Perini, 2010, p. 35)

From establishing basic working rights, respect for others, aspirations for the future, and space for collaboration in creating new products, New Management offered containment and working through of anxieties for their employees. The employees were expected to be active participants in the changes and take responsibility for themselves. To cope with the battering of constant change it helps to have a "knowing of thyself", as well as permeable boundaries to give flexibility and adaptability.

The Former Owner led his employees in a "dance of death" in which his psychic deadness determined the beat. New Management accepted that to achieve healthier engagement and high productivity, employees have their own rhythms, music to their souls, something unique and of value which they bring to the workplace, and that discord, as well as harmony, is part of the "rich" picture of organisational life.

REFERENCES

AcademicFOI.Com. Workplace bullying and harassment. (2011). Available from http://www.academicfoi.com/bullyingharassment/index.htm.

Adams, A. (1992). *Bullying at Work. How to Confront and Overcome It*. London: Virago.

Agervold, M. (2007). Bullying at work: a discussion of definitions and prevalence based on an empirical study. *Scandinavian Journal of Psychology, 48*: 161–172.

Agervold, M. & Mikkleson, E. G. (2004). Relationships between bullying, psychosocial work environment and individual stress reactions. *Work and Stress, 18*: 336–351.

Aquino, K. (2000). Structural and individual determinants of workplace victimization: the effects of hierarchical status and conflict management style. *Journal of Management, 26*: 171–193.

Aquino, K. & Thau, S. (2009). Workplace victimization: aggression from the target's perspective. *Annual Review of Psychology, 60*: 717–740.

Archer, D. (1999). Exploring "bullying" culture in the paramilitary organisation. *International Journal of Manpower, 20*: 94–105.

Arkin, A. (2010). Leadership is unbelievably important in tough times. *People Management*, 2 September 2010, pp. 18–21.

Armstrong, D. (2002). Making present: reflections on a neglected function of leadership and its contemporary relevance. *Organisational and Social Dynamics, 2*: 89–98.

Armstrong, D. (2005). *Organization in the Mind*. London: Karnac.

Arnaud, G. (2012). The contribution of psychoanalysis to organization studies and management: an overview. *Organization Studies, 33*: 1121–1135.

Arsenio, W. F. & Lemerise, E. A. (2001). Varieties of childhood bullying: values, emotion processes and social competence. *Social Development, 10*: 59–73.

Ashford, B. (1994). Petty tyranny in organizations. *Human Relations, 47*: 755–778.

Asser, J. (2004). Working with the dynamics of shame. *Organisational and Social Dynamics, 4*: 88–106.

Assland, M. S., Skogstad, A., & Einarsen, S. (2008). The dark side: defining destructive leadership behaviour. *Organisations and People, 15*: 20–28.

Atlas, R. S. & Pepler, D. J. (1998). Observations of bullying in the classroom. *Journal of Educational Research, 92*: 86–99.

Audard, C. & Grosz, S. (2000). Recognition. Available from http://www.psychoanalysis.org.uk/recognition2.htm

Baillien, E., Neyens, I., De Witte, H., & De Cuyer, N. (2009). Towards a three way model of workplace bullying: a qualitative study. *Journal of Community and Applied Social Psychology, 19*: 1–16.

Baillien, E., Rodriguez-Muñoz, A., Van den Broeck, A., & De Witte, H. (2011). Do demands and resources affect target's and perpetrators' reports of workplace bullying? A two-wave cross-lagged study. *Work & Stress, 25*: 128–146.

Bauman, Z. (2003). *Liquid Love*. Cambridge, UK: Polity Press.

Bauman, Z. (2004). *Wasted Lives*. Cambridge, UK: Polity Press.

Baumeister, R. F., Heatherton, T. F., & Tice, D. M. (1993). When ego threats lead to self regulation failure: negative consequences of high self esteem. *Journal of Personality and Social Psychology, 64*: 141–156.

Beddoes-Jones, F. (2012). Authentic leadership: the key to building trust. *People Management*, pp. 44–47, (August).

Benjamin, J. (1988). *The Bonds of Love*. New York: Pantheon Books.

Berke, J. H. (2012). *Why I Hate You and You Hate Me*. London: Karnac.

Berthold, K. A. & Hoover, J. H. (2000). Correlates of bullying and victimization among intermediate students in the Mid Western USA. *School Psychology, 21*: 65–77.

Bettleheim, B. (1982). *Freud and Man's Soul*. London: Penguin.

Bing, D. (2012). The weakness of strong leaders: crowding out space for collective purpose. *People Strategy, 35*: 36–41.

Bing, D. & Sullivan, C. (2009). Managing the movement of conflict in complex organizations. Paper presented at the International Society for the Psychoanalytic Study of Organizations 2009 Annual Meeting, Toledo, Spain.

Bion, W. R. (1961). *Experiences in Groups*. New York: Basic Books.

Bjorkqvist, K. & Osterman, K., (1999). Finland. In: P. K. Smith, Y. Morita, J. Junger-Tas, D. Olweus, R. Catalano, & P. Slee (Eds.), *The Nature of School Bullying. A Cross National Perspective* (pp. 56–67). London: Routledge.

Bloch, C. (2012). How witnesses contribute to bullying in the workplace. In: N. Tehrani (Ed.), *Workplace Bullying. Symptoms and Solutions* (pp. 81–96). Hove: Routledge.

Bollas, C. (1985). Loving Hate. *Annual of Psychoanalysis, 12/13*: 221–237.

Bollas, C. (1997). *Cracking Up: The Work of Unconscious Experience*. London: Routledge.

Boulton, M. J., Trueman, M., Chau, C., Whitehead, C., & Amatya, K. (1999). Concurrent and longitudinal links between friendship and peer victimization: implications for befriending interventions. *Journal of Adolescence, 22*: 461–466.

Bowes, L., Maughan, B., Caspi, A., Moffitt, T. E., & Arseneault, L. (2010). Families promote emotional and behavioural resilience to bullying: evidence of an environmental effect. *Journal of Child Psychology and Psychiatry, 51*: 809–817.

Bowlby, J. (1968). Separation and loss within the family (1968–70). In: J. Bowlby (Ed.), *The Making and Breaking of Affectional Bonds* (pp. 99–123). Abingdon, UK: Routledge, 2005.

Bowlby, J. (1984). Violence in the family as a disorder of the attachment and caregiving systems. *The American Journal of Psychoanalysis, 44*: 9–27.

Boydell, L. (2005). The defensive function of inter-organisational partnerships. *Organisational and Social Dynamics, 5*: 225–241.

Branch, S., Ramsay, S., & Barker, M. (2007). Managers in the firing line: contributing factors to workplace bullying by staff—an interview study. *Journal of Management and Organization, 13*: 264–282.

Brodsky, C. M. (1976). *The Harassed Worker*. USA: Heath.

Broussine, M. (2008). *Creative Methods in Organizational Research*. London: Sage.

Brunning, H. & Perini, M. (2010). *Psychoanalytic Perspectives on a Turbulent World*. London: Karnac.

Bryne, B. (1999). Ireland. In: P. K. Smith, Y. Morita, J. Junger-Tas, D. Olweus, R. Catalano & P. Slee (Eds.). *The Nature of School Bullying: A Cross National Perspective* (pp. 112–127). London: Routledge.

Burgoyne, J. (2011). Leading thinkers offer their game-changers. *People Management*, October 2011, p. 35.

Campbell, D., Coldicott, T., & Kinsella, K. (1994). *Systemic Work with Organizations: A New Model for Managers and Change Agents*. London: Karnac.

Cangarli, B. G. (2010). Individual and organizational antecendents: how relevant are they perceived to bullying? Paper presented at the Seventh International Conference on Workplace Bullying and Harassment 2010, Cardiff, UK.

Cardona, F. (2003). The manager's most precious skill: the capacity to be "psychologically present". *Organisational and Social Dynamics, 3*: 226–235.

Carr, A. (2004). The psychodynamic conception of the "death instinct" and its relevance to organisations. *Journal of Psycho-Social Studies, 2*.

Carr, W. (2009). The Eric Miller Memorial Lecture 2009. The beautiful journey: reflections on group relations. *Organisational and Social Dynamics, 9*: 249–268.

Chan, J. H. F. (2006). Systemic patterns in bullying and victimization. *School Psychology International, 27*: 325–369.

Chapman, J. & Long, S. (2008). Role contamination. *Organisations & People, 15*: 40–48.

Christie-Mizell, C. A. (2003). Bullying: The consequences of inter-parental discord and child's self concept. *Family Process, 42*: 237–250.

Chynoweth, C. (2011). Up for discussion. *People Management*, June, 2011, pp. 44–46.

Cilliers, F. (2012). A systems psychodynamic description of organisational bullying experiences. *SA Journal of Industrial Psychology, 38*: 1–15.

Clarkson, P. (1996). *The Bystander: An End to Innocence in Human Relationships*. London: Whurr.

Clutterbuck, D. (2011). Don't be blinded by HR bling. *People Management*, 26 September 2011.

Collinson, D. L. (1992). *Managing the Shop Floor: Subjectivity, Masculinity and Workplace Culture*. Berlin: Walter de Gruyter.

Coupland, C. (2009). Research topic: fairy-tale conflict resolution. *People Management*, 19 November 2009, pp. 42–43.

Cowie, H. & Berdondini, L. (2002). The expression of emotion in response to bullying. *Emotional and Behavioural Difficulties, 7*: 207–214.

Coyne, I., Seigne, E., & Randall, P. (2000). Personality traits as predictors of workplace bully–victim status. *European Journal of Work and Organizational Psychology, 9*: 335–349.

Craig, W. M., Pepler, D., & Atlas R. (2000). Observations of bullying in the playground and in the classroom. *School Psychology International, 21*: 22–36.

Crawford, N. (1999). Conundrums and confusion in organisations: the etymology of the word "bully". *International Journal of Manpower, 20*: 86–93.

Crawshaw, L. (2007). *Taming the Abrasive Manager*. San Francisco, CA: Jossey Bass.

Cummins, A. -M. (2002). "The road to hell is paved with good intentions": Quality assurance as a social defence against anxiety. *Organisational and Social Dynamics, 2*: 99–119.

Davidson, C. & White, S. (2013). Bullying in the York's Plays: A psychosocial perspective. In: C. Davidson (Ed.), *Corpus Christi Plays at York: A Context for Religious Drama* (pp. 240–264). Brooklyn, NY: AMS Press.

D'Cruz, P. & Noronha, E. (2010). The exit coping response to workplace bullying: the contribution of inclusivist and exclusivist HRM strategies. *Employee Relations, 32*: 102–120.

D'Cruz, P. & Noronha, E. (2011). The limits to workplace friendship. Managerialist HRM and bystander behaviour in the context of workplace bullying. *Employee Relations, 32*: 269–288.

De Cuyer, N., Baillien, E., & De Witte, H. (2009). Job insecurity, perceived employability and targets' and perpetrators' experiences of workplace bullying. *Work & Stress, 23*: 206–224.

De Gooijer, J. (2009). *The Murder in Merger*. London: Karnac.

Eigen, M. (1996). *Psychic Deadness*. Northvale, NJ: Aronson.

Einarsen, S. (1999). The nature and causes of bullying at work. *International Journal of Manpower, 20*: 16–27.

Einarsen, S. & Mikkelson, E. G. (2003). Individual effects of exposure to bullying at work. In: S. Einarsen, H. Hoel, D. Zapf & C. Cooper (Eds.), *Bullying and Emotional Abuse in the Workplace: International Perspectives in Research and Practice* (pp. 127–144). London: Taylor & Francis.

Einarsen, S. & Skogstad, A. (1996). Bullying at work: Epidemiological findings in public and private organizations. *European Journal of Work and Organizational Psychology, 5*: 185–201.

Einarsen, S., Raknes, B. I., & Matthiesen, S. B. (1994). Bullying and harassment at work and their relationships to work environment quality: An exploratory study. *European Work and Organizational Psychologist, 4*: 381–401.

Einarsen, S., Hoel, H., Zapf, D., & Cooper, C. (2003). The concept of bullying at work: the European tradition. In: S. Einarsen, H. Hoel, D. Zapf & C. Cooper (Eds.), *Bullying and Emotional Abuse in the Workplace: International Perspectives in Research and Practice* (pp. 3–30). London: Taylor & Francis.

Eisold, K. (2009). *What You Don't Know You Know: Our Hidden Motives in Life, Business, and Everything Else*. New York: Other Press.

Elias, N. (1982). *State Formation and Civilization*. Oxford: Basil Blackwell.

Eliot, M. & Cornell, D. G. (2009). Bullying in middle school as a function of insecure attachment and aggressive attitudes. *School Psychology International, 30*: 201–214.

Elliot, A. (2002). *Psychoanalytical Theory: An Introduction*. Basingstoke: Palgrave.

Farrrington, D. (1993). Understanding and preventing bullying. In: M. Tonny & N. Morris (Eds), *Crime and Justice* (pp. 381–458). Chicago: University of Chicago Press.

Ferris, G. R., Zinko, R., Brouer, R. L., Buckley, M. R., & Harvey, M. G. (2007). Strategic bullying as a supplementary, balanced perspective on destructive leadership. *The Leadership Quarterly, 18*: 195–206.

Fevre, R. & Lewis, D. (2012). Why ill treatment at work is so hard to change. *People Management*, June 2012, pp. 30–35.

Fevre, R., Lewis, D., Robinson, A., & Jones, T. (2011). *Insight into Ill-Treatment in the Workplace: Patterns, Causes and Solutions*. Cardiff: Cardiff University.

Field, T. (1996). *Bully in Sight*. Wantage, England: Success Unlimited.

Flouri, E. & Buchanan, A. (2003). The role of mother involvement and father involvement in adolescent bullying behaviour. *Journal of Interpersonal Violence, 18*: 634–644.

Flynn, R. (2001). Impediments to organisational effectiveness—social defences and shame in the workplace. *Socio-Analysis: the journal of the Australian Institute of Socio-Analysis, 3*: 109–122.

Fonagy, P. (1999). Male perpetrators of violence against women: an attachment theory perspective. *Journal of Applied Psychoanalytical Studies, 1*: 7–27.

Fonagy, P. (2001). *Attachment Theory and Psychoanalysis*. New York: Other Press.

Forero, R., McLellan, L., Rissel, C., & Bauman, A. (1999). Bullying behaviour and psychosocial health among school students in New South Wales Australia: cross-sectional survey. *British Medical Journal, 319*: 344–348.

French, R. & Simpson, P. (2001). Learning at the edges between knowing and not-knowing: translating Bion. *Organisational & Social Dynamics, 1*: 54–77.

Freud, A. (1936). *The Ego and the Mechanisms of Defence*. In: *The writings of Anna Freud, Vol II* (1936). London: Hogarth & the Institute of Psychoanalysis, (1979).

Freud, S. (1917). Mourning and Melancholia. *S. E., 14*. London: Hogarth.

Gabriel, Y. (1993). Organizational nostalgia—Reflections on "The Golden Age". In: S. Fineman (Ed.), *Emotion in Organizations* (pp. 118–141). London: Sage.

Gabriel, Y. (1999). *Organizations in Depth*. London: Sage.

Gabriel, Y. & Carr, A. (2002). Organizations, management and psychoanalysis: an overview. *Journal of Managerial Psychology, 17*: 348–365.

Gale, J. (2007). Xenophon and psychoanalysis: lessons in management. *Organisational and Social Dynamics, 7*: 1–19.

Gay, P. (1989). *The Freud Reader*. London: Vintage.

Ginzberg, C. (1980). Morelli, Freud and Sherlock Holmes: Clues and scientific method. History workshop. *A Journal of Socialist Historians, 9* (Spring): 5–36.

Girard, R. (2010). *Battling to the End*. East Lansing, MI: Michigan State University Press.

Glasø, L. Neilsen, M. B., & Einarsen. S. (2009). Interpersonal problems amongst perpetrators and targets of workplace bullying. *Journal of Applied Social Psychology, 39*: 1316–1333.

Glasø, L., Ekerholt, K., Barman, S., & Einarsen, S. (2006). The instrumentality of emotions in leader-subordinate relationships. *International Journal of Work Organization and Emotion, 1*: 255–276.

Gold, S. (2010). The transfer of evil: the scapegoat as whistle blower in organisational life. Paper presented at the International Society for the Psychoanalytic Study of Organizations 2010 Annual Meeting, Elsinore, Denmark.

Goldman, A. (2008). The enigma of an unintentionally toxic leader. *Organisations and People, 15*: 55–62.

Gottlieb, S. (2002). The capacity for love. In: D. Mann (Ed.), *Love and Hate: Psychoanalytic Perspectives*. Hove, UK: Brunner-Routledge.

Gould, L., Stapley, L., & Stein, M. (2001). *The Systems Psychodynamics of Organizations*. London: Karnac.

Gorvig, A. (2011). Who bullies and who is bullied on line. *EU Kids on Line—Short Report*. LSE, London: EU Kids Online. Available from http:eprints.lse.ac,uk/39601/

Grady, V. M. & Grady, J. (2008). Winnicott's potential space and transitional objects: implications for the organisational change process and its previously defined relationship to an organisational loss of effectiveness. *Organisational and Social Dynamics, 8*: 278–297.

Grady, V. M. & Grady, J. (2013). *The Pivot Point*. New York: Morgan James.

Grotstein, J. S. (1990). The 'black hole' as the basic psychotic experience: some newer psychoanalytic and neuroscience perspectives on psychosis. *Journal of the American Academy of Psychoanalysis, 18*: 29–46.

Halton, W. (2010). Group relations: achieving a new difference. *Organisational and Social Dynamics, 10*: 219–237.

Hamilton, E. & Cairns, H. (1961). *The Collected Dialogues of Plato. Bollingen Series LXX*. Princeton: Princeton University Press.

Handy, C. (1989). *The Age of Unreason*. London: Business Books.

Hauge, L. J., Einarsen, S., Knardahl, S., Lau, B., Notelers, G., & Skogstad, A. (2011). Leadership and role stressors as departmental level predictors of workplace bullying. *International Journal of Stress Management, 18*: 305–323.

Henricks, R. G. (1989). *Lao-Tzu Te-Tao Ching: A New Translation Based on the Recently Discovered Ma-wang-tui Texts*. New York: Ballantine Books.

Hershcovis, M. S. & Barling, J. (2010). Towards a multi-foci approach to workplace aggression: A meta-analytic review of outcomes from different perpetrators. *Journal of Organizational Behaviour, 31*: 22–44.

Hinshelwood, R. D. (1991). *A Dictionary of Kleinian Thought*. London: Free Association Books.

Hirschorn, L. (1997a). *Reworking Authority*. Cambridge, MA: The MIT Press.

Hirschhorn, L. (1997b). *The Workplace Within: Psychodynamics of Organizational Life*. Cambridge, MA: The MIT Press.

Hodson, R., Roscigno, V. J., & Lopez, S. H. (2006). Chaos and the abuse of power. Workplace bullying in organizational and interactional context. *Work and Occupation, 33*: 382–416.

Hoel, H. & Cooper, C. L. (2001). Origins of bullying: theoretical frameworks for explaining bullying. In: N. Teharni (Ed.), *Building a Culture of Respect: Managing Bullying at Work*. London: Taylor & Francis.

Hoel, H. & Salin, D. (2003). Organisational antecedents of workplace bullying. In: S. Einarsen, H. Hoel, D. Zapf & C. Cooper (Eds.), *Bullying and Emotional Abuse in the Workplace: International Perspectives in Research and Practice* (pp. 203–218). London: Taylor & Francis.

Hoel, H., Glasø, L., Hetland, J., Cooper, C., & Einarsen, S. (2010). Leadership styles as predictors of self-reported and observed workplace bullying. *British Journal of Management, 21*: 453–468.

Hoggett, P. (1992). *Partisans in an Uncertain World: The Ppsychoanalysis of Engagement*. London: Free Association Books.

Hoggett, P. (2001). The love that thinks. *Free Associations, 9*: 1–23.

Honey, P. (2011). Is bullying the norm at work? *People Management*, 24 February 2011, pp. 16–17.

Honneth, A. (1995). *The Struggle for Recognition*. Cambridge, MA: The MIT Press.

Hopper, E. (2003). *Traumatic Experience in the Unconscious Life of Groups*. London: Jessica Kingsley.

Hugh-Jones, S. & Smith, P. K. (1999). Self reports of short and long term effects of bullying on children who stammer. *British Journal of Educational Psychology, 69*: 141–158.

Hutchinson, M., Vickers, M., Jackson, D., & Wilkes, L. (2010). Bullying as circuits of power: an Australian nursing perspective. *Administrative Theory and Praxis, 32*: 25–47.

Ireland, J. L. (1999). Bullying among prisoners: A study of adults and young offenders. *Aggressive Behaviour, 25*: 162–178.

Ishmael, A. (1999). *Harassment, Bullying and Violence at Work*. London: The Industrial Society.

Jacoby, M. (1996). *Shame and the Origins of Self-Esteem: A Jungian Approach*. Hove, UK: Routledge.

James, K. & Huffington, C. (2004). Containment of anxiety in organizational change: A case example for changing organisational boundaries. *Organisational and Social Dynamics, 4*: 212–233.

Jenkins, M., Winefied, H., & Sarris, A. (2011). Consequences of being accused of workplace bullying: an exploratory study. *International Journal of Workplace Health Management, 4*: 33–47.

Johnson, D. & Lewis, G. (1999). Do you like what you see? Self perceptions of adolescent bullies. *British Educational Research Association, 25*: 665–677.

Johnson, S. (2011). An ecological model of workplace bullying: a guide for intervention and research. *Nursing Forum, 46*: 55–63.

Kahn, S. (2012). Death and the city. Paper presented at the International Society for the Psychoanalytic Study of Organizations, 2012 Symposium, San Diego.

Kahn, W. A. (2001). Holding environments at work. *Journal of Applied Behavioural Science, 37*: 260–279.

Kaltiala-Heino, R., Rimpelä, M., Marttunen, M., Rimpelä, A., & Rantanen, P. (1999). Bullying and suicidal ideation in Finnish students: school survey. *British Medical Journal, 319*: 348–351.

Kane, M. (2008). Envy in organisational life. *Organisations and People (Toxic Leadership), 15*: 96–103.

Kane, M. (2011). She was a princess, I was a wee frog: Sibling dynamics at work. Paper presented at the OPUS conference 2011, London.

Katzer, C., Fetchenhauer, D., & Belschak, F. (2009). Cyberbullying: who are the victims? A comparison of victimization in internet chatrooms and victimization in school. *Journal of Media Psychology, 21*: 25–36.

Keashley, L. & Jagatic, K. (2003). By any other name: American perspectives on workplace bullying. In: S. Einarsen, H. Hoel, D. Zapf & C. Cooper (Eds.), *Bullying and Emotional Abuse in the Workplace: International Perspectives in Research and Practice* (pp. 31–61). London: Taylor & Francis.

Keashley, L. & Neumann, J. H. (2005). Bullying in the workplace: its impact and management. *Employee Rights and Employment Policy Journal, 8*: 335–373.

Kelly, P. (1999). Bullying in the workplace. A qualitative investigation of the experience of being bullied at work. Unpublished thesis for a doctorate in clinical psychology, Faculty of Science of the University of Birmingham.

Kets de Vries, M. F. R. & Miller, D. (1984). *The Neurotic Organization*. San Francisco, CA: Jossey-Bass.

Kirwan-Taylor, H. (2010). Suffering from cyber-disinhibition. *Management Today*, p. 16, (2010 April).

Klein, M. (1955). On identification. In: *Melanie Klein. Envy and Gratitude and Other Works 1946–1963*. London: Vintage (1975).

Klein, M. (1957). Envy and gratitude. In: *Melanie Klein. Envy and Gratitude and Other Works 1946–1963*. London: Vintage, (1975).

Knight, J. (2008). Organisational helplessness in the public sector. *Organisations & People, 15*: 87–95.

Kochenderfer-Ladd, B. & Skinner, K. (2002). Children's coping strategies: moderators of the effects of peer victimization? *Developmental Psychology, 58*: 267–278.

Kochenderfer-Ladd, B. & Wardrop, J. L. (2001). Chronicity and instability of children's peer victimization experiences as predictors of loneliness and social satisfaction trajectories. *Child Development, 72*: 134–151.

Kondra, A. Z. & Hurst, D. C. (2009). Institutional processes of organizational culture. *Culture and Organization, 15*: 39–58.

Kotlyar, I. & Karakowsky L. (2006). Leading conflict? Linkages between leader behaviours and group conflict. *Small Group Research, 37*: 377–403.

Krantz, J., (2001). Dilemmas of Organisational Change. In: L. Gould, L. Stapley & M. Stein (Eds.), *The Systems Psychodynamics of Organizations* (pp. 133–156). London: Karnac.

Krantz, J. & Smilansky, J., (2006). From occupation to collaboration: the organizational dynamics of mergers and acquisitions. Unpublished paper presented at OPUS conference 2006, London.

Ladd, G. W. & Kochenderfer-Ladd, B. (1998). Parenting behaviours and parent-child relationships: correlates of peer victimization in kindergarten? *Developmental Psychology, 34*: 1450–1458.

Laing, R. D. (1969a). *Self and Others*. Harmondsworth, England: Penguin.

Laing, R. D. (1969b). *The Divided Self*. London: Penguin.

Laplanche, J. & Pontalis, J. -B. (1967). *The Language of Psychoanalysis*. London: Karnac.

Lawrence, W. G., Bain, A., & Gould, L. J. (1996). The fifth basic assumption. *Free Associations, 6*: 28–55.

Lear, J. (1998). *Love and its Place in Nature: A Philosophical Interpretation of Freudian Psychoanalysis*. New Haven, CT: Yale University Press.

Lear, J. (2000). *Happiness, Death and the Remainder of Life*. Cambridge, MA: Harvard University Press.

Lewis, D. (1999). Workplace bullying—interim findings of a study in further and higher education in Wales. *International Journal of Manpower, 20*: 106–118.

Leymann, H. (1996). The content and development of mobbing at work. *European Journal of Work and Organizational Psychology, 5*: 165–184.

Leymann, H. & Gustafsson, A. (1996). Mobbing at work and the development of post-traumatic stress disorders. *European Journal of Work and Organizational Psychology, 5*: 251–275.

Liefooghe, A. P. D. & Mackenzie Davey, K. (2001). Accounts of workplace bullying: The role of the organization. *European Journal of work and organizational psychology, 10*: 375–392.

Liefooghe, A. P. D. & Mackenzie Davey, K. (2003). Explaining bullying at work: why should we listen to employee accounts? In: S. Einarsen, H. Hoel, D. Zapf & C. Cooper (Eds), *Bullying and Emotional Abuse in the Workplace: International Perspectives in Research and Practice* (pp. 219–230). London: Taylor & Francis.

Liefooghe, A. P. D. & Mackenzie Davey, K. (2010). The language and organization of bullying at work. *Administrative Theory & Praxis, 32*: 71–95.

Lipton, J. D. (2011). Combating cyber-victimization. *Berkeley Technology Law Journal*, 1104–1155.

Lister, E. A. (2001). Organizational change: tales of intergenerational and sibling rivalry. *Journal of Organizational Change Management, 14*: 452–467.

Lohmer, M. & Lazar, R. (2006). The consultant between the lines of fire: the dynamics of trust, mistrust and containment in organisations. *Organisational and Social Dynamics, 6*: 42–62.

Long, S. (2002). Organisational destructivity and the perverse state of mind. *Organisational and Social Dynamics, 2*: 179–207.

Long, S. (2008). *The Perverse Organisation and its Deadly Sins*. London: Karnac.

Low, K. S. D., Radhakrisnan, P., Schneider, K. T., & Rounds, J. (2007). The experiences of bystanders of workplace ethnic harassment. *Journal of Applied Social Psychology, 37*: 2261–2297.

Lutgen-Sandvik, P. (2008). Intensive remedial identity work responses to workplace bullying, trauma and stigmatization. *Organization 15*: 97–119.

Maier, C. M. (2008). Identifying sources of interpersonal workplace conflict: a qualitative study. Paper presented at the 6th International Conference on Workplace Bullying, 2008. Montreal.

Main, M. (2000). The organized categories of infant child and adult attachment: flexible versus inflexible attention under attachment related stress. *Journal of the American Psychoanalytical Association, 48*: 1055–96.

Mann, D. (2002). *Love and Hate: Psychoanalytic Perspectives*. Hove, UK: Brunner-Routledge.

Mant, A. (1977). *The Rise and Fall of the British Manager*. Basingstoke: Macmillan Press.

Manzoni, J. -F. & Barsoux, J. -L. (2004). Rescue Remedy. *People Management*, 14 October 2004, pp. 27–30.

Maturana, H. R. & Varela, F. J. (1987). *The Tree of Knowledge: The Biological Roots of Understanding*. Boston, MA: Shambhala.

Mawdsley, H. (2012). Trade Union intervention in workplace bullying: issues of employee voice and collectivism amongst union members and officials. Unpublished Doctoral Dissertation, University of Glamorgan, UK.

McConville, D. & Cornell, D. G. (2003). Aggressive attitudes predict aggressive behaviour in middle school students. *Journal of Emotional and Behavioural Disorders, 11*: 179–187.

McGivern, G. & Ferlie, E. (2007). Playing tick-box games: Interrelating defences in professional appraisal. *Human Relations, 60*: 1361–1385.

Meech, D. (2011). On my agenda. *People Management*, July 2011, pp. 29–31.

Menzies Lyth, I. (1970). The functioning of social systems as a defence against anxiety. In: I. Menzies Lyth, (Ed), *Containing Anxiety in Institutions: Selected Essays Volume 1*. (pp. 43–99). London: Free Association Books, 1988.

Menzies Lyth, I. (1989). *The Dynamics of the Social: Selected Essays. Volume 2*. London: Free Association Books.

Mikkelson, E. & Einarsen, S. (2001). Bullying in Danish life: prevalence and healthy correlates. *European Journal of Work and Organizational Psychology, 10*: 393–414.

Mollon, P. (2002). *Shame and Jealousy: The Hidden Turmoils*. London: Karnac.

Moran, E. T. & Volkwein, F. J. (1992). The cultural approach to the formation of organisational climate, *Human Relations, 45*: 19–38.

Morgan, G. (1997). *Images of Organization*. Thousand Oaks, CA: Sage.

Morgan, M. (2004). The Projective Gridlock: A form of projective identification in couple relationships. Available from: http://www.psychoanalysis.org.uk/gridlock.htm.

Morgan-Jones, R. (2010). The work group as an object of desire: the embodiment of protomental life. *Organisational and Social Dynamics, 10*: 79–98.

Mulder, R., Pouwelse, M., Lodewijkx, H., & Bolman, C. (2008). Emotional and helping responses among bystanders of victims of mobbing: the role of perceived responsibility and threat of contagion. Paper presented at 6th International Conference on Workplace Bullying, 2008, Montreal.

Munroz-Flores, H., Jaca, L. M., Medina, F. J., & Guerra, J. (2007). Coping with bullying as an intractable organizational conflict. IACM 2007 Meetings paper, Budapest.

Naylor, P. & Cowie, H. (1999). The effectiveness of peer support systems in challenging school bullying: the perspectives and experiences of teachers and pupils. *Journal of Adolescents, 22*: 467–479.

Neidl, K. (1996). Mobbing and well being: economic and personnel development implications. *European Journal of Work and Organizational Psychology, 5*: 239–249.

Oade, A. (2009). *Managing Workplace Bullying*. Basingstoke: Palgrave Macmillan.

Obholzer, A. (2003). Some reflections on concepts of relevance to consulting and also to the management of organisations. *Organisational and Social Dynamics, 3*: 153–165.

Obholzer, A. & Miller, S. (2004). Leadership, followership and facilitating the creative workplace. In: C. Huffington, D. Armstrong, W. Halton, L. Hoyle & J. Pooley (Eds.), *Working Below the Surface. The Emotional Life of Contemporary Organizations* (pp. 33–48). London: Karnac.

Obholzer, A. & Roberts, V. Z. (1994). *The Unconscious at Work*. London: Routledge.

O'Connell, P., Pepler, D., & Craig, W. (1999). Peer involvement in bullying: Insights and challenges for intervention. *Journal of Adolescence, 22*: 437–452.

Ogden, T. H. (1992). *Projective Identification and Psychotherapeutic Technique*. London: Maresfield Library, Karnac.

Ojala, K. & Nesdale, D. (2004). Bullying and social identity. *British Journal of Developmental Psychology, 22*: 19–35.

Olweus, D. (1993). *Bullying at School. What We Know and What We Can Do*. Oxford: Blackwell.

O'Moore, M. & Lynch, J. (2007). Leadership, working environment and workplace bullying. *International Journal of Organizational Theory and Behavior, 10*: 95–117.

Parkins, I. S., Fishbein, H. D., & Ritchey, P. N. (2006). The influence of personality on workplace bullying and discrimination. *Journal of Applied Social Psychology, 36*: 2554–2577.

Patchin, J. W. & Hindurja, S. (2012). *Cyberbullying Prevention and Response: Expert Perspectives*. New York: Routledge.

Paull, M., Omari, M., & Standen, P. (2012). When is a bystander not a bystander? A typology of the roles of bystanders in workplace bullying. *Asia Pacific Journal of Human Resources, 50*: 351–366.

Pellegrini, A. D. & Long, J. D. (2002). A longitudinal study of bullying, dominance and victimization during the transition from primary through secondary school. *British Journal of Developmental Psychology, 20*: 259–280.

Perelberg, R. J. (1999). *Psychoanalytical Understanding of Violence and Suicide*. London: Routledge.

Perini, M. (2010). "Si vis pacem para bellum" Psychoanalysis, peace education and conflict literacy. In: H. Brunning & M. Perini (Eds), *Psychoanalytic Perspectives on a Turbulent World* (pp. 17–39). London: Karnac.

Perren, S., Gutwiller-Helfenfinger, E., Malti, T., & Hymel, S. (2011). Moral reasoning and emotion attributions of adolescent bullies, victims, and bully-victims. *British Journal of Developmental Psychology, 30*: 511–530.

Piontelli, A. (1985). *Backwards in Time*. London: The Clunie Press.

Pitterman, H. (2005). "You're either with us or against us": Dominant discourse in health care practice. *Organisational and Social Dynamics, 5*: 15–37.

Power, J. L., Lee, T., & Brotheridge, C. M. (2008). A typology of perpetrators, targets and observer: difference in personal background, traits, and coping with workplace bullying. Paper presented at 6th International Conference on Workplace Bullying, 2008, Montreal.

Ramsay, S. (2008). Workplace bullying: social identity and perspectives of skilled migrants. Paper presented at 6th International Conference on Workplace Bullying, 2008, Montreal.

Randall, P. (1997). *Adult Bullying: Perpetrators and Victims*. London: Routledge.

Rayner, C. (1997). The incidence of workplace bullying. *Journal of Community and Applied Social Psychology, 7*: 28–38.

Rayner, C. (1999). From research to implementation: finding leverage for prevention. *International Journal of Manpower, 20*: 28–38.

Rayner, C., Hoel, H., & Cooper, C. (2002). *Workplace Bullying: What we know, who is to blame and what can we do?* London: Taylor & Francis.

Richards, V. & Wilce, G. (1996). *The Person Who Is Me; Contemporary Perspectives on the True and False Self*. Winnicott Studies Monograph Series. London: Karnac.

Rigby, K. & Slee, P. T. (1991). Bullying among Australian school children: Reported behaviour and attitudes toward victims. *The Journal of Social Psychology, 131*: 615–627.

Rorty, R. (1989). *Congtingency, Irony, and Solidarity*. Cambridge: Cambridge University Press.

Rosenfeld, H., (1987). *Impasse and Interpret*ation: *Therapeutic and Anti-Therapeutic Factors in the Psychoanalytical Treatment of Psychotic, Borderline, and Neurotic Patients*. London: Routledge.

Rutter, M. (2006). Implications of resilience concepts for scientific understanding. *Annals of the New York Academy of Sciences, 1094*: 1–12.

Rycroft, C. (1995). *A Critical Dictionary of Psychoanalysis* (Second Edition). London: Penguin.

Salamon, S. D. & Maitlis, S. (2010). How group members "gang up": An empirically grounded model. Paper presented at the Seventh International Conference on Workplace Bullying and Harassment, 2010. Glamorgan, UK.

Salin, D. (2003). Ways of explaining workplace bullying: A review of enabling, motivating and triggering factors in the work environment. *Human Relations, 56*: 1213–1232.

Salmivalli, C. (1999). Participant role approach to school bullying: implications for interventions. *Journal of Adolescence, 22*: 453–459.

Salmivalli, C., Lappalainen, M., & Lagerspetz, K. M. J. (1998). Stability and change of behaviour in connection with bullying in schools, *Aggressive Behavior, 24*: 205–218.

Salzberger-Wittenberg, I. (1970). *Psychoanalytic Insight and Relationships*. London: Brunner-Routledge.

Sandler, C. (2010). How to manage leaders' anxiety. *People Management*, 8 April 2010, p. 33.

Schneider, C. (1975). Organisational climates: An essay. *Personnel Psychology, 28*: 447–479.

Schneider, C. (1997). *Shame, Exposure, and Privacy*. Boston: Beacon Press.

Segal, H. (1973). *Introduction to the work of Melanie Klein*. London: Karnac.

Seigne, E. (1998). Bullying at work in Ireland. In: *Bullying at Work 1998 Conference Proceedings*. Stafford, UK: Andrea Adams Trust, Staffordshire University Business School.

Seigne, E., Coyne, I., Randall, P., & Parker, J. (2007). Personality traits of bullies as a contributory factor in workplace bullying: an exploratory study. *International Journal of Organization Theory and Behaviour, 10*: 119–132.

Shakespeare's Sonnets (1997). (Ed. K. Duncan-Jones). *The Arden Shakespeare*. London: Bloomsbury.

Sheehan, M. (1999). Workplace bullying: responding with some emotional intelligence. *International Journal of Manpower, 20*: 57–69.

Shruijer, S. L. (2009). The dynamics of collusion in multiparty interactions. Paper presented at the Annual Meeting of the International Society for the Psychoanalytic Study of Organizations 2009, Toledo, Spain.

Skogstad, A., Torsheim, T., & Einarsen, S. (2011). Testing the work environment hypothesis of bullying on a group levels of analysis: psychosocial factors as precursors of observed workplace bullying. *Applied Psychology: An International Review, 60*: 475–495.

Skogstad, A., Einarsen, S., Torsheim, T., Assland, M. S., & Hetland, H. (2007). The destructiveness of laissez-faire leadership behaviour. *Journal of Occupational Health Psychology, 12*: 80–92.

Slojne, R. & Smith, P. K. (2008). Cyberbullying: Another main type of bullying? *Scandinavian Journal of Psychology, 49*: 147–154.

Smith, P. K. & Ananiadou, K. (2003). The nature of school bullying and the effectiveness of school based interventions. *Journal of Applied Psychoanalytic Studies, 5*: 189–209.

Smith, P. K. & Myron-Wilson, R. (1998). Parenting and school bullying. *Clinical Child Psychology and Psychiatry, 3*: 405–417.

Smith, P. K., Parrot, W. G., Ozer, D., & Moniz, A. (1994). Subjective injustice and inferiority as predictors of hostile and depressive feelings in envy. *Personality and Social Psychology Bulletin, 20*: 717–723.

Smith, P. K., Singer, M., Hoel, H., & Cooper, C. L. (2003). Victimization in the school and the workplace: Are there any links? *British Journal of Psychology, 94*: 175–88.

Smith, P. K., Mahdavi, J., Cravalho, M., Fisher, S., Russell, S., & Tippett, N. (2008). Cyberbullying: its nature and impact in secondary school pupils. *The Journal of Child Psychology and Psychiatry, 49*: 376–385.

Sourander, A. & Helsta, L. (2000). Persistence of bullying from childhood adolescence—a longitudinal 8-year follow-up study. *Child Abuse and Neglect, 24*: 873–881.

Spenser, E. (1909). *The Poetic Works. Book 1.* Oxford: Clarendon Press (1964).

Spitz, R. & Wolf, K. (1946). Anaclitic depression: an inquiry into the genesis of psychiatric conditions in early childhood. *The Psychoanalytic Study of the Child, 2*: 313–342.

Stacey, R. D. (2007). *Strategic Management and Organisational Dynamics. The Challenge of Complexity* (7th Ed). Harlow, UK: Prentice Hall.

Stanislaus Kennedy, Sr. (2001). *Gardening the Soul.* London: Simon & Schuster.

Stapley, L. F. (2006). *Individuals, Groups, and Organizations Beneath the Surface.* Karnac: London.

Stein, H. F. (2008). From organizational meaning through splitting to organizational meaning through integration: Healing the great divide. *Organisational and Social Dynamics, 8*: 298–321.

Stein, M. (2011). The dark side of groups: A 'gang at work' in Enron. *Group and Organization Management, 36*: 692–721.

Steiner, J. (1993). *Psychic Retreats.* London: Routledge.

Stevens, L. E. & Fiske, S. T. (1995). Motivation and cognition in social life: a social survival perspective. *Social Cognition, 13*: 189–214.

Strandmark, M. & Hallberg L. R.-M. (2007). Being rejected and expelled from the workplace: experiences of bullying in the public sector service. *Qualitative Research in Psychology, 4*: 1–14.

Sutton, J., Smith, P. K., & Swettenham, J. (1999). Social Cognition and bullying: social inadequacy or skilled manipulation? *British Journal of Developmental Psychology, 17*: 435–450.

Syedain, H. (2012). Biased. *People Management*, November 2012, pp. 31–36.

Taylor, C. (2004). *Sources of the Self: The Making of Modern Identity.* Cambridge: Cambridge University Press.

Thylefors, I. (1987). *Synda-bockar; om utstotnings och mobbning i arbetslivet.* (About expulsion and bullying in working life). Stockholm: Natur och Kultur. (Translated for this edition).

Tracy, S. J., Lutgen-Sandvik, P., & Alberts, J. K. (2006). Nightmares, demons and slaves. Exploring the painful metaphors of workplace bullying. *Management Communication Quarterly, 20*: 148–185.

Tuckey, M. R., Dollard, M. F., Hosking, P. J., & Winefield, H. (2009). Workplace bullying: the role of psychosocial work environment factors. *International Journal of Stress Management, 16*: 215–232.

Turkle, S. (2011). *Alone Together.* New York: Basic Books.

Turquet, P. (1974). Leadership: the individual and the group. In: G. S. Gibbard, J. J. Hartmann & R. D. Mann (Eds.), *Analysis of Groups* (pp. 87–144). San Francisco, CA: Jossey-Bass.

UNISON (2009). Tackling bullies at work. UNISON guidelines. Available from http://www.unison.org.uk.

Van Heugten, K. (2010). Engaging bystanders as change agents. Paper presented at the Seventh International Conference on Workplace Bullying and Harassment, Glamorgan, UK.

Vartia, M. (1996). The sources of bullying—psychological work environment and organizational climate. *European Journal of Work and Organizational Psychology, 5*: 203–214.

Vince, R. & Broussine, M. (1996). Paradox, defense and attachment: Accessing and working with emotions and relations underlying organizational change. *Organization Studies, 17*: 1–21.

Waddell, M. (2007). Grouping or ganging: the psychodynamics of bullying. *British Journal of Psychotherapy, 23*: 189–204.

Webster's (1986). *Third New International Dictionary of the English Language.* Encyclopaedia Britannica. USA: Merriam-Webster Inc.

Western, S. (2008). *Leadership: A Critical Text.* London: Sage.

White, S. (1998). The Prevention of Bullying in the Workplace. Unpublished MBA Dissertation, Southampton University. UK.

White, S. (2001). A life cycle theory of bullying: persecutory anxiety and a futile search for recognition. *Socio-Analysis, 3*: 137–154.

White, S. (2004). A psychodynamic perspective of workplace bullying: containment, boundaries and a futile search for recognition. *British Journal of Guidance and Counselling, 32*: 269–280.

White, S. (2007). A psychodynamic perspective of workplace bullying scenarios. Unpublished Doctor of Philosophy Thesis, University of Western England, UK.

White, S. (2010). Exploring space in workplace bullying scenarios: boundaries, vacuums and black holes. Paper presented at the Seventh

International Conference on Workplace Bullying and Harassment. 2010, Cardiff, UK.

White, S. & Davidson, C. (2011). Bullying in the workplace: a dance of death. Paper presented at ESRC seminar series, Vulnerable Selves: Disciplining others. 2011, Birkbeck, University of London.

Wilton, M., Craig, W., & Peplar, D. (2000). Emotion regulation and display in classroom victims of bullying: characteristic expressions of affect, coping styles and relevant contextual factors. *Social Development, 9*: 226–245.

Winnicott, D. W. (1971). *Playing and Reality*. London: Tavistock.

Woods, J. (2006). Bullying, education and the role of psychotherapy. In: C. Harding (Ed.), *Aggression and Destructiveness: Psychoanalytic Perspectives* (pp. 150–164). London: Routledge.

Worrell, L. & Cooper, C. (2012). The quality of working life 2012: Managers' wellbeing. motivation and productivity. Executive summary, Chartered Management Institute.

Wren, B. (2012). Creating new spaces and having new conversations in NHS organisations. Paper presented at the OPUS conference, 2012, London.

Zapf, D. & Einarsen, S. (2003). Individual antecedents of bullying: victims and perpetrators. In: S. Einarsen, H. Hoel, D. Zapf & C. Cooper. *Bullying and Emotional Abuse in the Workplace: International Perspectives in Research and Practice* (pp. 165–184). London: Taylor & Francis.

Zapf, D. & Gross, C. (2001). Conflict escalation and coping with workplace bullying: a replication and extension. *European Journal of Organizational Psychology, 10*: 497–522.

Žižek, S. (2008). *Violence*. London: Profile Books.

INDEX